CAPTURED BY FIRE

CHRIS CZAJKOWSKI AND FRED REID

CAPTURED

Surviving British Columbia's New Wildfire Reality

BY FIRE

**HARBOUR
PUBLISHING**

To Katie and Dennis—as always, a port in every storm. —Chris
To Monika. —Fred

HARBOUR PUBLISHING CO. LTD.
P.O. Box 219, Madeira Park, BC, VON 2H0
www.harbourpublishing.com

Cover photos by Chris Czajkowski (front) and Fred Reid (back)
Cover design by Anna Comfort O'Keeffe
Edited by Emma Skagen
Text design by Shed Simas / Onça Design
Printed and bound in Canada

Canada Council   Conseil des arts
for the Arts   du Canada

BRITISH COLUMBIA
ARTS COUNCIL
An agency of the Province of British Columbia

Harbour Publishing acknowledges the support of the Canada Council for the Arts, which last year invested $153 million to bring the arts to Canadians throughout the country.

Nous remercions le Conseil des arts du Canada de son soutien. L'an dernier, le Conseil a investi 153 millions de dollars pour mettre de l'art dans la vie des Canadiennes et des Canadiens de tout le pays.

We also gratefully acknowledge financial support from the Government of Canada and from the Province of British Columbia through the BC Arts Council and the Book Publishing Tax Credit.

LIBRARY AND ARCHIVES CANADA CATALOGUING IN PUBLICATION
Title: Captured by fire : surviving British Columbia's new wildfire reality / Chris
       Czajkowski and Fred Reid.
Names: Czajkowski, Chris, author. | Reid, Fred, 1951- author.
Identifiers: Canadiana (print) 20190144815 | Canadiana (ebook) 2019014484X | ISBN
       9781550178852 (softcover) | ISBN 9781550178869 (HTML)
Subjects: LCSH: Czajkowski, Chris. | LCSH: Reid, Fred, 1951- | LCSH: Wildfires—British
       Columbia—History—21st century. | LCSH: Evacuation of civilians—British Columbia.
Classification: LCC SD421.34.C2 C93 2019 | DDC 363.37/9—dc23

Contents

PART TWO

YOU MUST EVACUATE NOW.

Register at the ESS Reception Centre at Williams Lake Secondary School or the ESS Reception Centre in Prince George at the College of New Caledonia, west entrance.

Close all windows and doors.

Shut off all gas and electrical appliances other than refrigerators and freezers.

Close gates but do not lock.

YOU MUST EVACUATE NOW!

    —West Chilcotin Search and Rescue, automated phone call.

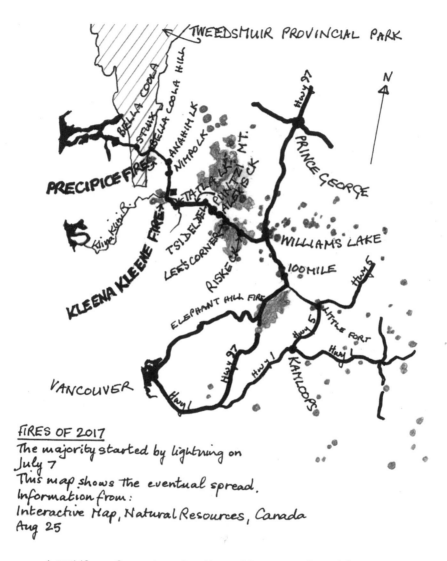

TWEEDSMUIR PROVINCIAL PARK

N

BELLA COOLA
STUIX
BELLA COOLA HILL
ANAHIM LK
NIMPO LK
Hwy 97
PRINCE GEORGE
PRECIPICE FIRE
Klinaklini R.
TATLA LK.
PUNTZI MT.
NAZKO CK
KLEENA KLEENE FIRE
TSI DELDEL
LEE'S CORNER
WILLIAMS LAKE
RISKE CK
100 MILE
Hwy 5
ELEPHANT HILL FIRE
Hwy 5
LITTLE FORT
Hwy 5
Hwy
VANCOUVER
Hwy 97
Hwy 1
KAMLOOPS
Hwy 1

FIRES OF 2017
The majority started by lightning on
July 7
This map shows the eventual spread.
Information from:
Interactive Map, Natural Resources, Canada
Aug 25

BC's Wildfires of 2017, based on Natural Resources Canada's
Interactive Maps, August 2017. Drawn by Chris Czajkowski.

Part One

The Strikes

KLEENA KLEENE, JULY 7

IT WAS EARLY AFTERNOON ON A HOT, RATHER DULL DAY. I WAS SITTING in a mechanic's office in Williams Lake, British Columbia, while some work was being completed on my van. I was told that the van was OK for now, but it was going to need a brake job soon. That, however, could wait until the next time I came to town. I was not sure when that would be. Williams Lake, population 11,150, is the nearest place to my home that is big enough to boast a bank, a supermarket, traffic lights, a bus station, a full-time mechanic, and cell phone service. But my home is three and a half hours' drive away.

Normally I would be out of town earlier, but that day I had to wait until 4:30 p.m. as a friend was arriving from Saskatchewan by bus. I was half dozing in the muggy heat and staring idly through the open door of the mechanic's office. The shop is in a light industrial area; the buildings across the street are unattractive and utilitarian. Behind them climbs a steep-sided slope covered in coniferous forest.

Traffic on the road in front of the garage was busy and noisy, and it all but drowned out a few rumbles of thunder. Nothing particularly loud; most people never heard it. I was staring straight at the hill when the lightning struck. Three broad stabs of white light, one after the other. Bang. Bang. Bang. There was a wind up there, and within minutes black smoke was roiling into the heavens.

I have lived for nearly forty years in this dry, flammable country—long enough to have considerable experience with forest fires. My first instinct was to run. To get away from potentially panicky crowds. But Miriam's bus wasn't due for another couple of hours. It takes days to travel from Saskatchewan by bus and I could not abandon her.

People coming into the office were hyped up and talking.

"108 Mile is burning," some said. (About an hour south of Williams Lake. The bus would be coming through there. Would it be delayed?) "It started there yesterday." "Rumour has it that some kids were shooting at targets in a quarry." "Doesn't take much of a spark to set things off in these conditions." "It is already out of control and the community is being evacuated." People seemed oblivious to the smoke above their heads. The drama, for them, was elsewhere; they had not yet registered that it was also in their backyard.

The bus indeed was late. Smoke continued to boil from the hill east of the city. Finally, the Greyhound coach eased in behind the bus station, and there was Miriam, shouldering her backpack. She excitedly showed me pictures she had taken on her phone of the 108 Mile fire. I barely looked at them. I wanted to be gone.

"I just need to go to the supermarket," she said. "I have everything I need for our backpacking trip except food."

Hanging about to shop was the last thing I wanted to do. "I have plenty of suitable food at home," I told her. "We need to get out of here."

Fortunately our route took us directly away from the Williams Lake Fire. We would be heading west along Highway 20, the thin ribbon of road that runs all the way through the Chilcotin to Bella Coola. The highway first climbs over a ridge then drops down to the Fraser River. The following steep scarp, Sheep Hill, needs a couple of hairpin bends to gain elevation. As we climbed, we caught glimpses of the black smoke pluming up behind us; the fires must have coalesced as there was only one column now. It rolled along with the wind but was topped by a towering dense white mass of pyrocumulus. Pyrocumuli, or fire clouds, happen only when the burn is very hot. They are created by steam from a living forest and fierce heat from flames boosted by a high wind. The forces within are similar to those in thunderclouds, which is why they resemble their tight, cauliflower structure. Pyrocumuli over the wildest fires may even create their own lightning storms.

At the top of Sheep Hill, we were on the high, open country of the Chilcotin Plateau. At first there is little evidence of the mountains that hover just below the horizon, but they will draw closer as we head west. Once on the plateau, as very often happens when coming out of town, we drove beyond the overcast. The sky here was cloudless. The van thermometer was registering twenty-nine degrees Celsius.

We were now faced with a narrow, comparatively empty road. Due to our late start, the sun was already ahead of us. The sky was a blue so pale it was almost white. The land stretched wide on either side. But was that something on the horizon ahead of us? A smudge? A cloud? A fly splat on the liberally bespattered windshield? As we drove steadily on, we could see it was another fire. No: a series of fires, stretched in a line.

From the way the highway twisted, it was impossible to tell if these fires were going to be a problem. One moment we seemed to be pointing straight toward them—the next they would be off to the right. We drew closer and the smoke columns grew bigger. The sun glared through my dirty windshield, causing me to squint. Was that an obstruction ahead? Someone was parked in the middle of the road—a truck pulling a horse trailer. The driver, wearing a cowboy hat and a gunslinger moustache, was out of his vehicle, talking to the

Four fires burn near Lee's Corner on July 7. Photo by Chris Czajkowski.

driver of a pickup coming the other way. "I know that guy," I said. "He's one of my neighbours." I stepped onto the hot, windy road as he walked toward me.

"That's it," he said. "We're not allowed through. We've got to go back. I have a daughter in Riske Creek—I guess I'll head back there."

I could not believe this. They could not be stopping us from going home. Surely there was a way through. We drove cautiously forward. We were about an hour out of Williams Lake and approaching a rest area perched on the top of a hill—two concrete outhouses, bear-proof litter bins, a couple of picnic tables. To the south a steep drop tumbles to the Chilcotin River, beyond which a rugged wall of rock and forest steeply rises. It is usually a pleasant spot to stop for a break.

Now several vehicles were parked sloppily around the outhouses, and below us rose a black tower of smoke from the southernmost of the string of fires. Everyone had bits of information. "All the other fires are north—that one's south of the highway and the wind's right behind it. That's why they won't let us through." "It started at Yunesit'in (Stone Reserve)." "The wind's been screaming down there all day."

A cop was doing his best to turn us back. He was on his own and getting more and more frustrated. He jabbered angrily into his radio while driving to and fro, trying to round people up like a sheepdog attempting to control a bunch of excited goats. He would have been from the detachment at Alexis Creek half an hour west, one of only two RCMP stations along the whole of the Chilcotin.

We milled around getting photos, mostly ignoring the cop. Although the bottom of the hill was invisible from our viewpoint, I knew that the junction with the Nemiah Road lay there. It ran south for several hours, dead-ending at Xeni Gwet'in (Nemiah) and Chilko Lake.

At the junction, there was a restaurant. Although the current building was not the first to occupy that site, one had existed there for many years. In the unadorned dirt yard reposed a gas pump, and four small, very basic frame cabins that did duty as a motel. The location was known as Lee's Corner, which was part of Hanceville, population three.

The place had already been ramshackle when I had first come across it thirty-five years ago, and though owners had come and gone since, not much had changed. Half a set of horse hames worked as a handle for the heavy door, and a clattery cowbell announced entry. Inside, despite the roaring, rattling fan, the place reeked of years of ancient grease. A new flat-screen TV blared and the coffee was execrable—but the baking was superb. I can no longer eat wheat or sugar without regretting it, but was always tempted by what had to be the best carrot cake in the world. I often complimented the baker—bent over with arthritis, she was unable to stand upright— and she shyly acknowledged my praise. "You know," she confessed one time, "I hate making it."

I would also stop there for a caffeine boost to cope with the last slog homeward after a long day in town, and if I had passengers, we would get something to eat. It was the only place along our journey that could be relied upon to serve meals late in the afternoon. Miriam and I had looked forward to having a break there.

Still unable to believe that we wouldn't be able to go home, or even get as far as Lee's Corner, we reluctantly turned back. "There's a field about twenty kilometres east where you can wait," we were told. I did not know who had arranged for the gate to be open but a dozen assorted vehicles were spread haphazardly over a small, stony field. The land was desperately dry; what little grazing had existed had been mashed to dust under the tires. Some people were strangers, but others I knew. Friday is town day for many of my neighbours. One pickup belonged to the owners of the restaurant so near but so unutterably out of reach. They had been to town to get supplies. Their load consisted exclusively of pop and chips. "Sorry I don't have any carrot cake," said the baker sadly, trying to smile. They were expecting the wind to die, as it very often did when the sun went down, so they would be able to go home. The restaurant was licensed, and the owners were worried about looters.

No one believed this would be anything more than an inconvenience. There were fires every year on the Chilcotin. True, the dryness was on the extreme side this year, but drought and thirty-degree temperatures in July were not unusual. A month previously I had set off on a road trip to the Yukon. Green was all I saw on that trip, for I had been dogged by deluges of rain and snow and hail. But on my return to the Chilcotin only three weeks later, my jaw dropped.

The land was as crisp and brown as it would normally be after the heavier frosts of September. The sparse weeds and grass amid the stunted forest were brittle as cornflakes, disintegrating into dust as I walked on them. Fenced areas were bared to the earth, the stalks probably destroyed by animals' feet as much as their hungry mouths. Beyond the pastures is open range. Open range in this country means forest. Huge parcels of pine and Douglas fir hold pockets of grazing around ponds and sloughs, on old burned areas, and in clear-cuts. The cows are put out there at the end of May and rounded up in dribs and drabs through November.

What had caused the rapid drought of 2017? The summer of 2016 had been unusually wet; the subsequent winter's snow cover not particularly heavy, but fairly average for the area. No one I knew had ever seen such a short green season, or such a rapid change to brown.

The restaurant owners had their little lapdog with them; their half-wild white tomcat would be sleeping off the heat somewhere near home. Their only close neighbour, forced to evacuate with no real warning, sat in his pickup, scowling. The hot wind coursed through the open windows of his cab. Two large dogs of indeterminate breed were sprawled across his lap; he had been unable to find his third.

My nearest neighbour, Dillon—who lives four kilometres farther along my bush road—was also in the field. He and his soon-to-be wife, Tamara, were heading west, but only as far as Tsi Del Del (Redstone Reserve), where Tamara's mother owned the store. Their plan was to stay the night and gas up before they went home the following day.

Other people in that stony field were strangers, but we talked, all a bit bewildered. Some had families and livestock on the Nemiah Road. No one wanted to be in the field but we didn't know what to do. Maybe the wind would die and we would be allowed through. Someone said there was a series of logging roads going north; they would detour us around the fires. But rolling walls of black smoke lay in that direction. It looked as though we might run directly into the flames if we went that way.

A truck towing a trailer pulled into the field. The driver worked for Forestry. He confirmed that there was indeed a way round and he knew where to go. "It's pretty rough," he said, eyeing my van. "And

I won't be going slow, so it will be very dusty. It'll take about an hour and we'll end up at the Forestry building at Alexis Creek." I thanked my lucky stars that I had splurged on truck-quality tires for the vehicle that spring. My four-kilometre driveway is pretty rough, and prior to that, flats had been common. I ran and told Dillon. He hoped he had enough gas. He unearthed a half-empty can from the jumble of chainsaws and tools in the back of his truck and topped up his tank.

Off we went. Instantly we were plunged into a rooster tail of dust and could see almost nothing either ahead or behind. I lost sight of the trailer but kept following the dust cloud. Occasionally the road forked—I followed the direction in which the dust cloud hung and hoped the wind hadn't moved it. I had no idea if Dillon was behind us. We met other vehicles roaring the other way, all rushing to get around the fire before someone got smart and closed this route as well. The road was so narrow we were often forced to the very edge where the gravel was coarse and piled into a little ridge.

The dust grew darker; it was now mixed with smoke. Cows wandered in forlorn groups. Miriam was taking pictures. "I see flames," she kept saying, pointing to both sides of the road. (They were only small flames.) We hurtled on. A guy coming the other way flagged us down and told us to watch out for a cattle guard ahead—one man already had a flat tire from it. He must have hit it wrong, for it wasn't a problem for us, crossing in the middle and going slowly.

At a major fork, our guide was waiting for us. We stopped for a while to see whether Dillon was behind us, but there was no sign of him. I hoped he didn't have a flat. He and Tamara were both experienced in the bush—I knew they could look after themselves, and the presence of other drivers meant someone would stop if they needed help. Our guide was anxious to move.

The smoke was now high in the sky, like a lid above our heads. But the flames were behind us and the scruffy, brittle forest ahead was clear in the hot, late sun. Now, however, the road was even rougher. On we flew, following the dust plume, rocks the size of tennis balls sliding under our wheels. And then suddenly, down a hill, there was the Forestry building and the tiny town of Alexis Creek, seemingly deserted like a city abandoned in a disaster, which I guess it pretty much was. Two hours after we were first turned round, we were back on Highway 20. We were only twenty kilometres from the aggressive column of smoke at Lee's Corner, but we were on the right side of the fire. The sky was clear, and now it was calm. Not because it was later in the day, but because the fire wind wasn't blowing here. This country is famous for the contrast between gales that roar wildly through mountain passes and dead calm areas elsewhere. It was now about 8:00 p.m.—still full daylight at this time of year. Two hours to go. We stopped in at the Tsi Del Del store to let Tamara's mother know that she and Dillon were hopefully behind us, then continued steadily along the empty highway. Logging trucks had been forced to quit hauling just the day before. Logging always has to stop when the fire hazard is high: too much risk of iron hitting rock and causing sparks. Logging trucks constitute the majority of traffic this far west, and without them the road was eerily quiet.

Twilight suffused the land about the time we drew close to the mountains. It was cool enough to close the van windows. The nights never get truly dark at this time of year and only the brightest stars were visible. Our headlights cut a lonely swath through the dimness.

Past Tatla Lake—forty minutes to go. Not far west, the road bends sharply to cross a river. As I slowed for the turn, I suddenly smelled it. Smoke. *Oh! No!* It was like a blow to the stomach. I could see no sign of it—the dark ridges against the summer night sky seemed clear and sharp. The river captured the light and gleamed faintly. But the smell was unmistakable—not a chimney fire or campfire (neither would have been present in that unpopulated spot in any case) but the distinctive reek of a burning living forest.

It was another ten minutes before we saw them. Just two or three small fires, gentle and seemingly innocuous; one would hardly notice them if it wasn't for the darkness. They were high on a forested ridge behind downtown Kleena Kleene.

Downtown Kleena Kleene used to boast a ranch house, a mechanic's shop, a store and a school, but no one lives there now. The only thing of note is a state-of-the-art sprinkler system, recently installed to irrigate several hectares of prime hayfields. Tame hay is a rare species in the Chilcotin. Most of the country is scrubby forest, either rocky or silty depending on what the glaciers dumped during the last ice age, pockmarked with bogs that provide coarse "wild hay" composed mostly of weeds and sedges. The sprinkler system was idle and tucked against the highway fence, no doubt pulled off the fields in preparation for haying.

To our amazement we could see that the road here was wet. It had rained. The fires burned quietly but steadily. Small red candles in the night. We drove on; I stopped at the old cabin that does duty as a post office to pick up mail from the ancient shabby green boxes. Mail comes to the Chilcotin by truck, three days a week. I had no way of knowing that I would not see that post office again for nearly a month. A few more kilometres and we turned off the highway onto the bush road that Dillon and I share. We marvelled at the puddles on it and the weird way that the van's headlights reflected off them into the scruffy trees. I had not seen water on the road since breakup in May. The summer dark was soft and cool and calm. Although the drive had been twice as long, the fire was probably five kilometres away from my house as the crow flies. There was no sign of it from my yard.

Day Two

KLEENA KLEENE, JULY 8

THE FOLLOWING MORNING WAS CALM, HAZY WITH SMOKE AND ALREADY hot, even though the sun had not been up very long. It was shaping up to be another thirty-degree day. What were the fires doing this morning?

The BC Wildfire Service Active Wildfires website is useful for a quick glance. New fires are red, less active ones are amber, and those under control or out are yellow. Serious fires boast a little icon representing flames. These are designated "Wildfires of Note." There were groups of these around Williams Lake and Lee's Corner, and several more were scattered throughout the province. The Riske Creek area, halfway between Lee's Corner and Williams Lake, was already blowing into quite a big fire, though we had seen nothing of it while driving by. The 108 Fire had its little bunch of flames, as did another serious-looking one north of Ashcroft, which would be a major player during the season and become known as the Elephant Hill Fire. I heard later that ninety-seven fires had started on the same day, all from lightning strikes.

The fire positions are presumably automatically loaded from a satellite and are usually fairly accurate. One is supposed to be able to click on the little flame icons and get an update, but in my experience

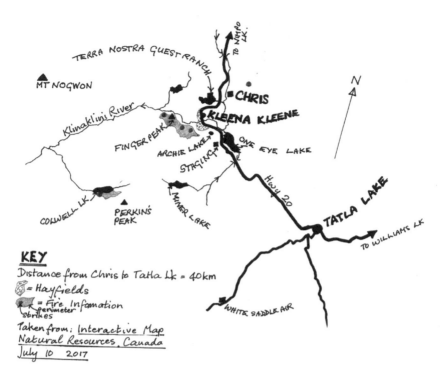

This is a map of the local Kleena Kleene area. It is based on Natural Resource Canada's Interactive Maps, July 10, 2017. Drawn by Chris Czajkowski.

these pages are all but useless. One can make the excuse that, in 2017, the Cariboo Fire Centre was overwhelmed, but every fire I have been involved with in the past has shown the information to be arbitrary and often many days out of date.

The USDA Forest Service Fire Detection Maps have the same colour coding, but they show the shape of the fires superimposed on a satellite map. The area around Williams Lake, Riske Creek, Lee's Corner, and for some distance north and south showed splotches of yellow heavily spotted with amber and red. Farther west, and north of the highway, there was another group of fires and, close to home, was a small blob representing our local Kleena Kleene blaze. Nearby, quite a way back from the highway, was a small red dot at the head of Colwell Lake, a glacier-fed body of water buried in a deep trench. I had once looked down upon it from a nearby mountain and knew it to be a startling turquoise blue.

Another red dot was of some concern to me. It was not big enough to be a "Wildfire of Note" so there was no additional information available, but it was, as far as I could judge, only two kilometres north of my house. Winds did not often travel at great speeds from that direction, but there was no natural barrier between us and the fire; no road, river, swamp or large area of water. In highly incendiary conditions, a blaze smaller than a campfire can grow very rapidly.

Strings of bald sand hills bracket my property. From these dunes there is quite an extensive view of the country toward the mountains. The McClinchy Creek runs below the hills; Highway 20, backed by forested foothills, lies parallel half a kilometre away. The mountains behind them are not all that high, but a good portion of them is above the treeline and they never quite lose all their snow.

Miriam and I trudged up the loose, silty slopes of the dunes to where we could see the view uninterrupted by trees. Haze-filtered sunlight cast pale shadows. Two or three grey plumes from where we had seen the flames the evening before were contributing to the poor visibility, but now we were high enough to see more smoke coming from between the next two ridges; they would be on either side of Colwell Creek. In the distance we could hear the rhythmic beat of a helicopter. Just looking and assessing, or was it doing actual firefighting?

Behind us, the land was only slightly hilly; small, forested swells eventually culminated in a gentle rise of land on which old logging scars were visible. The red dot on the BC Wildfire Services site showed that the lone northern fire should have been well in front of the old clear-cuts, but we could see no indication of it. However, as we stood there, the heli-noise increased and a Bell 407 detached itself

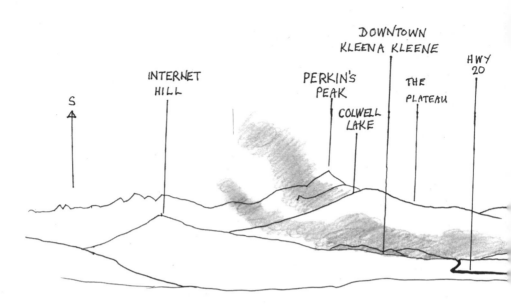

Diagrammatic Representation of the View from My House, South to West

This is a diagram of Chris's view at Kleena Kleene during the early part of the fire. Drawn by Chris Czajkowski.

from the main fire area and flew within binocular range. It bore the insignia of White Saddle Air, a thriving helicopter business south of Tatla Lake, and was likely piloted by Mike King. The chopper was slinging a large red bucket on a long cable. The lip of the bucket trailed a comet-tail spray of water that glittered in the smoke-veiled sunlight. The pilot headed directly toward where I had estimated the north fire to be, hovered low, and despite the thick haze, we could see an upward spray of smoke, ash and steam. So a fire *was* there. The pilot had brought his first load of water from a lake south of the highway, but now he hunted around the nearby country for swampy pockets that contained puddles big enough for his purpose, and to my surprise he found a few. Despite the rapid browning and crisping of the country, rivers and ponds were still relatively high.

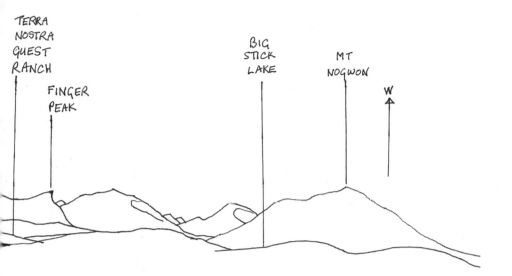

TERRA
NOSTRA
GUEST
RANCH

FINGER
PEAK

BIG
STICK
LAKE

MT
NOGWON

W

Not to Scale

The motion a helicopter makes when it picks up water reminds me of nothing other than a broody hen settling on her eggs. The pilot dumped several loads on the site; steam and ash flew every time, but eventually he headed back to the main fire. Although he disappeared into the distance and smoke, we could hear that he was repeating the exercise at various other locations. White Saddle was operating two choppers that day, but alone they would make very little impact. We would not be able to expect much assistance from farther afield for a while. The firefighting machine generally takes at least a week to get going, and any firefighters that might be mobilized this year would be deployed around the much bigger centres. The choppers droned steadily throughout the day; later we heard one coming back overhead. No sound of the bobbing and lifting associated with the bucketing, just circling, then returning from where it had come. That tiny fire was out. We never saw any activity there again. I was to thank our firefighters time and time again for that propitious intervention.

ONE MORE FIRE WAS OF CONCERN TO ME. IT WAS BETWEEN MY PLACE and the coast. Lightning had struck a bluff beside the Atnarko River, near Stillwater Lake. I had built my first cabin beside that river, a half-day's walk south of the lake (there are no roads in there). It had been destroyed in the 2004 Lonesome Lake Fire. By then I had long since ceased to live there and the cabin's destiny had been to return to nature; it just happened sooner than expected. The area around the Stillwater, at that time, had remained unburned. I zoomed in on the USDA map and could see that the strike was right above where the Hotnarko River spills into the Atnarko.

The Hotnarko is spawned in the Chilcotin and runs into a steep, wild canyon before reaching the valley bottom. Steep hillsides act as chimneys; eagles, condors and hang-gliders make use of these updrafts; they welcome nature's helping hand. But fires love them also; they are the most likely climate conditions to send a blaze out of control.

The direction of the Hotnarko valley is northeast to southwest. In this country, southwest winds are the wildest and most violent. (It was a southwest wind that was blasting through Lee's Corner as we drove by.)

Friends of mine lived above the Hotnarko Canyon in a place where the valley widened enough to support a ranch and a market garden. The distance between them and the strike was only ten kilometres. In 2004, the southwest wind had driven the Lonesome Lake Fire along the upper Atnarko River twenty kilometres in two days. My friends' properties could be in very great danger.

The Precipice / Stillwater / Hotnarko Fire

PRECIPICE, JULY 7–8

MONIKA AND I LIVE AT THE VERY WESTERN EDGE OF THE CHILCOTIN, where the Hotnarko River drops steeply through the Coast Mountains toward Bella Coola and the Burke Channel. Our valley is called the Precipice because of the organ-pipe basalt columns—evidence of the Chilcotin's volcanic origins—that rim its northern edge. The valley is a bit of an oddity in this country, which is otherwise wild and mountainous. Six kilometres long and an average of half a kilometre wide, it is hung at an elevation of 800 metres. This puts it roughly halfway between the harsher Chilcotin and the lush coast in altitude, and it has a climate somewhere in between. Right below our property is the boundary of the Tweedsmuir Provincial Park.

Our home is off-grid, and isolated from the interior of British Columbia by thirty-five kilometres of bush. A rough tote road and a logging road get us to the small community of Anahim Lake. From there it is another three hundred kilometres of lonely highway to the city of Williams Lake. We like our isolation and use the internet only sporadically so it is understandable that we would not be immediately aware of the number of fires that broke out on July 7.

When Monika noticed the plume of smoke to the west of us, I was not much interested and did not encourage her to report the

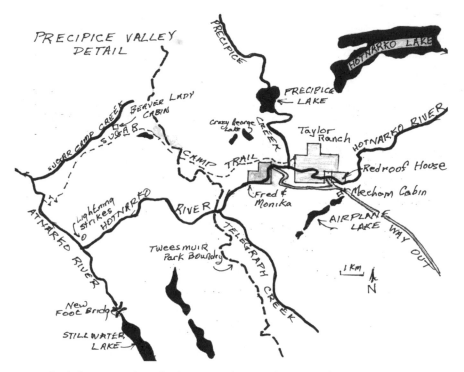

The lightning strikes of July 7 were directly downriver from our properties in the Precipice Valley. Drawn by Fred Reid.

fire, saying that it was probably already called in. Monika was more concerned than I. She had to make a few phone calls before connecting with the wildfire office in Bella Coola. They had not in fact been informed of the fire and wanted to know the colour of the smoke and how big it was. We estimated it to be two to four hectares but really had no idea of the actual size (in fact it was likely much smaller). The smoke was pale grey. Thus our fire became VA0778, the Precipice/Stillwater Lake/Hotnarko Fire. It probably would never have received the name "Precipice" if Monika had not explained where she was calling from.

I am not sure why this fire did not concern me from the outset. I should not have been so cavalier or naive about it. I had experienced fires before, the first going back to my childhood in Saskatchewan. My dad and uncles had lit a stubble fire in the spring after a heavy fall harvest. There was too much dry straw to work into the soil so they decided to burn it before cultivation. The fire was lit on a calm spring morning, on a small rise over a kilometre from my uncle's house. Siblings and cousins were assembled to help. We each had burlap grain sacks to fan or beat the flames as needed—an exciting outing for a child of ten years.

The fire occasionally flared in the deeper straw and then crawled lazily between swaths until it reached more dry material and again sprang into life. For an hour or so it spread slowly within the perimeter of our wet sacks. But winds like fire and fires love wind. The field sloped from the crest of land where we had started down toward my uncle's homestead, which was nestled behind a ring of aspen and spruce trees. The stubble was much thicker on the lower slopes, where more retained moisture resulted in greater yields. At the same time as the flames found more fuel in the denser straw, the winds picked up and began driving the fire toward the homestead.

Gentle laughter and conversation was replaced by shouts and screams of alarm. We could not attack the front of the fire as the smoke quickly robbed our breath, yet I remember rushing in to do what I could whenever I spotted a weak spot at the front of the fire. Voices came and went depending on the whim of the blaze as it captured our words in mid-air and sent them skyward with the smoke.

The adults, in a desperate panic, tried to create a fire-break between the raging stubble fire and the ring of trees. My uncle drove our tractor, pulling a disc plow between the flames and the homestead in order to try to mix some of the straw into the ground and thus reduce available fuel. However, the ground was much too wet. The tractor got bogged down halfway across the swale at the bottom of the long slope. Not only was the homestead in danger, but now we had a tractor stuck even closer to the advancing flames. I think it was the sense of panic and worry in adults that so firmly embedded such a memory into the mind of a child. I can still feel the intensity of the adults' fear more than my own fear of the fire.

But the flames weakened as they descended the slope where there was more shelter and less wind. It was also combatting wetter soils and straw. We were able to move in with our charred and ragged sacks to stop the fire before it reached the stranded tractor. I had a huge sense of pride in having contributed to the defeat of that fire.

I had three other brushes with out-of-control blazes. The first was when I tried to burn down an old house on my farm in the Fraser Valley. I had started dismantling the house piecemeal, but it seemed such a lot of work, and I thought putting a match to it would be easier. The garden hose I had readied for emergencies proved utterly useless. The flames flew high into the sky and started to spread to a nearby tree. I was able to dampen the fire as it licked up the branches, but I had to let the house burn out of control. Fortunately, it was over within an hour. I didn't fear the fire itself, only worried about the repercussions of authorities descending on the farm, giving me holy shit and fining me an outrageous amount of money.

Twice in the Precipice we had land-clearing fires get out of control. There is only a very narrow window—sometimes a matter of days—between it being too wet to burn because of the snow, and too dangerous because the forest is tinder dry. On both occasions, by dint of a great deal of panicky exertion, we were able to subdue these fires, not without some damage to my pants, socks and long underwear as I attempted to stamp out the flames.

It was not these experiences that made me so indifferent to the Precipice Fire, however. I was not arrogant, thinking that I could fight any fire. I put it out of my mind just because I did not want to be bothered by it, especially when it seemed so far away.

Monika and I had been slowly creating a small farm in the Precipice. We engaged volunteers to help us with the chores and to build some infrastructure. Over the years we had constructed a barn, a chicken coop, a greenhouse, a recreational building (called the "pool room" because it housed a pool table), two cabins, and three sheds. In July 2017 we had two volunteers from a French wood engineering school who had arrived a couple of weeks earlier, and a couple who had been on our farm in the past and returned for two months. The four young people were bonding well and I planned on using their help to build a machine shed and a new root cellar. I wanted to get on with the summer and, as far as I was concerned, a fire was not a part of the equation.

Monika, a recent German immigrant to Canada, in her early sixties, grey hair, cool eyes, and classically German in her concern for detail, was aware that the winds of summer blew predominantly out of the southwest—putting us in a direct line with fire VA0778. She phoned Lee Taylor, the rancher who owned most of the valley. Lee, in his early seventies, had severely injured his right knee in the spring, and had been lifted out by helicopter. He was undergoing rehab in Vancouver under the close supervision of his wife, Pat. Lee—the most knowledgeable about the area and very proactive—phoned two helicopter services and the BC Wildfire Service to see if anyone was doing anything. West Coast Helicopters (with a base in Bella Coola) had seen the smoke but had not been able to get authorization to attack the fire. Whether they could have stopped it on that first day would be debated most of the summer. Lee desperately wanted to be in the valley to help protect our homes, but Pat wanted to ensure he recovered sufficiently from his injury before he returned.

The next day I continued to try ignoring the fire. We had just completed a first cut of hay on the meadow next to the house. Matilda and Florian, the French couple, were beginning the strawberry harvest. Tabi and Katie had arrived four days earlier and were settling in to one of the cabins. We have a greenhouse built in terraces against the slope of a hill, and I spent the morning watering, tying tomatoes

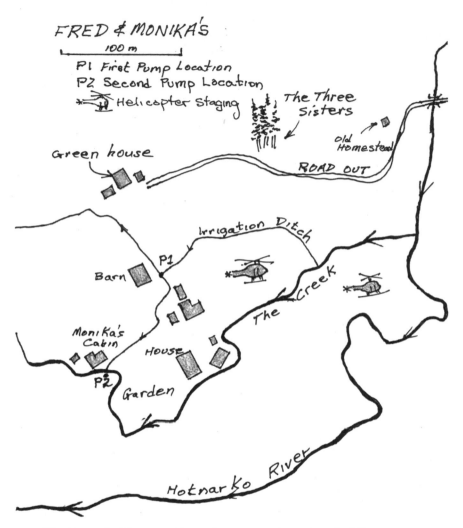

The Hotnarko River runs through our property and our buildings are scattered among green meadows. *Drawn by Fred Reid.*

and generally putting things in order. I planned to have Tabi and Katie look after the crops in there throughout the summer.

I heard a soft whine, an alien sound that I could not place. I exited the top of the greenhouse to search for the source. Tabi and Katie had purchased a small drone just before coming to the Precipice and were down in the meadow below the greenhouse, doing trial flights. They were trying to capture pictures of the plume of smoke that hovered on the western horizon. I was annoyed by the strange mechanical sound that had interrupted my work. Little did I know that mechanical sounds were to dominate our summer.

Late in the afternoon we heard the dull throbbing of a helicopter from White Saddle Air approach from the west, circle our meadows and begin a descent. At the time this was not a common event, and Monika and I walked with some excitement to the edge of the swirling downdraft. Two red-shirted Forestry people and the pilot came to greet us.

"Are you Monika who reported the fire?" asked one of the two women. "I'm Kerry from Forestry's field office in Bella Coola, and this is Sally from the Cariboo District."

"I'm Jim," said the pilot. "This is my second trip to the Precipice this year. I was the one who airlifted Lee in the spring."

We were never to have an unfriendly visit from the people involved with this fire. There would always be great concern for us, often with stern warnings about the dangers—the fire's heat, its speed and its smoke. This first visit was typical. They had just flown around the fire and they asked who was in the valley. We told them that there were four volunteers with us, and Caleb was caretaking the Taylor Ranch four kilometres to the east. They advised us to leave. We explained that we and Caleb would not likely be going. Caleb had worked at the Precipice for many years but had recently left; however, due to Lee's injury, he had been contracted to come back for the spring to feed the cows and keep the ranch running smoothly. He was reclusive, independent and resourceful, with a healthy disrespect for authority and an unbridled contempt for incompetence.

The third and easternmost property in the valley was occupied by Jade and Ryan, who had two small children. They were caretaking for the absentee owners but had left for holidays a few days before. That house, at the moment, was empty.

VA0778 suddenly made its presence felt. We turned to the west as one. A dark column of smoke rose dramatically in front of the declining sun, building rapidly and arching with the soft west wind. It was immediately captivating and alarming, yet foreign to Monika and me. It was our first encounter with one of the characteristics of wildfires—the "afternoon run." The afternoon's spiking heat, coupled with increasing winds, can drive a slumbering fire into a frenzy of fuel combustion within minutes.

"We'd better have a look at that, but we will also check in on Caleb," Kerry said as they scrambled to the helicopter.

"The smoke can be horrific," Sally warned. "If it gets very bad you should stay as close to the ground as possible and go into the water if necessary." She nodded to the pond that had been built into our meadow.

The helicopter made its rattling takeoff, leaving Monika and me standing and staring at the dark, billowing plume of smoke. Any hope of quickly stopping the fire was gone. My chance of ignoring it also vanished.

We began taking some rudimentary precautions against a possible onslaught. We had the volunteers help fill sixteen-litre buckets with water and place them around the house, barn and hay shed. I connected garden hoses to the house and a standpipe by the barn, and checked that they could reach all sides of the buildings.

In the evening I went on the internet to try to find out what was happening. The wildfires dominated the headlines in British Columbia. A low-pressure weather system continued to cause dry lightning strikes, starting new fires. Strong winds fanned the existing ones. Two hundred and twenty wildfires were burning in the province, ninety-seven sparked on July 7 alone. Nearly ten thousand people were ordered to evacuate their homes in or around the towns of 100 Mile House, Ashcroft, Cache Creek, Princeton and Williams Lake. It was especially devastating to find that Lee's Corner had been completely destroyed. It had been a popular stop for us on our trips to Williams Lake. We would rest and collect ourselves before continuing to town and a day of hectic shopping. However, I never had the carrot cake.

I phoned friends near 100 Mile House to ask about their status, for there were fires very near them. As I chatted with Jerry, I could hear Nicola shout from the door, "Jerry we got to go. The truck is loaded." The second time she called out, Jerry sighed that he had to go. They were evacuating to a friend's place at Green Lake.

Our fire—the Precipice Fire—was of little consequence in the general scheme of things. It was designated a Wildfire of Note but was described as being in a remote part of the province and not threatening urban structures—i.e., not an "interface fire." It was also a considerable distance away from any of the other fires. By a random stroke of a pen years ago on someone's desk, all the other Chilcotin fires were under the auspices of the Cariboo Regional District (CRD). We, however, came within the boundary of the Central Coast Regional District (CCRD). Next morning, the CCRD phoned asking who was in the Precipice, what properties were involved and what travel out of the valley entailed.

Our early structural protection efforts soon ran into problems. During the night our three cows drank out of some of the buckets and knocked others over. Monika and I, with the help of the French volunteers, refilled them. We rerouted the electric fence to separate the cows from the house but had to leave them access to the barn. We moved the buckets near there into a corral to keep them from the cows but I did not like the idea that I would have to step over and around an electric fence if I had to fight a fire. Katie and Tabi had gone to the Taylor Ranch to help Caleb move tractors and equipment into an open space away from the buildings and other combustible material.

That afternoon two new Forestry personnel clad in heavy red shirts arrived by helicopter. Mark Petrovcic introduced himself as the incident commander responsible for the Precipice Fire. Mark exuded confidence, telling us our fire was the only significant one of the Coastal Division, and they were putting together a team (called Incident Command, or IC) to fight it. He warned us that resources were in short supply since they were competing with all the other fires in the province. Across Mark's chest was a shoulder harness hung with numerous pouches holding pens, a radiophone, notepads and maps. He was friendly but officious as he handed us an evacuation order from the CCRD, and firmly stated that we should leave. The BC Wildfire Service, he added, could handle the fire and would protect our buildings. If we left, we would not be allowed to return until the evacuation order was lifted. The BC Wildfire Service might indeed protect our buildings, but who would look after the garden and livestock? We had little understanding of any of the issues regarding fighting a forest fire but were of the belief that they could not force us to leave. We countered that we were not likely to go.

We took an immediate liking to Arlen, fair and tall with a bashful but easy smile. He also had an easy confidence about the fire—casual but reassuring. "It will burn!" he said casting an eye across the slopes that surrounded our meadows, "but your buildings are probably safe surrounded by all this green grass. If I were you I would probably stay too."

From the outset the fire had a capricious nature. Winds that blow from the Pacific often change direction as they sort out which valley through the Coast Mountains offers the least resistance. The fire, which had headed directly up the Hotnarko Canyon yesterday, had now begun a run up the Atnarko Trench toward Stillwater Lake. But it still crept in our direction on the slopes above the Hotnarko River. It was difficult from our perspective to determine where the fire actually was. Smoke was billowing up across the entire western horizon without a dominant discernible column. The BC Wildfire Service website stated that the fire had grown from 15 hectares yesterday to 134 hectares. But this information was actually one day out of date.

Mark and Arlen later shared maps showing that there were five lightning strikes near the confluence of the Hotnarko and Atnarko rivers on July 7—three west of the Atnarko River and two on the east side (on the slopes of the Hotnarko Canyon). It was the two above the Hotnarko River that started the Precipice Fire and combined to contribute to its rapid expansion.

In addition to phoning the Wildfire Service and helicopter companies, Lee Taylor had called our scattered neighbours. Everyone jumped into action. By Saturday, David J and David D (nicknamed Hoss, because of his resemblance to the character on *Bonanza*) came with a pressure pump, hoses and sprinklers from Anahim Lake. On Sunday, Troy and Lorrein, long-time friends associated with the Precipice by way of the Mecham Cabin a little way up the south side of the valley, and a man called Hans, arrived from Bella Coola with more hoses and sprinklers. (Most of them came without permits, therefore defying the evacuation order.) It was chaotic as we scrambled to set up minimal structural protection around the properties.

In the early afternoon the fire began travelling fast—an afternoon run in two directions. Mark flew in for a second time. He was with Kerry, not Arlen, this time, and once again he urged us to leave, reporting that the fire was moving our way at half a kilometre an hour and was now within five kilometres of us. He was angry that not all our volunteers were near the house. He quickly returned to the helicopter and flew to the Taylor Ranch. They landed in the midst of the buildings and found Katie and Tabi with Caleb. Caleb had not made himself available on Kerry's first visit, and now she was very agitated. She warned the three of them that they were under evacuation order and urged Katie and Tabi to return to our place and find a way to leave the valley.

Our heads were down, focusing on the task of making our property fire safe. Each day we learned more in a numbing struggle to prepare for the arrival of the fire. Fortunately we had cut the hay in the meadows near our buildings earlier. They had been flooded for regrowth and were very wet and green. We set David J's pump at a central location between the house and the greenhouse, drawing water from an irrigation ditch. We laid one mainline hose to our home (a log house built in the early 1980s) and another to the greenhouse. The greenhouse was at the very edge of our property right next to the forest. David J had fought forest fires in the past and suggested we fall trees above the greenhouse. I cast my eyes across the slope of well-spaced pine sprinkled with the statelier Douglas fir. It was an area that I was very attached to, having spent nearly eight years removing beetle-killed trees, building log fences and cutting trails. I knew there was a danger to the greenhouse but I decided to leave things as they were. The hose extended just beyond the greenhouse. With the proper nozzle, the system could throw water thirty metres into the forest. In my naïveté, I figured that was protection enough. David J allowed that if I kept the forest floor wet I might be able to get away with it. I had brief visions of standing firm against a raging blaze. My ten-year-old self was rising to the challenge. But when I tried using the hose, I realized how difficult it was going to be manipulating it single-handedly through stumps, fence and trees, while fighting the pressure of the water.

Monika and I were dazed by the pressure. We had nothing but our green meadows to protect us. We had no idea how we would save our place if the fire came upon us as, driven by the westerly winds, it surely would. Our four volunteers huddled in a group next to the garden, debating whether to stay or to abide by the evacuation order. Their loyalty to us was evident, and their emotions torn. Katie's dad

On July 9, Fred practises with the fire hose while David J and Monika stand by the pump and volunteers Florian, Matilda and Tabi look on. Our dog Fossie stands in the foreground. Photo by Katie Iveson.

was a firefighter from Manchester, England, who had already been apprised of the wildfires in British Columbia and had seen pictures of the destruction. He was unequivocal. "Get the hell out of there," he had emailed her. "It's not your decision to make."

Hans was returning to Bella Coola, and he offered the volunteers a ride to Anahim Lake where we arranged for them to stay with friends in case the situation calmed down and they could come back. Hoss remained to help make our place more fire safe. David J returned to Anahim Lake to locate more structural protection equipment. Troy and Lorrein spent the night at the Taylor house. By late afternoon the violent plume of smoke from the fire began to settle and a degree of calmness came with it.

Fire Smart

KLEENA KLEENE, JULY 9

MIRIAM, THE FRIEND I HAD PICKED UP IN WILLIAMS LAKE, IS NO STRAN-ger to fires. She and her husband, Quincy, live near Lac La Ronge in northern Saskatchewan. The province used to fight fires diligently, but now enormous conflagrations are left to burn unless they directly threaten communities. "Our fires," Miriam told me, "are not meas-ured in hectares, but in square kilometres. Because of your hills," she added, "you can see your fires and have a much better idea of where they are. In flat land, a plume of smoke might be two kilometres away or twenty kilometres—it is impossible to judge."

Miriam and Quincy had built a cabin on an island in another lake, twelve kilometres from the nearest road. In June 2015, a friend of theirs was staying in the cabin, which had no phone or internet. Quincy and Miriam had checked out the fire maps and noted that one of a series of fires was less than ten kilometres from the cabin. Next thing, they received a tearful phone call from their friend, who had been evacuated to a hotel. She had been so scared that she had not dared fall asleep in case she did not wake up. The friend was safe, but the next day's fire map showed the cabin had been engulfed. Miriam later wrote to me, "Our kayak, the cabin, the dog yard, the outhouse, the woodshed, the staircase down to the lake, the jack pines, the spruce trees, the Labrador tea, the grasses by the shore, the grouse sitting on her eggs, the little owl hunting mice, the lichen on the rock, the deep green moss—they were all left behind.

"I stare at the fire map, [our lake] surrounded by red, but I can't believe what I see. And I couldn't believe it until we stood on the scorched soil and sifted through the grey ashes of what used to be the dream of a wilderness home."

Quincy maintains water bombers, and as their house had not been in the fire's path, he had returned to work. His sister came and looked at the trees surrounding the house. "That one, that one and that one has to go," she said.

"No!" Miriam replied. "The fire won't come here." But she kept staring at the tall balsam fir that was right behind her bedroom window. She tied a rope as high as she could on the tree, and with straps she tried to pull it away from the house. She knew that straps alone would not work well, but she didn't have a come-along. She cut down the tree with her chainsaw. It hit the roof and tore a few shingles off. She trailered away brush load after brush load to a nearby gravel pit and cut down more trees. She knew it was futile, there were just too many, but she could not sit and do nothing. She kept working, pulling away grass and twigs close to the house. In the end the fire was diverted from their property and the house was saved.

After our hike on the dunes on July 8, Miriam stepped into her sister-in-law's shoes and looked critically at my home. "The biggest problem," she allowed, "is the open sides around the deck. Sparks can be blown underneath and ignite the dry sawdust and debris under there." Some parts of the deck are over a metre off the ground. It is not a regular shape, but built in a bit of a curve. I did not have much in the way of materials suitable for walling it in at such short notice, but then I remembered the tarps. Over the years I had accumulated a large pile of woven, blue plastic tarps, now badly frayed and full of holes. I have lived so long without money and far from services that

The deck is surrounded by tarps to deflect wind-blown sparks.
Photo by Chris Czajkowski.

I have a very hard time throwing anything away. The tarps were in such bad condition, though, that every time I noticed them stuffed under the guest cabin I kept thinking I really *must* take them to the dump. Now I dragged them out and we stapled and nailed them to the deck, weighing down the skirts with rocks. By doubling them up we were able to obviate the worst of the holes.

The woodshed attached at the other end of the house was also open at the bottom, designed that way to allow air to circulate and dry any wet wood that might be stored in there. We swathed the lower regions with more tarps. Plastic isn't going to stop a flame, but winds often gust furiously around the house and it might just be enough to deter a swirling spark. Miriam also carted away interesting roots I have collected to decorate the area. This is the sixth cabin I have built, but the only one in which heavy machinery was used.

The silt dug out to make the basement was piled around the hole and, though a lot of what was left was removed, a wide circle of ground surrounding the house is as barren as the Sahara Desert. Year after year I have tried to grow something on it to stop the flying dust, but I don't have enough water in my paltry well to nurture it, and little has survived. Hence roots and rocks for decoration. This sterile apron, however, now had a great advantage. There was a large open space free of vegetation around my home.

When I logged the small hill to create the building site, I had left a few pines for shade. I had taken down anything that had leaned toward the place where the house was going to be, partly because I knew how strong the local winds could blow, and partly because, should the unthinkable happen and I had to cut down trees to save the building, each could be toppled easily, with no danger to the faller. I didn't want to annihilate my shade unnecessarily though, so I left these pines standing for the time being.

In the afternoon, we drove to downtown Kleena Kleene. A couple of other locals were parked beside the hayfields. The wind was not all that strong and, though the fires had spread a little, they still seemed unthreatening. One onlooker made a living operating heavy machinery, and he talked about trying to rustle up a water tank and some pumps, and a couple of skidders to build fireguards. The government frowns upon lay people taking problems such as fires into their own hands, but the government, as we well knew, was busy elsewhere. I would not be much use. I could use a chainsaw well enough, but bad knees meant it was difficult for me to scramble over rough country, and I had never driven heavy machinery.

Back home, I didn't really think the situation too serious; even if the southwest wind got up, it would likely blow the fire away from me. Still, I figured that it wouldn't hurt to start thinking about packing. I had been threatened by forest fires twice before, both times while I was still living at Nuk Tessli, the fly-in resort I had constructed nearly thirty years before. There, my only way out was by float plane. This vastly restricted the amount of things I could bring when evacuated, especially as, on both occasions, guests and volunteers took up plane space. And, each time, I had only about half an hour to pack.

Here, at my current home in Kleena Kleene, I had much greater vehicular capacity and the leisure to think about it. I was not sure that I was going to leave; still, it was better to get things together now. Items that I would not want to put into the van until the last minute would go on a list.

The first consideration was food. I have chemical sensitivities and would quickly become very run down on the canned and packaged "staples" found in any of the Chilcotin stores. Most of my food is purchased in bulk from far away, often by mail. Into plastic totes went organic rice; wild rice; oats; baking soda; raw, sulphite-free vinegar, etc. I left the fresh food in my basement for the time being as it was cool. I would have to leave room in the van for my two largish dogs and their paraphernalia, as well as some personal gear of my own, like a sleeping bag and clothes. The passenger seat was left free—it would hold my computers and cameras and all their accessories. (Who said laptops were portable?) Water jugs were placed ready to fill. Camping gear. Who knows, in a state of emergency, what one might need? An axe and chainsaw resided in the van permanently. A wave of pine bark beetle killed a lot of trees here twenty years ago, and they often blow down onto my four-kilometre driveway. The government has decommissioned the road (it used to be Highway 20), so the only people who maintain it are my neighbour Dillon and me. We plough it in the winter and cut it out every time there has been a blow.

The hiking trip that Miriam and I had planned was to have been at Nuk Tessli. Although I had sold the resort, I had agreed to guide clients for the owner that summer. Miriam and I had arranged to fly in early and hike for a few days on our own before the paying guests arrived. But road closures were now prevalent throughout BC. The clients that I was supposed to guide could not drive north. Also, there was no way that I was going to leave my place under these circumstances unless forced to, so the hiking trip was out. Miriam's presence at this time was very useful, however. As well as the van, I own a small pickup truck and a trailer. Having an extra driver meant that I now had a lot more options of what to take. First the ATV went into the trailer. Then the snowplow, chains and ramp, followed by a second chainsaw. These things could all be replaced, but they amounted to quite a lot of money and I was not covered by fire insurance. Few people are around here. The population is scattered and we live far from a fire truck; there is no fire suppression service for hours in any direction. Any insurance, therefore, is expensive.

Because I live forty minutes away from a gas station, I keep cans of fuel handy. I tipped the contents into the vehicles' tanks; empty cans would be far less flammable. Propane tanks would explode, whether they had gas in them or not, so all four were put into the trailer. Behind the seats in the pickup's half cab went a few winter items—a couple of excellent wool blankets, my best winter boots, down coats, and a few out-of-print and irreplaceable plant reference books. A couple of thick sweaters. My favourite huge cast-iron frypan.

And what about all my personal stuff? Years of memorabilia from around the world; albums; art work, both mine and countless items from friends, either bought or traded; skull, fossil and shell collections—the copious attic was stuffed to the brim. I rescued a few documents like my birth certificate and journals, but as for the rest, I didn't know where to start. The task seemed so overwhelming that in the end I packed none of it. Was there a sneaking feeling of relief in the back of my mind? Before I came to Canada in 1979, I had travelled for a decade round the world with a backpack. I'd had no possessions, very little money—but I was rich. Now I have property, vehicles, taxes and boxes of essentially useless stuff that I can't really bear to throw away. It was as if it was no longer me who owned these possessions, but the possessions that owned me.

At some point during the day we lost the internet. I phoned a neighbour who received a signal from the same tower, but his signal was also down. Christoph and his wife, Corinne, own the Terra Nostra Guest Ranch on Clearwater Lake. Their resort is two kilometres southwest of my place (although it is a ten-kilometre drive to get there). His power was also out but he had a generator backup and was functioning with that. I hadn't realized that bc Hydro had failed, for I have solar power. Christoph told me that a long string of power poles had burned near Lee's Corner when the restaurant had been destroyed. I pictured the owners where I had last seen them in the temporary parking lot, waiting for the wind to drop so they could go home and guard their property. All they had left of their twenty-year Chilcotin life was their old pickup, a load of pop and chips, their little dog, and the clothes on their backs.

Still not a lot of wind, and we went to bed with a certain amount of reassurance. But how quickly things can change.

Evacuation

KLEENA KLEENE, JULY 10

KATIE HAYHURST AND DENNIS KUCH ARE FRIENDS FROM WAY BACK living at Stuie in the upper part of the Bella Coola Valley. They'd had their fair share of fires to deal with and were cognizant of my situation. They had already emailed me with an offer to go down to their place. They live in what had been a resort, and there were several old cabins on the property. I had stayed in one or another of them many times.

I checked the internet first thing the following morning. It was still not functioning. I tried the phone (there is only a land phone here; no cell phone service) but it was dead as well. Suddenly we were cut off from all information except whatever we could deduce with our eyes. Fine as long as we could see, but if the smoke got worse…

I have lived in the bush for nearly forty years. At first I had no power at all, and my sole communication tool was a very unreliable, battery-operated radiophone. It has only been in the last fifteen years that I have been able to afford the internet. I didn't miss what I didn't have, but now I don't know how I'd live without it. With its sudden cessation in this time of potential disaster, I felt vulnerable and powerless.

Miriam and I had planned to fly to Nuk Tessli from the float plane base at Nimpo Lake. Tweedsmuir Air had a different internet provider, and the pilots, with their eyes in the sky, might also have some information, so it seemed a good idea to go there. Nimpo Lake is forty minutes' drive west.

When we turned up, the owner of the float plane company, Duncan Stewart, asked us if we were going into the mountains. Nuk Tessli was well out of the fire zone, but I certainly did not want to be up there and then find that my home had been burned while I was away. I had already emailed details of the road closures to the new owner of Nuk Tessli, but he had not yet experienced a bad fire season and replied something to the effect that things might change in the five days before the clients were due. "Good luck with that one," I thought.

Nimpo Lake had both phone and internet. We caught up on email, checked the fire sites (not huge changes at Kleena Kleene and the Precipice but a veritable chaos farther east) and made a few calls. Katie and Dennis in the Bella Coola Valley were glad to hear from us.

There had been a thin haze of smoke when we left home, but now the wind was freshening. As so often happens, the stronger breeze cleared the air. The lake beside the float plane base was blue and sparkling, and the low, snow-streaked mountains over which one would have to fly to reach Nuk Tessli were sharp and smoke free. A strengthening wind would likely stir up the fires, but as the winds varied tremendously from valley to valley, there was always hope it wouldn't amount to much at home. But as we turned back south we could see the smoke beginning to build over Kleena Kleene. We drove on past my driveway and called in at the Terra Nostra Guest Ranch to give Christoph and Corinne the information we had gleaned while in Nimpo Lake. They told us the good news that the internet had just come back on.

Our internet provider is a local husband and wife team. They had set up a tower on Tatla Hill as a hub to bounce signals in several directions. This tower acquired the internet from the Telus phone line, a fibre-optic cable that had been strung on the same poles as the power lines. When the poles burned, the wires all lay on the ground. It was found, however, that the fibre inside the phone cable was still functioning; the only reason the internet was down was that the power source was out. When our local providers discovered this, they rounded up extra solar panels—and we were back online.

The Terra Nostra Guest Ranch looked over Clearwater Lake toward the burning ridges. Black plumes of smoke were beginning to roll, and we could see more smoke pouring from the Colwell Creek Fire. "If only," said Corinne exasperatedly, "they had dropped retardant on it yesterday! Just one plane load—what a difference that would have made!"

I just laughed. Corinne and Christoph had bought Terra Nostra three years ago and, like the owners of Nuk Tessli, had yet to experience a serious fire season. "I bet that's what at least ten thousand people are saying about their own fires right now," I said. "I've seen a lot of this stuff over the years. Any available personnel and machinery—and that won't be a lot at present—will be concentrated around the cities. And with so many lightning strikes all at once, it must be chaotic in the fire centres. I bet it will be a couple of weeks before we get much outside help."

Christoph was worried about his horses. "They are so quiet with people but some of them have never been boxed. I would never be able to take them out of here." Terra Nostra was much closer to the fire than my place and, being south of the river and highway, they did not have these barriers to protect them. They had the lake, but it was not that big, and given the right wind, a fire could whip around the edge in no time. "The *Williams Lake Tribune* had an online article I looked at when I was in Nimpo," I said. "Ranchers are opening gates and cutting fences to let their livestock have a better chance out there. I guess if you have to go, that's what you will need to do."

Before we went home, we drove down to the hayfields. Huge towers of black smoke now poured into the sky. We plunged under the smoke. Below it, the thick black shadow was a stark contrast to the hot, bright world outside. The state-of-the-art irrigation system stood tucked against the highway fence. "Why isn't he running the sprinklers?" Miriam asked. I wasn't sure at the time but of course the system needed electricity; besides, the owner lived an hour and a half east and he had his own fires to deal with.

The power of the fire close up was terrifying, even though I knew this one was comparatively small. We saw trees flare sporadically within the black smoke. There was no wall of flame like the one I had witnessed in 2004, when being evacuated by float plane from the Lonesome Lake Fire. Then, each lake had a tree-high ribbon of fire burning along its shore, and the front of the fire was many kilometres long.

A red-tailed hawk was perched on the phone line (which was still standing here). Predators know that animals will flee from the flames and this behaviour is standard practice for hawks at such times.

It wasn't until we reached the open space around my house that we were presented with the awful sight of my home backed by a massive wall of boiling brown smoke. It was not, however, blowing directly toward us. Equidistant between the fire and my place is the hill that now holds the Kleena Kleene internet tower. The hill is on the same side of the highway as my house but on the far side of the river. It was to become a marker for me; if I could see it, I had two kilometres of visibility. If flames ever reached it, my place would likely be toast.

I emailed Katie to let her know the internet was working but we still had no phone. I checked the fire sites—not a lot of change, but it would take a few hours to register anything on most of them. The billowing smoke was frightening and we packed with greater urgency. I ticked off last-minute items on my list. But still we hung

An RCMP officer serves me an evacuation order on July 10. Photo by Miriam Koerner.

in there. Was it really necessary to leave? Christoph and Corinne were going to stay.

Then one of my dogs barked—but only the old one, Badger. This meant a vehicle was coming; if a wild animal or range cow had been close, both dogs would have made a racket. Sure enough, a Suburban appeared, nosing its way along the dusty ruts of my driveway. As it drew into the yard, we could see that it was embellished with the colours of the RCMP. It would be from the detachment at Anahim Lake, half an hour north of Nimpo. My heart sank. I knew what they had come for. The policeman was accompanied by a Fisheries officer. Police are shuffled around every couple of years and few know the area, so the passenger was acting as a guide. I had met him before. The policeman handed me a slightly grubby piece of paper.

CRD Evacuation Order

Kleena Kleene One Eye Lake Area

Monday, 10 July, 4:00 p.m.

Pursuant to the BC Emergency Program Act, an Evacuation Order has been issued by the Cariboo Regional District.

Due to immediate danger to *life safety* due to fire [*Who writes these things?*], members of the RCMP or other groups will be expediting this action.

The Evacuation Order is in effect for the following areas... Map attached...

WHAT YOU SHOULD DO:

- You must leave the area **immediately**.
- Follow the travel route provided, and register at the ESS Reception Centre at Williams Lake Secondary School or the ESS Reception Centre in Prince George at the College of New Caledonia, west entrance.
- If you need transportation assistance please advise the individual presenting this notice or call 250-398-(****).
- Close all windows and doors.
- Shut off all gas and electrical appliances, other than refrigerators and freezers.
- Close gates (latch) but do not lock.
- Gather your family. Take a neighbour or someone who needs help.
- Take critical items (medication, purse, wallet, keys) only if they are immediately available. [*How can you leave if you don't have your car keys?*] Take pets in pet kennels or on leash.
- Do not use more vehicles than you have to.
- Do not use the telephone unless you need emergency services.

CRD Evacuation Order
Kleena Kleene One Eye Lake Area

EVACUATION ORDER ISSUED

Monday, 10 July 2017 4:00 PM

Pursuant to the BC Emergency Program Act, an Evacuation Order has been issued by the Cariboo Regional District

Due to immediate danger to **life safety** due to fire, members of the RCMP or other groups will be expediting this action.

The Evacuation Order is in effect for the following areas:

> From Highway 20 North of Clearwater Lake, East 13 km, South 15 km to Highway 20, South 16 km, West 23 km, North 31 km, and East 9.5 km, including Clearwater Lake, One Eye Lake, Big Stick Lake, the community of Kleena Kleene and Dowling Road, Bittner Road and Colwell Road

> Map attached

WHAT YOU SHOULD DO:

- You must leave the area **immediately**
- Follow the travel route provided and register at the ESS Reception Centre at Williams Lake Secondary School or ESS Reception Centre in Prince George at the College of New Caledonia – West Entrance
- If you need transportation assistance from the area please advise the individual providing this notice or call 250-398-████
- Close all windows and doors
- Shut off all gas and electrical appliances, other than refrigerators and freezers
- Close gates (latch) but do not lock
- Gather your family: take a neighbour or someone who needs help
- Take critical items (medicine, purse, wallet, and Keys) only if they are immediately available. Take pets in pet kennels or on leash.
- Do not use more vehicles then you have to.
- Do not use the telephone unless you need emergency service.

YOU MUST LEAVE THE AREA IMMEDIATELY

For more information contact: CRD call center/info line at 250-398-████

Al Richmond

X _____

Al Richmond, CRD Chair

This is the scruffy evacuation order that was handed to me by the RCMP *on July 10. Photo by Chris Czajkowski.*

YOU MUST LEAVE THE AREA IMMEDIATELY

For more information contact: CRD call center/info line at 250-398-(****)

—CRD Chair

"We're pretty much ready to go," I said to the cop. "We can be out of here within the hour."

He repeated the information on the paper: "You have to go east to Williams Lake and then north to Prince George."

"Nope," I said. It was my first rebellion against the fire authorities. "I'm going west. To Bella Coola."

"You won't find any accommodation there," the officer warned tiredly. He was parroting what he had been told to say, but without conviction. I was likely not the first person who had countermanded his edicts. The Fisheries officer had a very tiny smile on his face.

"Oh yes, I will," I retorted. "A friend has already offered us a cabin."

The cop shrugged resignedly. Before he left, he tied a piece of red flagging tape to my house. "It means you have left," he said. "Yellow means the place has been visited but no one was home"—I told him that the neighbours beside the river were not living on the property at the moment—"and blue means people are staying. We'll put these symbols on the house numbers by the highway as well." "Well," I thought. "That's good news for looters."

I emailed Katie and informed her we had been told to leave. I wrote that it was now getting late so we would probably spend the night at Stewart's Lodge in Nimpo Lake, where the float plane company is based. Duncan likely wouldn't mind under the circumstances. Still no phone. Duncan is not a happy user of the internet so I didn't bother to contact him. I packed up the computer stuff and put it on the van's seat. I shut the greenhouse vents and door, and screwed a piece of plywood over the dog door. Strong gusts of wind sometimes flap it open and sparks could fly inside. All windows were fastened tight. I even locked the door, which I very rarely do, even if I am away overnight. But who knew when I would return?

Our last job was to nail and staple a tarp over the opening to my porch that surrounds the main door. Scraps of useful wood are stacked in there; if a spark got among them it would have a field day.

The sun was going down as Miriam started the truck and began to move along the road. The dogs were already inside the van. I jumped out to take a few last photos. The garden, which was just starting to produce nicely, looked fresh and innocent beside the house. Without water, it would die. Then there was that small hitch, that small lurch of the heart that was now familiar to me. Would I ever see this house again? All the bits and pieces I had saved were conveniences, but amounted to nothing. The house was a different story. For my whole life I have been short of money. I have lived without power and conveniences in cramped, rough-built cabins. Over a period of many years I scrimped and saved and I had finally built myself a decent home. I don't enjoy building, but have spent a quarter of my life doing it. I was now seventy years old. If this house was destroyed, I would have neither money nor energy to start again.

I could not dwell on such thoughts and I pushed them away. Miriam was already disappearing around the first corner. I climbed into the van and turned the key. For the third time in my life I was running from a fire.

Preparing for the Fire

PRECIPICE, JULY 10–14

I TURNED MY BACK ON THE FIRE IN SOME FORM OF DENIAL, ANGRY with myself that we were so unprepared for such an event, living as we were deep in a forest so dependent on a cycle of fire. Evidence of past burns was all around us. Evidence that we had ignored. The densely packed pine we hiked through on outings to Crazy George Lake, a small lake we named after a hermit who had lived in the bush near our valley in the seventies, was regrowth from a fire seventy years ago. The charred remains of logs along the ridges of our hikes, and the darkened bark of the mighty Douglas fir that grow at the very edge of our meadows, stared us in the face at every turn. How could we have ignored these warnings?

In the afternoon Arlen flew in with two Initial Attack crews (IAS) of three firefighters each, a handful of sprinklers bought at the hardware store in Bella Coola, and some two-centimetre hoses that would be connected to the mainline. Arlen explained that they were not trained for structural protection but felt it was necessary to do whatever they could, because if the winds picked up, the fire could reach us in a day. The Bella Coola Forestry field office had limited resources on hand but expected a Canadian Air Force plane to fly into Bella Coola at any time with a container of structural protection equipment. I followed Arlen around like a puppy dog, anxious to learn what I could about how to protect our place. He asked what buildings were of highest priority. Monika and I accepted that some would be lost (the sauna and lumber shed had wooden roofs and the greenhouse was covered in plastic). We decided the house and the pool room should receive the protection of sprinklers. We would try to protect the barn with our own hoses and nozzles, drawing water from a standpipe near the barn. By early afternoon the IA crews had added three sprinklers to our system (two on the house and one on the roof of the pool room) then left for the Taylor Ranch to place their remaining five sprinklers. This was grossly inadequate for all the buildings, but we were very grateful that they showed such concern for us and were willing to do whatever they could.

Arlen pointed out that falling embers were the biggest danger. They could find their way into cracks and onto piles of fuel in the form of dried wood, grass or other combustibles. After Arlen left, Monika, Hoss and I began removing firewood from our sheds by the house and the greenhouse, dumping the piles onto the green meadow at a distance from the buildings.

Everyone had much more fire experience than we did. Hoss told of a ride out of the mountains driving his pack horses ahead of a wildfire with the embers falling around him. David J was steeped in firefighting, as if weaned on it very early in the forests of British Columbia. And there was Arlen, so nonchalant about the fire, acknowledging that "it would burn" but doing all he could to protect us and our buildings.

The Precipice Fire smouldered in the distance but was not growing quickly on this day. By late afternoon Mark flew in and told us the fire had increased only from 650 hectares to 680 hectares—but it was now only three and a half kilometres from us, on a point jutting out along the north slopes of the Hotnarko Canyon. He again urged us to leave. We were too tired to consider leaving and too busy to take pictures—the western horizon was a featureless wall of smoke in any case.

Tuesday, July 11, was one of the darkest days of the fire. David J phoned in the morning. The Kleena Kleene Fire was raging and they needed all the resources they could muster to fight it. The folks of Anahim Lake were concerned because new fires were breaking out and the existing ones were expanding rapidly. Although it was thirty kilometres away, Anahim Lake was directly downwind from the Precipice Fire. People felt that the hoses, sprinklers and pumps that had been lent to us were needed to protect their own homes and ranches. David J was coming in to pick up his pressure pump. I was stunned by this turn of events. We were the closest to the fire and directly in the path of its most likely onslaught. It had to come through us to get to Anahim Lake. If it could be stopped at our place, Anahim Lake would be safe. We were the first line of defence and in the most need. How could David J consider such a thing?

Monika was in tears with the news. She phoned Lee immediately. I walked to the pump uttering a continuous string of expletives. Hoss stumbled after me.

I shouted, "If I had a gun I would go to the gate and not allow him on the property." Then I turned to Hoss, a friend of both David J and me, and said more softly, filled with dejection, "But I don't have a gun and I probably wouldn't do that anyway. It is his pump after all."

Hoss and I stood next to the pump as Monika approached. "Lee phoned back. He talked with David. He will not be taking the pump."

But David's call had added to my stress and mixed emotions about those helping us. My confusion and numbness would continue in the following days as we scrambled to improve our protection and waited for the fire to come.

For the second straight day the fire was quiet. We could hardly see evidence of it—only small plumes of smoke from time to time. On these days my fear lessened, but we were warned that it was still out there and that it could not be stopped. Mark and Arlen flew in daily after circling and assessing the fire's activity and growth. With each return of the helicopter we would drop whatever we were doing and walk to the edge of the propeller's downdraft. Arlen, always smiling: "It's just bubbling away." Mark, confident and concerned, continued telling us that we were under evacuation order and that we should leave, assuring us that they could protect the buildings. We appreciated the constant updates, eager to learn all we could of the fire's movement and proximity to us.

Our gratitude and confidence in the Coastal Division of the BC Wildfire Service was being cemented. They were putting together an Incident Command (IC) to fight the fire but were competing for resources within the BC Wildfire Service because of the other fires raging in the province. Many ICs are groups of professionals that move as a unit. With VA0778, Mark, the incident commander, and Kerry from the Bella Coola field office were drawing resource people from within the Wildfire Service to form the IC. The number of people in the IC and their responsibilities can and often did vary. Basically it consisted of an operations chief responsible for ground and air activities (Arlen); logistics personnel (those who had to locate and obtain resources for fighting the fire: this included everything from chainsaw fuel to helicopters to crews of firefighters to bulldozers); a plans chief; a financial officer; and an information officer. In this IC, the desperate search for resources necessitated four people working in logistics.

Four days into the fire, Mark had still been unable to acquire the resources he needed. He wanted helicopters to bucket the fire and firefighters to battle it on the ground. One of the problems was that VA0778 had started in the centre of Tweedsmuir Provincial Park. We understood that it was policy not to fight fires in provincial parks and ours was considered a remote area. We were surprised that they were doing anything for us. Mark and Arlen assured us that they would fight the fire and improve our structural protection; it was just a matter of when the resources would arrive.

The lack of strong winds was giving us time. The fire was moving on two fronts. In the Atnarko Trench at the bottom end, close to the strikes, it was creeping both north and south, threatening a walking bridge across the river. (The bridge had recently been rebuilt after the previous one had been destroyed in the 2010 flood.) It was also heading up the Hotnarko Canyon toward us. We remained lucky that it stayed on the ground, finding its way around rock bluffs. It was constantly burning and advancing, but it was unable to access the tree crowns and move rapidly. Our concern increased when the fire, which had so far been active only on the north slopes of the Hotnarko Canyon, jumped the river. Now we were threatened along both sides of our narrow valley. Mark was trying to determine where his resources could best be deployed—once he had them.

The structural protection at our place and the Taylor Ranch was still grossly inadequate. The cheap garden sprinklers that Arlen had brought to our place—they were all he had been able to get— were already beginning to malfunction. At the Taylor Ranch, the five sprinklers were on a single line serviced by a small backpack Forestry pump. There was not enough pressure to drive all the sprinklers at the same time. The Taylors' house was some distance away from the ranch buildings and was not close to a good water supply. A couple of sprinklers provided by Troy had been set up there. The house at the top of the valley where Jade and Ryan were living, known by the firefighters as the Red Roof House, and the Mecham Cabin had no protection at all. Caleb asked for help from other friends in Anahim Lake. Lee and the owners of the Red Roof House bought two smaller pressure pumps each and more water hoses. It was a wonder that they found any. Pumps in British Columbia were rapidly being bought up and the price of them was rising. The pumps were flown to the Anahim Lake Airport and ferried down by the volunteers.

Others also brought pumps and hoses. I took a spare hose from our place to the Taylor Ranch, where they were jerry-rigging hoses to fit pumps, and nozzles to fit hoses. David J, still committed to us, was in Anahim Lake installing a large tank onto his forwarder to provide water to protect both the Taylors' and the Red Roof House.

There was news of imminent relief from our trepidation when Mark flew in with Gord from Comox Fire Rescue. They asked to look around to assess our structural protection. The roller coaster of emotion I had been on since the beginning of the fire had brought me to near collapse. I did not bother to accompany them, and instead waited aimlessly for their return to the helicopter. They explained that there was still some difficulty getting the supplies into Bella Coola but assured us that they would have things worked out and they would come into the Precipice by truck the next day.

Our lives were turned inside out. We had to undo much of our work of late spring. We placed plywood over the open entrances to two sheds and moved loose hay away from all outbuildings—raking the ground to bare soil. We removed wood from our woodsheds. We moved equipment, vehicles and fuel containers out of the buildings and onto the meadow where they had less chance of being consumed. Piles of fire-hazard debris were randomly scattered over our once tidy meadows. The meadows would normally be drying out at this time to encourage second growth, but we had to leave the irrigation ditches open to provide water for the pumps.

The barn remained our biggest concern. We had been happy to have baled the first crop of hay early and to have it nicely stored in the loft, but now it presented our biggest fire hazard. The loft was consciously well ventilated by a slab cladding with many open spaces. These spaces were an invitation for hot embers. We did not want to remove all our hard-gotten hay but we did not want to lose the barn either. We elected to leave the hay, and Hoss and I set to work stapling tarps and plastic over the gable ends to cover the openings. As we neared the apex of the north end, a barn swallow flew out of a large gap. We would have to be very unlucky for the fire to find this spot—it would have to arrive from the opposite direction—and we left the opening so the swallows could continue to feed their fledglings.

We had been dazed since the beginning of this ordeal. Our brains were in a fog thicker than any smoke we would ever experience from the fire itself. In fact, on some days you would not even know that the fire was out there. We were on a steep learning curve. With legs of rubber we climbed the curve, unsure of where the crest of the hill would be.

As topsy-turvy as our routine became, our emotions were more so. We felt gratitude for all that was done for us, but I was also confused. I was still very shaken by the fact that David J had wanted to take the pressure pump even though he continued to work diligently at the Taylor Ranch and Red Roof House. I felt inadequate, overwhelmed by all the decisions that now faced me and the various opinions regarding evacuation, structural protection and forest firefighting. I just wanted to be left alone rather than be confronted by conflicting ideas and loyalties. Monika was the opposite. She embraced all the help. She smiled from ear to ear when she heard a helicopter coming in. She rushed out to the edge of the meadow just beyond the swirling grass, anxious for any news. I dragged a little behind but usually joined her by the time the propellers stopped.

Our next helicopter brought bad news. There had been problems flying the structural protection equipment into Bella Coola. The truck and container were too big to fit into the military transport plane that had been designated for the job. Everything would be delayed for another day. However, they had contracted Rob, a seasoned pilot with a mid-sized helicopter, to begin bucketing the fire. Monika and I had been reluctant to take pictures of the helicopter Mark and Arlen had flown in on. We felt that doing so would be intrusive to their work that we were so grateful for (and a bit embarrassed about). We watched as

Rob prepared to bucket the fire. He seemed a bit standoffish, barely pausing to wave as he rushed around the helicopter unloading line, bucket, net and retardant, then leaving quickly with bucket in tow. He began drawing water from a lake less then a kilometre from the blaze, making swift one-and-a-half-minute returns to the fire's front.

Many friends had heard of the fires through Chris's blog or Pat Taylor's and others' Facebook posts. We had maintained a Facebook page for some years but had in fact rarely put anything on it. On July 12, I wrote: "I guess it's time we said something. No pictures though. It is tough to send a picture of a wall of smoke. That is all there has been for three days now. Each morning we look into that wall trying to determine where the monster is—no flames, just more smoke. But it stays away from us. The air quality is actually quite good for most of the day.

"We have had lots of support. Friends from Anahim Lake have supplied equipment and well wishes, and the Wildfire Service drops in twice a day to give us a report and provide us with infrastructure to protect what we can.

"Each day that the fire has stalled has given more time to prepare. We have more worry than fear. When I asked Monika how she was feeling she responded, 'I feel like I would just before a big exam.' It rang so true. That sinking feeling low in the stomach right down to the intestines. Have I studied enough? (Have we done all we can to protect the buildings?) What questions will be asked? (From which direction will the fire approach?) We are hoping that classes will be cancelled."

On Thursday, July 13, almost a week after we reported the fire, the Comox Fire Rescue team drove down our bumpy tote road and gave our structural protection a major overhaul. They replaced some of the sprinklers that Arlen had installed. They made loops of hoses around the house and greenhouse. Gord explained that sprinklers placed within a circuit would have equal water pressure. The house and greenhouse now each had five sprinklers protecting them. More were added to the chicken house, snow machine shed and Monika's cabin, an exquisite little two-storey structure next to a channel of the river we call the creek that runs through our property. It has two rooms on the lower floor and an upstairs bedroom over one half. Monika had done most of the construction herself. It had taken her over three years to complete and we were very proud of it.

Monika sheepishly showed Gord how we had put plastic on the barn's gable ends. Gord smiled and showed her the roll of plastic inside their pickup. "That is exactly what this is for. You have done a good job."

When they placed a powerful Wajax pump next to David's I felt a pang of mixed emotions—we had gone from the possibility of having no pump to having a backup. The pumps were set side by side. With a simple transfer of the mainline we could use either one.

I liked David's: it had a Honda four-stroke engine that I was familiar with—they do not require a mix of gas and oil and are very easy to start. Its drawback was that it did not have enough power to drive all the sprinklers at once. This limitation had been overcome by running half the system at a time. The powerful Wajax could easily power the whole system but we were warned that it was not easy to start and had to be fed a mix of oil and gas drawn from two gas cans. One of the structural protection people began dramatically pulling on the cord and fiddling with the choke and throttle, but was unable to get it going. A second crew member gave it a try—he squeezed a suction bulb situated between the gas cans and the pump in addition to pulling the cord and fiddling with throttle and choke. The engine sputtered but did not start. A third person finally brought it to life. David's pump looked more desirable to me with each passing minute.

Our place became a hub of activity with two helicopters flying in and out and structural protection people buzzing around. I began to embrace this new energy. By late afternoon the Comox crew left, promising to come back the next day to work on the Taylor Ranch and the Red Roof House.

Fred works with the two pumps. David J's is on the left, the Wajax on the right. Drawing by Chris Czajkowski, from a photo by Monika Schoene.

After they left, the west wind picked up, clearing some of the smoke from our valley and blowing it toward Anahim Lake. At times I felt that my gloom was related to the amount of smoke as much as anything else. The afternoon was clear and hot. But VA0778 never let us enjoy a sunny afternoon for very long. There were soon dramatic plumes of smoke across the western horizon. Rob constantly dumped water by helicopter in front of the part of the fire closest to us, keeping it cool and slowing it down. As Arlen would say, "We want it to bubble but not to boil." The plumes of an afternoon run were frightening but they were also beautiful—greys and blacks were mixed with yellow and deep orange as the sun descended behind them. By evening the fire—and the smoke—settled, resting for the night. We ran the sprinklers for half an hour to make sure I could start the Wajax—assurance so we would sleep better.

Flight

KLEENA KLEENE, JULY 10–12

BOTH MIRIAM AND I, DRIVING ALONG THE ROAD IN OUR SEPARATE vehicles, realized we had been foolish to leave when we did. When the sun went down, the wind died, and the smoke dropped with it, shrinking into a brownish fog over the fire site. It was as calm and safe an evening as one could wish for. We could have spent a comfortable night in our own beds.

We drove into Tweedsmuir Air's yard well after 10:00 p.m. The whole place was quiet and dark. There was still a greenish glow along the mountain horizon but it was barely light enough to find our way to the waterfront to give the dogs a drink. "I think there's going to be a frost tonight," I said. A frost in July is not uncommon here. The Chilcotin Plateau is not that far north, but it lies between 1,000 and 1,300 metres in altitude, and the climate is dry enough to encourage temperature extremes between night and day.

We spread our sleeping bags in our vehicles. Modern cars don't have that long front seat like the old pickups used to have. In the van I had a box of tools between the two seats and attempted to cushion the bumps with a small foamie. It was a very uncomfortable night; in addition to the uneven surface, the van was not wide enough for me to stretch out properly. I had spent many a night this way at different times so knew I would survive. There was no room for me in the back. The dogs had only just enough space for themselves. I could have tied them up outside, but the last thing I wanted was for them to start barking and being a nuisance.

I am an early riser and even in the summer am usually up at first light. But I didn't want to disturb anyone—and there was indeed a sharp frost—so I stayed buried in my sleeping bag for as long as I could. When I emerged it was to find that Miriam had given in to the cold long before and was already in the lodge with a cup of coffee. The cook and Duncan were about, and we learned that Duncan's wife, Angela, had in fact sat up late and waited for us. As soon as Katie in the Bella Coola Valley had received my email telling her we were on our way, she had been on the phone to them and said we might end up there. These people live forty minutes and two hours away respectively, but a neighbourhood like ours stretches many kilometres.

Duncan steered us toward the staff shower block and the cook plied us with a gourmet breakfast. Duncan and Angela waited on us as if we were rich paying guests. Duncan would take no money for our stay. "Business is one thing," he said. "But this I am doing for a friend." I felt drained and empty. Everyone was being very kind. As a supremely independent person, I find it hard to accept kindness gracefully.

We did the email/phone thing so Katie would know when to expect us. It would take at least two hours to drive to Stuie. We left the pickup and trailer in Duncan's yard.

It is a spectacular journey across the divide of the Coast Mountains. The road turns to gravel past Anahim Lake then climbs gently to its maximum height of 1,600 metres. From there, the landscape crashes down in waves of cliffs; the road clings to the mountainside and loses height through a series of hairpin bends. There are no barriers, and sometimes it is only a single lane wide, with fresh washouts taking bites off the edge. This is the famous Bella Coola Hill. But locals have no fear of this road; given the terrain, it is very well maintained. Sometimes it is closed for a few days in winter due to avalanches, and in the fall of 2010 it was cut off for six weeks due to horrendous flooding. But most of the closures have been due to fires. Between 2003 and 2010 (before the flood) we had year after year of fires. The top of the Hill is a favourite target for lightning strikes and, as we headed west, we drove through several areas of tree skeletons in various stages of disintegration.

Going down the Hill takes one into a completely different world. Great coastal fir, cedar and hemlock over a metre thick at the butt dwarf the string of buildings that Katie and Dennis call home. The land drops down a bank in front of the buildings, then soars up great craggy mountain faces to an altitude of about 2,000 metres. Sir Alexander McKenzie was the first recorded person to cross the North American continent (beating Lewis and Clark by twelve years) and he ended up a short distance downriver from Stuie. As he breasted the pass to come down into the valley, he saw in front of him "a stupendous mountain." Thus Stupendous Mountain received its name.

Miriam and I chose our cabins and settled in. Out with the laptop and a check on the fire sites and news. The *Williams Lake Tribune* now had more stories. The 108 Fire had started south and west of the subdivision. A shallow, grassy valley separated the burning forest from the houses, but the fire didn't let that stop it. It licked over the grass and consumed two homes. More houses had been lost in the Riske Creek area between Lee's Corner and Williams Lake. There was a story about the tow-truck driver's house near Riske Creek. He has occasionally fetched my vehicles for repair in Williams Lake, there being no other BCAA tow truck closer. They managed to save the house but the unclaimed vehicle yard discreetly hidden behind trees was not so lucky. "The gas tanks all exploded like bombs," a witness stated.

Another article showed smoky pictures of cows, driven by grim-faced cowboys on horseback. They were escorted by a phalange of police cars. Only a fraction of the livestock had so far been found; their summer feed and most of the hayfields had been lost. There were more pictures of the ravaged Lee's Corner; the empty hole where the restaurant had been. Both north and south of Williams Lake several different fires were causing problems. One moment evacuees were told to go north to Prince George, the next they were steered south to Kamloops. The Elephant Hill Fire had blasted through Nlaka'pamux (Ashcroft Reserve), destroying many homes, and was travelling rapidly north.

The Precipice lightning strikes were about twenty kilometres east of Stuie. According to the fire websites, a steep rocky wall had steered the flames away from the river five kilometres from Fred and Monika's, and it seemed to have eased off a little. It was not moving much downriver toward Katie and Dennis.

The Central Coast Regional District was already issuing reports about the Precipice Fire. (There had been none from the CRD regarding Kleena Kleene.) The CCRD iterated that, despite a great difficulty in rounding up resources, twenty-two firefighters, three sprinkler experts and three helicopters had been deployed on the Precipice Fire. There was a heliport forty minutes down valley from Stuie, and helicopters flew back and forth over our cabins several times a day. Most of them trailed buckets and slings of equipment. Fred told me later that he had not observed them at the Precipice itself, so they must have been working closer to the bottom end of their fire at the Stillwater.

MIRIAM AND I WERE NOW WELCOMED AND COMFORTABLE IN KATIE and Dennis's beautiful home. The fire and its possible consequences, though looming large in my mind, were now remote. But we had a more immediate problem. How was Miriam going to get home?

Large stretches of Highway 20 were of no danger to anyone. Even through the fire zones it was being kept open for emergency responders and for evacuees heading east. All non-official westbound traffic, however, was blocked. This meant that I could take Miriam to Williams Lake, but I would not be allowed back home. It was possible I could arrange another ride for her, via someone who was not returning, or even the RCMP, but it would not be very useful as Williams Lake itself was now being evacuated and her bus would therefore not be running.

Two other travel options were to fly or to go by ferry. Pacific Coastal Airlines offered two flights from Bella Coola to Vancouver every day. From there, Miriam could catch a bus whose route would be well away from the fire zones. Miriam got onto the airline's website. The company offers random seats for as low as two hundred dollars, though the normal price is twice as much. When she saw that a seat for two hundred fifty dollars was available in two days' time, that seemed ideal. Darn, she had left her credit card in her cabin. By the time she had retrieved it and signed on again, the cheap seat had gone. The only place left would cost her four hundred fifty dollars. "I guess everyone's trying to get out of here as fast as they can," Katie commented.

The ferry was a sporadic service in 2017, but one was slated to leave the following day to Bella Bella, which is ninety kilometres west of Bella Coola. From there one has to go either north to Prince Rupert or south to Vancouver Island; the destination depends on which way the Inside Passage ferry is sailing. Wherever she arrived, Miriam would have to find overland transport to link her with a bus route. Either trip would take two or three days and would not be cheap. As well as the boat fares, she would also have to find food and accommodation.

The BC Ferries website is hard to fathom and Katie spent some time assisting Miriam to navigate through it. It turned out that the

Inside Passage ferry was heading north. She would arrive late in Bella Bella and leave early the following morning. She would also arrive late in Prince Rupert and have to be at the railway station early to catch the train. Where would she stay on those nights? She would need taxis to get to and from hotels. But Katie put her thinking cap on and came up with a couple of people who might help. She did not know them well, but under the circumstances... Of course everyone was delighted to accommodate a stranded traveller, and that was how Miriam was able to return to Saskatchewan. She had come to visit me for an adventure. She got one, all right—just not the kind of adventure she had expected.

The Battle Begins

PRECIPICE, JULY 14—15

ON FRIDAY, JULY 14, ROB ARRIVED EARLY AND BEGAN DROPPING BUCK-ets of water mixed with retardant in front of the fire. It had become trapped behind a bend of the Hotnarko River but was still festering in the rock bluffs above it. His efforts were concentrated on the upper edge of the front. Incident Command was intent on keeping the fire as low on the slopes as possible. Their main fear was that if it crested onto the plateau, the westerly winds would drive it toward Anahim Lake. Twenty firefighters representing one unit crew had finally arrived to fight the fire on the ground. They and an IA team of five were deployed in the Atnarko Canyon to prevent the fire from crossing to the west side of the Atnarko River. They were also battling to keep the fire from reaching the walking bridge that crossed the river at the foot of the Stillwater. We were disappointed that they were not fighting the front closest to us, but recognized that the terrain there was too difficult for a ground assault.

Over the next couple of days we continued to make minor improvements to our structural protection. The Comox Fire Rescue team laid a large loop next to four of the major Taylor Ranch buildings—extra sprinklers were added to the loop. There were ten buildings that had to be protected in all. A second line fed a large nozzle that Caleb had to manoeuvre to protect the remaining buildings, including his house, a fuel shed and the first cabin built in the valley around 1912—a lineman cabin to service the original telegraph line that connected Bella Coola to the rest of British Columbia. The sprinklers were served by one of the pumps that Lee had purchased. A second pump was connected to a large line and nozzle that Caleb had to drag around to areas not reached by the sprinklers. He complained bitterly about the way everything had been laid out. He would never have faith in the structural protection personnel from that time onward.

Caleb asked me for any spare plumbing fittings I might have. There were problems attaching the hoses borrowed from our friends in Anahim Lake to the new equipment. I threw all the fittings I had into a tub and lashed it to the ATV, then grabbed a second tub and added more short hose lengths. The ATV had been difficult to start all spring and it stalled regularly. That morning it sputtered to life. When I arrived at the Taylor Ranch, Caleb was working with one of the structural protection technicians to weld two metal fittings together to make a specialized coupler. He was focused on the repair. I sensed that his coworker was already impressed with his ingenuity so I just nodded and dumped the parts and hoses next to the work bench.

Jade had phoned a few days earlier asking if we could retrieve some important documents from her office in the Red Roof House; since I was already halfway there I decided to get the stuff. I hated being away from our farm with the fire so close and Monika all alone to defend it. A yellow smoky haze and the misfiring ATV added to my dread. The smoke thickened as I drove up the final steep hill. The normally yellow arnica that grew at the forest's edge next to the buildings glowed orange in the smoky haze as if the fire was already there. I increased the throttle on the ATV to prevent it from stalling while I rushed into the house with the two tubs. There were three accordion files, a box of papers and a camera on the shelves I had been directed to. I never bothered to try to sort anything out. I stuffed the tubs and grabbed the camera. The ATV was still running when I re-emerged into the smoke. I didn't stop at the Taylor Ranch. Both the smoke and my heart eased when I entered our first meadow.

The biggest limitations for protecting buildings threatened by wildfire is the availability of water for the sprinklers and fuel for the pumps. We and the Taylor Ranch buildings were close to the river and would have plenty of water as long as the river remained high. We had, however, only a limited amount of gas in the valley.

The Taylor house, though, was about four hundred metres away from the river, and it presented major difficulties. On the weekend of July 8 and 9, David J and Troy had dammed a spring above the Taylor house, creating a reservoir of water to supply sprinklers on the house. However, the flow from the spring was so weak that the pump had to be run at low idle to avoid drawing air. David J had completed the installation of a large water tank on his forwarder and drove it into the valley with the idea of filling it from the river and alternately hauling water to the Taylor and the Red Roof Houses. This required yet another pump.

The structural protection crew installed a twenty-thousand-litre bladder that resembled a plastic backyard swimming pool, a large Forestry pump and a loop around the Taylor's house with five sprinklers to keep it, the woodshed and a cabin that had been built in the 1920s protected. The bladder was filled from David's forwarder and the trickling spring. A barn, below the house and thirty metres away, was only poorly protected with two weak sprinklers.

By late afternoon, the crew's work shifted to the Red Roof House. It and the neighbouring shed presented serious problems. The house was a beautiful structure located on steep slopes one hundred metres above grassy meadows that had not been cut for a year. We had learned and witnessed how fires like to rage up slopes. If the Precipice Fire were to reach the dry meadows below the house,

Hoss directs David J's forwarder to the Taylor house. Photo by Fred Reid.

it would be very difficult to protect the buildings. Also, the house and shed were closely surrounded by pine and Douglas fir, and had large piles of combustible material—scrap lumber and the like—in proximity. We were amazed that the Comox crew would attempt to protect these buildings, but they welcomed the challenge. They installed another twenty-thousand-litre bladder and Forestry pump to service a loop of sprinklers. David J had to fill both the bladder and an old cistern above the house to keep everything going. If the fire was to get this far there would be only one shot at protecting this property. It would be too dangerous to go through an inferno to refill the gas or water—whichever ran out first.

The battle with the fire began to escalate. Two IA crews had established a number of helipads and a staging area in the Atnarko

Valley. Mark brought a contract for me to sign authorizing the Forest Service to use our meadow as a staging area. I gladly gave my signature and he offered me a loonie. "You have to take it," he said. "Our financial officer will insist that you have it to make the contract valid." The loonie sat on the coffee table in our porch throughout the entire summer.

A second mid-sized helicopter, which pilots and firefighters referred to as a "medium," was contracted and piloted by Randy. He and Rob began cycling in a synchronized dance over the leading edge of the fire. Rob had become more sociable and we visited whenever he had some downtime. He cautioned us that a helicopter could not put a fire out. They were only keeping it cool until they could get firefighters on the ground.

Monika and I began to feel that we were in very good hands. We were at last able to relax a little.

Back up the Hill

KLEENA KLEENE, JULY 13–18

I LOVE VISITING THE BELLA COOLA VALLEY. I HAVE BEEN FRIENDS WITH Katie and Dennis for nearly forty years and I stay with them to enjoy the wonderful spring flowers on the forest floor, and the bears. It is such a vastly different ecosystem from the Chilcotin that it is sometimes hard to believe they are both on the same planet.

The weather on this occasion was postcard perfect. The sky was blue, the mountains were majestic, the air was fresh and clear of smoke. I could not have wished for a better place to be evacuated to. I had my own cabin, communication facilities and welcoming friends.

But paradise is meaningless if you don't want to be there. Apart from the fact that I was away from home, the main disadvantage, as far as I was concerned, was having neighbours. A lodge was operating next door. When Katie and Dennis first bought their property, the lodge was laid-back and fairly quiet; now it was owned by a big business corporation and was noisy with clients and helicopters. I am not used to living within sight and sound of others. The mental freedom of being truly alone is impossible for most people to understand. I need social contact just like anyone else, but I don't function to my full emotional capacity without long periods of solitude. When people are within sight or sound of my personal space, I am always aware of them and can never properly relax.

Another problem was the dogs. They had to be tied full-time by the cabin, and walked on leads, something none of us enjoyed. I could usually let Harry loose once I got away from the buildings but Badger had to be kept on a long rope. His back legs were very stiff and not well co-ordinated, and if he fell into a hole he could not always get out of it. One time we walked on a narrow trail beside the river; Badger tried to get a drink and fell in. The bank was half a metre high; the river wide; the current swift and swirling—had it not been for the rope, I would have lost him.

Because Katie suffered from asthma and was very allergic to dogs, I never brought them inside, not even into the cabin in which I was staying. They were normally outdoor dogs, so except for being tied, this was no hardship. Sometimes I drove down valley to a logging road where Harry could get a good burst of speed. It was stinking hot, and periodically he would dive down through the forest and plunge into the river below. Apart from these jaunts, we simply trudged, tethered to each other, back and forth, several times a day, along the driveway and a short stretch of road. For many city dogs, this is all they get; for us it was tedious and frustrating.

Constant checking of the internet gave me a virtual picture of the fire, and the terror of the flames was still very fresh in my mind, but the cushioning of distance was almost worse than being in the thick of it. The websites couldn't give me a real feel for the situation. And then there was the garden. Without water, it would die. When I left home, I assumed that my abandonment would be the end of it. But the idea of a fire on my doorstep was now becoming more acceptable. Isolated by distance, it seemed less fearsome. If I were to get home soon, I might just be able to save the vegetables. As far as I could gather, the only barrier preventing people from going into the Kleena Kleene area was in the east. It had not yet occurred to the fire planners that there might be people sneaking home from the west.

On July 13, I packed everything in the hopes that I might be able to stay home, but I left early so I would have time to drive up there, turn the drip hoses on for a few hours, then drive back down before dark. The Hill was sunny but I ran into smoke fairly quickly on the Chilcotin; at first this was from the Precipice Fire, but that was fairly high and no more than a thickish haze. Through Anahim Lake, and then Nimpo Lake... From a hill not far before my turnoff, I looked down into a dense brown soup. The smell of smoke was strong; visibility was maybe two kilometres. Max.

Just past my turnoff is a bridge. A cop car was parked there. The officer was leaning in a bored way against the parapet. At seeing me coming, he roused himself. It must have been quite a while since another vehicle had come by. "Oh no," I thought. "He's going to turn me back." I didn't stop but instead dived into my driveway, waving at him as if I had permission to be there. It worked, because he gave a half wave back and subsided to his post once more.

I have only a slow trickle of water in my well. The garden is set up with drip hoses but they cannot be left running all the time. Also, there is not enough pressure to operate all the hoses at once. Usually I turn on a quarter of them at one time, running each section for an hour. I would normally spread this activity over a couple of days but this time I would run all four hoses, one after the other, and hope that the water supply lasted. The tap was outside and I started the first section immediately. It had been four days since the plants had received a drink. A lot of the early vegetables had bolted in the heat and other plants looked very wilted, but they were still alive. The poor potatoes were blackened to the ground. They would have been zapped by the frost on the night we had shivered in our vehicles at the float plane base. The frost did not kill the plants but it knocked them back. It is a struggle to grow potatoes here.

There was a steady, light wind coming from the fire area, bringing thick smoke my way. I could barely make out Internet Hill, and this confirmed my visibility estimate, but of the main mountains I could not see a thing. Somewhere up above the sun was shining, but here everything was swallowed in a dense brown fog. I removed just a small corner of the tarp covering the back porch, and ducked underneath to get inside. I set up the laptop and checked the websites—the internet was working fine now. There had been some fire growth at Kleena Kleene since I had left Stuie that morning, and new red spots were dotted about within the yellow masses, but it still looked as though it hadn't spread a great deal. However, the wind direction was not good. It was not only blowing the smoke my way, it had the potential to bring the fire closer as well.

I lifted the phone. It was working. A series of beeps told me I had a message. *This is an automated call from the West Chilcotin Search and Rescue. Evacuate now! Shut all windows and doors, turn off appliances except fridges and freezers, shut but do not lock your gate... You must evacuate NOW.*

It was dated the day I had left. I erased it and called Christoph at the guest ranch to see how he was making out. Like me, at the moment he couldn't see anything of what was going on because of the smoke. He had been a firefighter in Switzerland and was a general fix-it sort of guy. He had acquired a pump and a hose long enough to reach his lake, and was ready to set up sprinklers around his lodge. As an owner of livestock he was able to get an official licence to stay, though he wasn't supposed to move off his property without a permit specific to the day and destination of travel and to the names and number of the people riding with him.

The steady wind, the thick gloom, and the unpleasant taste of the smoke did not make me feel at all comfortable. (I was to learn later that there had been a crucial flare-up on that date.) The watering finished, I decided to go back to Bella Coola. The dogs, at least, had had a bit of freedom.

The cop was still by the bridge, and this time I drove up to him. "We're worried that the fire might cross the road," he said, "so we're stopping all traffic except first responders." I told him I had just been home to water the garden but was going back down to Bella Coola. It was not the same cop who had given me the evacuation order, and as long as I was heading away from the fire he didn't seem to care what I was doing. I left him to his contemplation of the smoke.

So back I went to Stuie. The valley was not quite so paradisiacal now as the change of wind was bringing smoke down the Atnarko from the Precipice Fire. Stupendous Mountain was hazing over and by the following morning we could barely see it. I shared the garden veg I had brought with me: Katie's garden had some salad greens and kale in it, but most of her space was devoted to an incredible crop of raspberries and what might have been a decent crop of strawberries if it hadn't been for the squirrels. Like most people who expect to grow fruit in the valley, Katie and Dennis have surrounded the garden with a pretty skookum electric fence attached to the original split cedar rails. It did a good job of keeping the bears out, but it couldn't stop the squirrels. They would run along the top rail, fat strawberries in their mouths, and stop and stare at us, knowing there was nothing we could do.

Life in the lowlands got back into its routine. Picking raspberries, dog walking, surfing the internet. The USDA Forest Service map showed the yellow blob of the Kleena Kleene Fire had indeed crossed the highway, but DriveBC—although it had four specific closure locations for Highway 20—showed none there. Everyone I contacted in my area had heard nothing about it. I assumed it was because the USDA satellite recorded heat. It was very likely, given the wind direction, that the heat had certainly crossed the road, even if the fire itself had not.

Katie and Dennis were well aware that though their property was in a safe zone at the moment, things might not stay that way. They'd had pretty close encounters with fires in the past. They needed to make their buildings more fire-smart. The cabins were dwarfed by the giant trees—very attractive aesthetically, but in a crowning fire, the buildings would be gone in a flash. Something could be done to help prevent a ground fire taking hold, however. Although the cabin roofs were all metal, fallen branches and needles had accumulated on them, at times so thick that the metal could not be seen. Not all the buildings had eavestroughs, but those that existed were choked. So we got up there with ladders and rakes, and slowly pulled all the debris down. Despite the steep slope of the roofs, the mats of needles had stuck quite hard, and they often needed scrubbing to remove. Not easy while standing on a ladder and working with extra-long-handled tools. Then the debris had to be raked away from the cabin walls. Katie started to pile some of that using the wheelbarrow but there was really nowhere to put it. A large pile of incendiary matter would also be a danger.

During an email exchange while trying to find out what was happening at Kleena Kleene, an interesting bit of information popped up. I was told to get hold of the Tatla Lake Command Centre. This was the first I'd heard of such a group. The phone number that my contact gave me was for the motel.

"Tatla Lake Command Centre," said a voice. I recognized Karin Sartre. I told her that I was in Bella Coola and that I was planning to go home periodically to water the garden. "That's fine," she said. "Because we have such a low population here, it is easy to keep track of people. As long as we know where you are, that's all we need. I have your Kleena Kleene number; give me your Bella Coola number. Let us know if you go home, and let us know if you leave again."

This was great news. I had been down at Stuie for another four days. The weather there was a cloudy, smoky and a bit drizzly. The forecasts showed no cloud or rain expected on the Chilcotin, but damp air masses rarely cross the mountains. Many times I have started to drive up the Hill in rain or falling snow, and ended in sunshine. Karin confirmed that there had been no sign of precipitation at Tatla. She also confirmed that the fire had not crossed the road, though it had touched it in a couple of places. "Stay safe," she said as she signed off. It was the first time I had heard that expression, but it was to become the signature to every activity connected with the fire. It was the new *Have a nice day.*

The drizzle stopped overnight and the morning of July 18 was clear and sharp in the Bella Coola Valley. Just above the bottom of the Hill, one normally has a good view up the Atnarko River trench, where its course veers away from the road. I used to hike along there to reach my first cabin at Lonesome Lake. On this day, however, the trench was absolutely clogged with smoke, even though the tops of the mountains above it were clear. No doubt when the day warmed and the air stirred, the smoke would be spread around again.

Along the Chilcotin, the smoke was already thick and the filtered light had an orange cast. Swaths of foxtail barley lining the road had sprouted into a mass of feathers that were burnished bronze in the eerie light. Red clumps of Indian paintbrush glowed like coals.

I phoned both Katie at Stuie and Karin at the Tatla Command Centre to inform them I was home. I started the watering routine, opened the windows of the house, and settled down to enjoy the feeling of being in my own space again. It was so peaceful. No logging trucks on the highway, only the distant drones of two helicopters. Birds were still singing. Many of the migrants quit vocalizing around the middle of July when they concentrate their energies on rearing their broods, but white-crowned sparrows were still performing their plaintive little airs, song sparrows were whistling and warbling, and a few hummingbirds buzzed around the newly filled feeder. There were not as many as usual, for the males had already taken off for their bachelor parties, and several birds would have moved on because the feeder had not been kept topped up. I marvelled that all these creatures were calmly going about their daily lives, oblivious to the drama around them. It was a sobering perspective on the human animal's place in the scheme of things.

Smoke hazed the air around home, but it was much thicker over the fire area. The two helicopters working over it were perfectly audible but invisible. I could, however, see a few of the mountains directly across the river from me: Finger Peak, an old volcanic core; Middle Mountain (it probably has an official name but I don't know what it is); and Mount Nogwon.

The watering done, I thought I'd drive closer to the fire and try to see what was going on. There was no cop by the bridge this time. The smoke grew thicker toward downtown Kleena Kleene and soon I was ensconced in a thick brown gloom through which the white flowers of the Russian chamomile along the roadside gleamed weirdly. Normally they would have been mowed by now, but none of that kind of activity was going on.

The red-tailed hawk was gone from his perch, but just past the hay meadows, where the forest drew close to the highway again, a bunch of ravens were frantically cawing and wheeling. Ground fire was smouldering there, throwing up a bunch of smoke. Something must have died; whether it had succumbed to the fire or other causes was impossible to know. It must have been quite a large something, for there were at least a dozen scavengers. The ravens swooped down then shrieked as they charged up again, wings windmilling. They were desperately trying to get a feed, but it was obviously too hot for them. They weren't about to give up this largesse unless they absolutely had to, however. I imagined their feathers singeing as they dived and screamed.

I drove cautiously on through the end-of-the-world gloom. The two helicopters were very close now, their battering rattle plain over the noise of my van's motor. Where the forest reached the road, a rough, sandy scar had been newly bulldozed parallel to the highway. Up and down the contours of the land it snaked. The bare earth would easily be jumped by a strong blaze, but it would stop a ground fire. The road climbed a small hill. At the top was a tiny, shallow pond in which, several years ago, some wag had put a sign that said *Wreck Beach*. (That is the name of a naturist beach in Vancouver.) A less likely place for one to want to strip off is hard to imagine. The water recedes to the centre during the summer and the shores are bottomless sludge. And the bugs! However, there was apparently enough water for a helicopter's bucket. The rotors clattered loudly, the machine swayed into view through the smoke and squatted to lower its bucket. This close, the bucket was huge. As the heli climbed, the bucket swung like a pendulum toward me; I had a sudden horror of being sideswiped by it; full of water, it was big and heavy enough to knock my van clean across the road.

Of course I should not have been there. The last thing firefighters needed was a tourist to watch out for. I was utterly amazed that the pilots could find their way to do any meaningful work with such poor visibility. The wind was getting up a bit, too. It would add tremendously to the difficulty of their work.

Back home, though the wind was strengthening, it was still blowing the fire away from my house. I began to think that it might be possible to spend the night. But there was a phone message waiting for me. I was advised to call the Tatla Command Centre forthwith.

"You've got to get out of there," said Karin, her voice breaking with emotion. "The fire's getting away from them. They don't think they can prevent it from crossing the road this time. You have to meet at staging in Peter Weiler's yard. Then everyone will be escorted to Williams Lake."

"Peter Weiler's!" I exclaimed. "But I would have to go right through the fire to get there." I thought guiltily of my illicit drive into the fire zone—I had indeed been very close to the danger point. "Surely it makes much more sense for me to go to Bella Coola."

Karin didn't know where I lived. People east of Kleena Kleene rarely have reason to come this way; sometimes I think they look on my area as their *ultima Thule*. I heard Karin confer with someone else in the centre. "OK, we'll put you down as going to Bella Coola," she said. "Stay safe!" Her voice still shook with the drama.

I hadn't unpacked anything except the laptop. I stopped long enough only to grab more veggies and re-secure the tarp over the porch. Harry, my younger dog, didn't want to get in the van. He knew he would be subject to a hateful life on a lead once more. It took a few minutes to catch him. As I hurtled out onto the driveway I was almost run down by an SUV coming the other way. It contained a couple of local Search and Rescue (SAR) members. "We just wanted to make sure you're leaving," they stated. Everyone seemed just below panic level. And yet the fire was still being blown away from me and wasn't a problem to Tatla yet. Only a few properties, which lay directly in the path of the fire, would be in serious danger. It occurred to me that the occupants of the car would have had to drive right through this zone to get to me. "I'm on my way," I said resignedly. And back down the Hill I went.

Back Burning

PRECIPICE, JULY 15—19

EVACUATION ALERTS OR ORDERS WERE ISSUED THROUGHOUT BRITISH Columbia almost daily. Highways 97 and 20 were constantly closed, with only emergency or essential service vehicles allowed through. Homes had been lost and cattle had died or been forced out of their summer ranges. The province was setting up programs to help ranchers. We got a call from the British Columbia Ministry of Agriculture offering assistance if needed. The federal government was adding the military and other federal assistance to the province, which was now declared to be in a state of emergency. The Red Cross was activating relief programs and the province offered six hundred dollars per household that was required to evacuate. (We were not much interested in this.)

Lee Taylor was desperately trying to increase his strength from the spring accident by doing physiotherapy, and at the same time he was working through the Cattlemen's Association to get a pass so he and Pat could travel north through the various roadblocks between Vancouver and the Precipice.

Adding to our emotional turmoil was word that Katie, the volunteer who had been relocated to Anahim Lake, now had to go back home to England for medical reasons. Katie was enthusiastic, fun and above all, dedicated to those around her. She and Tabi had arranged their second trip to the Precipice three years ago. Their plans had been severely interrupted when Katie suffered an injury at work in England. A shelf loaded with heavy boxes gave way, falling on her head. The concussion that resulted was not immediately apparent and she continued working. Symptoms of confused words and disorientation became apparent later. As her situation deteriorated, Katie took her complaint to the company and government compensation board. The company intimidated her fellow workers and they said there had been no such accident at work. She was denied any compensation or help from the company or government. Katie and Tabi struggled for two years to overcome the effects of the head injury. When they felt Katie was safe and well enough, they had purchased tickets to Vancouver and Anahim Lake. They had been in the valley for only four days when the Precipice Fire started. Although she was perfectly safe up at Anahim Lake, the stress had caused Katie once again to develop signs of disorientation and confused speech. She and Tabi had invested a lot of money and time for their trip to British Columbia only to have it ripped away by the fire. Their foreign status made them ineligible for compensation. Their story was one of hundreds of similar instances in which people's lives were disrupted at this time.

For a while, the fire remained quiet with only two helicopters continuously dropping water in front of it. We were told constantly that helicopters can't put a fire out, only mother nature or ground crews could do that, so we were delighted to hear that a second unit crew of twenty firefighters had arrived from Pemberton. They began working on a fireguard ahead of the front that was creeping toward us, but we would have both unit crews only for a couple of days, because the first was preparing to transition out.

There was talk of a back burn. A back burn is one of the most controversial methods of fighting a wildfire. The firefighters establish a guard in front of the fire and then start a controlled burn toward it by hand lighting or dropping flames from a helicopter. The man-made blaze is designed to establish a large fuel-free zone. Many back burns are completed successfully, but if they go wrong, they can be disastrous.

Arlen was dropped into the forest near the historic Sugar Camp Trail. He hoped to expand the trail to create a guard for the back burn.

The Sugar Camp Trail is one of many grease trails that were used by the Ulkatcho and Nuxalk First Nations as a trade route between the coast and BC's interior. The Ulkatcho supplied dried moose, deer meat, animal pelts and obsidian (volcanic glass for making arrowheads) to the coast, and brought back fish products—one being the much-prized fermented oolichan oil. The oil was carried in woven cedar baskets that leaked, leaving a greasy ribbon along the path, and these routes became known as grease trails. With the arrival of early white settlers and gold seekers, the Sugar Camp Trail became an important pack train route. I have heard various stories of how the trail got its name, but my favourite is Clayton Mack's description in *Ulkatcho Stories of the Grease Trail*: when a pack horse of Antone Capoose's brushed against a tree, causing a small rip in a hundred-pound sack of sugar, then the sugar dribbled out all the way up the hill.

Monika and I honoured the history of this trail, and we worked every year to keep it clear of windfall—an onerous task after the pine bark beetle killed so many trees a decade ago.

The twenty firefighters frantically worked on the fuel-free guard next to the Sugar Camp Trail as the fire bubbled through the rock bluffs to our northwest. Helicopters flew in pumps, cans of fuel, bladders, hoses and sprinklers to dampen and protect the guard. Two helicopters dropped tons of water mixed with retardant on the hottest spots to prevent the fire from reaching a large area of dry forest.

If the fire got into these fuels it would rapidly advance onto the guard and the people working on it.

The Coastal Wildfire Service had a weather specialist stationed at its head office in Parksville on Vancouver Island. He accessed weather information from as far away as a service in Norway. He was in contact with IC by video calls when modelling fire behaviour and forecasting weather. This synopsis was an important part of all Incident Action Plans (IAPs), which contained briefings of the fire's activity and the co-ordinated plan to fight it. New IAPs were printed daily. They were small booklets containing weather synopses; communication information; command structure; safety tips; and forms for describing individual encounters with the fire. IAPs were considered confidential but Monika and I craved them in our attempt to learn about the fire.

Although we were unaware of much of the complexity of the fight against the fire at the time, we were entranced by the battle. We made a point of having coffee and fresh strawberries always available for the firefighters and helicopter pilots who had to be on the ground for their scheduled downtime. Our screened porch became a haven away from the mosquitoes and blackflies that persisted in our meadows. We listened intently to the communications over the radios that our visitors held, and watched the airborne helicopters circle as they delivered a constant stream of water against the fire. Everything seemed to be going according to a well-thought-out master plan. As our building protection improved and cooler temperatures stalled the fire, we were lulled into a false sense of security.

But the fire was oblivious to those fighting it. Like water or wind, it was seeking the path of least resistance. In the afternoon heat of July 16 it dramatically opened up a second front. It had found some dry fuel on the south side of the Hotnarko Canyon and rapidly climbed the slopes. Its plume of smoke was instantly huge and it continued to grow at an amazing speed as it arched with the wind.

It was heading toward Telegraph Creek (named for the telegraph line established in 1912). Our complacency was shattered. We were threatened anew, worried now that the fire might close in from both sides of the valley. I could not determine how far away the fire was by the size of its plume. Large plumes always seemed closer than they were. The direction of the smoke trail was more important—I was relieved that this one trailed away toward Charlotte Lake rather than coming directly overhead.

Arlen and Mark did not seem concerned. They had a contingency plan involving reopening an old guard installed to protect the Anahim Lake and Nimpo Lake communities from the 2004 Lonesome Lake Fire if our fire moved rapidly toward these communities from the south side of our valley, but they didn't have the resources to fight it at this time. They were concentrating on the preparation of the back burn to our northwest.

That evening we were confident that the fire was contained for the night, so we accepted Caleb's invitation for supper. We thought all the flying had finished, but when we were halfway through the meal and darkness was falling, we heard a helicopter pass low over the valley. We guessed that it was descending toward our place. We became anxious that we were missing some important news and returned home immediately.

The helicopter had left, but a note from Arlen was on our door. He had been concerned that we would be nervous about the flare-up and he had called in to ensure us that everything was under control. But we also had a big shock, for we found Fossie, one of our dogs, dead in front of the door. She had died only minutes before. She lay on her side as if falling over in mid-step. Old and faithful, it was her time. I was relieved to see no signs of pain in her limbs or face. We curled her into a sleeping position inside a box. She looked as pretty as ever. Both missing Arlen's visit and finding Fossie accelerated our growing anxiety.

A week of cool night temperatures had helped to keep the fire at bay. That night it dropped to three degrees Celsius. I awoke, still feeling uneasy, but was grateful that I was spared the worst of the smoke that had been settling overnight. Fossie would normally be lying at the base of our stairs. I would miss her more on future mornings but today I was up early to bury her, eager to have the task done before the chaos of the coming day.

In response to several messages of concern on Facebook, I wrote, "It is a waiting game. We are under evacuation order. If we leave we are not allowed to come back—although I imagine that we could sneak in and out of Anahim Lake if we wanted to. We have been told not to expect the order to be lifted for another four weeks at the least. This is very disappointing news."

We tried to keep busy with our daily routine—milking the cow, weeding the garden and picking strawberries—but it was tough to keep focused on menial tasks. We had lots of food of course but our propane was getting low. After an unusually wet fall last year, the culverts on our bush road had plugged with ice. The spring runoff in May and early June had eroded many portions and severely washed out a thirty-metre stretch. Using a shovel and grub hoe I had been able to make a path wide enough for a small vehicle, but our trips to town had been greatly restricted. We had never managed to get into Anahim Lake to have our propane tanks filled. Amid the smoke and heat with a wildfire approaching, it was surreal to think of washed-out roads. We had the option of taking one of Lee's or Jade's tanks if we actually ran out.

As the time for the back burn approached, we were on the edge of our seats. IC brought in a seasoned pilot to do it. He was grey haired, crusty and distant. After a brief introduction, he returned to his helicopter and pulled out a lawn chair, placing it in the shade of his machine, to wait until the conditions were right. Back burning is a very exact science. For it to work properly, temperatures have to be high enough, humidity must low enough and of course the winds have to be just right.

Throughout the day the unit crew worked on the fuel-free line next to the Sugar Camp Trail setting up sprinklers and laying hose while two helicopters bucketed water between them and the fire. Another helicopter freighted in eight barrels of fuel and stashed them on our meadow. Four more were dropped at staging in the Atnarko Valley at the lower end of the fire. By 4:00 p.m., Mark felt that conditions were right. The unit crew was airlifted off the line. Meanwhile three firefighters were on standby in our yard, preparing the barrels and a gun that ignites the fuel as it leaves the barrels.

Mark took to the air to fly above and direct the pilot doing the fuel drops (no one other than the pilot is allowed in a helicopter towing a sling—especially a sling full of fire starter). All other helicopters were grounded. At 4:20 the first barrel was lifted off our meadow on the end of a long line. The pilots and remaining firefighters returned to our porch to watch the show. We made popcorn and coffee to supplement the ever-present strawberries. Our porch was packed as we listened intently to the communications between Mark and the grey-haired pilot. Releasing the ignited fuel, they coaxed the back burn toward the head of the Precipice Fire. We could see the flames drop toward the forest on some of the helicopter's passes. Ten to twelve barrels were used to draw the back burn from the guard to the fire itself. As the flames came together, the combined heat created the desired thermal updraft. The fires exploded into a huge orange, black and grey column. Mark's helicopter hovered close to the crown of the plume and we heard his announcement that the back burn had been successful. The operation had taken nearly six hours. A young female firefighter, who had been connecting the fire-gun to the fuel barrels, had to call for permission to override safety rules and be flown back to Bella Coola after dusk. It was nearly 10:00 p.m. when she left.

Ash fell in the night and we were blanketed by thick smoke all morning. It took a couple of attempts before Arlen could get to us. Eventually he was able to circle wide around the fire and approach our place from the east. It was too smoky to put people on the ground near the fire, but Arlen hoped that visibility would improve before long and they could have a closer look.

The back burn might have been a success from the aerial point of view, but hidden by the veil of smoke, the fire stubbornly gnawed at the guard, burning hoses in a couple of places. This shut down the sprinklers and allowed the fire to work its way across the guard. David P, head of the unit crew from Pemberton, was warned that some of their caches of equipment might be affected. He shrugged, grumbling that this might be his worst loss ever. He wished he'd had a few more hours to strengthen the defences. But on the whole he had the same relaxed attitude as Arlen, and shared many stories with us. He had driven through sixteen checkpoints (representing eight fires) on his trip from Pemberton to Bella Coola to join the fight against our fire.

The thick smoke persisted through July 18. The fire was like that. There were days that you would look west and there would be no smoke, no evidence that there was a fire at all. On other days there would be a single giant plume as if the fire was stationary and in one small area. Then there were days like this, when the area was blanketed and the fire could have been anywhere. The IAP for July 18 estimated the fire to be around one thousand hectares, but there was no way of knowing for sure because of all the smoke.

Daytime highs of twenty-five degrees and minimum relative humidity of 18 per cent were approaching the highly dangerous "30/30/30": when afternoon temperatures above thirty degrees with relative humidity below 30 per cent combined with winds of over thirty miles (approximately fifty kilometres) per hour result in highly volatile wildfire conditions. Arlen kept reassuring us but the synopsis was not good. The smoke was predicted to persist. Only the forecasted mild winds were in our favour. By the afternoon two helicopters were able to drop water in front of the fire, but the situation was deteriorating.

Many well wishes flooded to us over the internet about the loss of Fossie. We began to realize that a large community of support was following our ordeal. By late afternoon I posted about the back burn and its consequences, and added that the Beaver Lady Cabin was probably gone. This was a small, one-room, pioneer structure near Sugar Camp Creek built in the 1930s for a baroness from the Netherlands. The baroness got her nickname because she wanted to re-establish beavers in the area. The cabin was used periodically into the 1970s but remained a relic of the past with its candles, hand-crafted wooden table, pot-belly stove, weak spring cots and old tools. When we discovered it a few years ago, the roof had withstood most of the rain, but the walls and floor sagged badly.

Caleb's frustration with the structural protection around the ranch continued. The bladders at both the Taylor house and the Red Roof House had leaks. They were able to repair the tear in the Taylors' bladder but would have to replace the other. The crew came in daily and ran the sprinklers. Caleb felt this was unnecessary. David J had to make many trips with his forwarder to refill everything. On one trip he forgot to disconnect the intake hose as he pulled away from the river. The hose caught on some branches and ripped a coupler apart. It was a tricky weld for Caleb to fix. The thick smoke, Caleb's grumbling and the lack of progress on fighting the fire led to a long, disappointing day.

The fire continued to creep among the rocks at night. New helipads were being built in an attempt to get a unit crew near enough to fight the fire on the ground. The nightly descent of smoke prevented them from getting in early but by the afternoon of July 19 the air quality improved and everyone seemed much more optimistic because they could actually work. They seemed to be throwing everything at the fire, but that one lost day proved to be critical. Other fires in the Chilcotin were raging so viciously that helicopters and ground crews were of no use to them, so IC seized the opportunity to engage as many of both as they could for the Precipice. They concentrated on the hills nearest us, keeping the fire at a distance of two kilometres, trying to steer it farther north. The terrain was deemed too difficult for work on the ground. Along the Atnarko River, the unit crew had contained the fire and they maintained that the Tweedsmuir Provincial Park walking bridge was protected. IC began developing plans to deploy these firefighters to our southwest.

AS HARD AS THEY TRIED TO FIGHT IT, THE FIRE FOUGHT BACK. THERE were now major plumes rising from many locations and it was spreading aggressively. When the smoke cleared enough to allow aircraft to fly its perimeter, they found the fire had more than doubled in size to twenty-five hundred hectares. David P from the structural protection unit was able to get into the helipads close to the back burn, which contained the pumps, gas, hoses and sprinklers. Although they had lost a lot of equipment it was not as bad as he had first thought.

Four helicopters bucketed the fire from noon until dusk. They worked in pairs, attacking the fire on two fronts. Because of the fire's advance, they were now getting water from lakes nearer to us and we could hear the constant pounding of the machines. A fifth helicopter had to fly above them to monitor and co-ordinate the traffic. At one point one of the pilots became agitated by the amount of traffic, deeming it too dangerous, and pulled out of the cycle to fly to Anahim Lake.

The expression "two steps forward and one step back" seemed appropriate, but it felt more like one step forward and two back, because near dusk we saw flames for the first time. Trees candled as the fire moved in from the southwest. I posted on Facebook: "It is approaching Telegraph Creek. Another old cabin exists there—it is bound to be lost. So far we have concentrated all our emotional energies on the north side. Now this."

Pat added from her watchpost in Vancouver: "Winds are due in tonight. Rain may come, too, but no guarantees. Lee and I watch and wait from our urban distance. Wishing everyone a much needed reprieve."

The Fascination with Firefighting

PRECIPICE, JULY 20–22

DURING THE NIGHT OF JULY 19 THERE WAS A VIOLENT THUNDERSTORM. We worried about more lightning strikes but were delighted when we began to hear the rain pelting our roof. Mark had installed a rain gauge on his second visit to our valley. I got up very early and messaged Arlen and Mark: "seven millimetres of rain last night!"

"Thanks, Fred," Arlen quickly responded. "That changes our strategy… I was feeling pretty deflated until this email. You made my day."

We had heard a lot of criticism of the BC Wildfire Service and how they fight fires. Some of the people of Anahim Lake were getting impatient with the fire and made accusations that those fighting it were just farming the fire. Many people thought they were not fighting it at all because it was in a provincial park. These comments trickled through to us, causing some dismay, because we saw nothing but the firefighters' dedication to protecting us with the limited resources they had. News services enjoy highlighting dissatisfaction, and they dwelled often on conflict between the public and the Wildfire Service. Since the beginning of the fires, I had been shaken by such negative comments. Statements about lack of communication, poor management, out-of-control back burns and the reticence in using local resources were common. Our experience was very different. We understood and accepted the work the professional firefighters were doing, and received copious information from Mark and Arlen. We were learning so much about fighting wildfires—the utility of helicopters, the mechanics of a back burn, the risks to firefighters on the ground.

Our place had become the major staging area and was a hive of helicopter activity. Helicopters were guaranteed a minimum of four hours' airtime and the IC tried to share it equitably. We welcomed the pilots who were grounded during the day and fed hungrily on their stories of past battles and strange encounters. Monika and I were very happy with the Coastal Fire Centre and the Incident Command.

David J phoned to ask about the rain. He was concerned about the flames we had seen on the south side of the Hotnarko Canyon. He had lived in the Precipice for three years and had hiked to more places than most. He knew the area well and felt that the rain would give them a chance to put a fireguard on our south flank parallel to Telegraph Creek to block the flare-up from a couple days before.

I emailed Arlen with David J's proposal. "There is an old road above our place that leads to Telegraph Creek and a trail that goes next to the creek for a ways. David J thinks there is maybe a chance for a fireguard there. I cleared the road a while back but have not been up there for three years. David says he wants to get in there and fight that thing."

Arlen responded. "Thanks Fred for the update, I passed on the info to Mark and he said that he is aware of that area. Please do not let David 'get in there.' After what I've been seeing the past couple days it is way too dangerous for anybody. Also, I went for a quick flight this morning and couldn't see anything because of the smoke, I will try again at 11:00 and stop in. Take care and see you soon."

The bucketing helicopters started to roll in at 2:00 p.m., another late start because of a mixture of fog from the new moisture and smoke from the constantly smouldering fire. Arlen came by in the early afternoon and for the first time he tried really hard to convince us to leave. The fire was very large now, and displaying a lot of erratic behaviour. Even with the rain they had lost control of most of it. Flames were again creeping along the Atnarko Trench and they had to redeploy twenty firefighters to prevent it from crossing the river and surging up the steep slopes to the west (a priority for BC Parks). The IC was struggling to model what the fire was doing and to develop a plan to fight it. They were now besieged on many fronts and we worried that they might have to divert their attention to other areas of the fire. Arlen consoled us somewhat with the assurance that protecting us and our property was a priority. He also had some good news. The Beaver Lady Cabin was still standing.

By the end of the day over ten millimetres of rain had fallen. The last helicopter left for Anahim Lake at 9:00 p.m. The fire remained active but it settled for the night.

Although one could never rely on it, the saving grace for VA0778 was that it continued to burn at an elevation below the strong winds of the plateau. It sputtered mostly on the ground. Helicopters were effective at keeping it cool and directing it to areas of lesser harm, but it was now nearly two weeks since we first reported the fire, and there were still only twenty-five firefighters on the ground. Meanwhile, by July 18, professional firefighters were starting to arrive at the Puntzi fire camp between Tsi Del Del and Tatla Lake, to fight the Kleena Kleene Fire. We still had a growing faith in the Coastal Fire Centre and the professional firefighters but shared their frustration with the inability to obtain more resources to battle the expanding fire.

I woke early after a night of bad dreams. Since the rain, I had begun communicating morning weather reports to the Wildfire Centre in Bella Coola as well as directly to Mark and Arlen. The morning was beautiful—no smoke, no wind, no firefighters and no helicopters. Birds were singing. I vaguely wondered if they sang every morning or had I been too involved with the fire to notice. Maybe I was just up earlier than usual. The low sun's light was filtered through a haze of smoke, magnifying the beauty of the valley. But though I recognized its wonder, it was not enough to bring me out of my funk as I trudged toward the rain gauge.

Upon my return, there was a message from Mark. "Good morning Fred. Today is Arlen's last day, and David P will be taking over for him. If you could include your morning, and any afternoon/evening weather updates to everyone listed above that would be greatly appreciated. I will also be transitioning out Sunday afternoon, and Kate M will be taking over the IC [Incident Commander] role. I will be flying up shortly and having a visit with both you and Monika to ensure you have a formal introduction. The phone number here at the office is ***-***-**** if you need to get hold of myself or Kate M. Kind Regards."

I had come to rely on Mark and Arlen's leadership so this news was disheartening. But I made no mention of my feelings when I emailed Arlen: "Cloud cover is relatively high, no smoke, calm, ten degrees. No rain in the night. Getting more calls from local people wanting to come down and fight that thing."

"Thanks Fred. We are having discussions right now on how to utilize local help but it's challenging from a safety and supervision perspective. I'll be out there by around 10:00."

I struggled to stay positive throughout the morning. I felt that we were on the cusp of losing something special, be it the Precipice itself, trust in the Wildfire Service, or loss of local friends—the latter because they disagreed with our defence of the Wildfire Service.

It was a hectic day. Helicopters were flying in and out. We were introduced to many new people. Two members of the RCMP arrived on ATVs—just doing a check in. They brought Monika, Caleb and me treats of candy bars, beef jerky and cashews. They were surprised that the air in the Precipice was less smoky than at Anahim

Monika poses with Arlen, the initial operations chief for the Precipice Fire. Note the two radiophones—a common feature with operations chiefs. Photo by Fred Reid.

Lake. They didn't ask us to leave. We knew it was frustrating for ranchers and other resource people who wanted to move around the interior of British Columbia. The RCMP were responsible for people in an evacuation zone and thus received a lot of the public's scorn. However, they were so nice to us and we felt privileged by their kind gestures toward us.

By the late afternoon I was able to pull partway out of my funk and tried to sort out the conflicting ideas about fighting wildfires. Anahim Lake folks were supportive and so anxious to help. They were in the Cariboo Regional District and frustrated by all the news—or lack of it—about the fires; they did not have the close communication with the Wildfire Service that we did. I felt we were undeserving of so much attention. I buried my internal conflict in what had now become a nightly Facebook post: "The news—what can I say about the news—just 'fuck off' I guess. So much on the negative. So sensational. Still only twenty-five firefighters on the ground and we have not met many of them. They will be rotating out soon. We are very grateful to them because they are truly the front line. Arlen and David P are hopeful that we could be up to forty ground crew by next week. The fire was very quiet today. Cool temperatures and high humidity with a little bit of rain is doing wonders. Five helicopters dropped water and retardant on two hot areas of the fire, one being the front nearest to us. The last helicopter to leave dropped its water bucket on our meadow at 7:50 p.m."

We had a tearful goodbye with Arlen. Somehow I managed to hold it together. We loaded him up with strawberries, cheese and fresh milk. He was able to squeeze Monika in on one of the flights to monitor the fire. She was so surprised and excited that she forgot to take a camera.

The Soaker

KLEENA KLEENE, JULY 22−24

THIS TIME, MY STAY DOWN THE VALLEY WAS A LITTLE DIFFERENT. AT first the sky was merely dull above the smoke but then dark areas of the mountains visible through the murk took on the sullen bluish cast of impending precipitation. Soon the first drops fell. Rain takes a while to filter through the tall, dense trees here, rather like one of those toys where a small ball starts at the top and gradually zigzags down, until it finally rattles into a container. The branchy baffles also make it impossible to know when the rain has actually stopped. The last drop is released some time after a shower has ceased.

The rain settled the smoke somewhat, but clouds clogged the valley, giving only vapour-swirled glimpses of the valley walls. On the third day of my stay, the rain was more noticeable. Not heavy, but steady. Even the Chilcotin forecast was for a 30 per cent chance of showers. I phoned the Tatla Lake Command Centre. "Any rain up there?" I asked.

"Is there ever!" Karin exclaimed excitedly. "We've got a real soaker."

I wasted no time returning home again. The bottom of the Hill was choked with fog—hard to tell if it was still actually raining—but this time the lack of visibility was due to water vapour instead of smoke. At the top of the Hill I drove into a landscape lidded with heavy, grey clouds, beneath which the air was completely clear. It had stopped precipitating, but the evidence was everywhere—puddles on the road and wet-looking cows. (These animals were not fire refugees; the area west of Tatla Lake is open range. There are no roadside fences and it is normal to see cattle along the road in summer.) I wondered if I would run into smoke closer to home, but even the area around Kleena Kleene was clear.

Before turning into my driveway, I drove to downtown Kleena Kleene. Every ridge above the hayfields was sharply delineated. Where we had seen the flames in the dark on July 7 was now starkly black and brown. The burn stretched for a considerable distance on either side of the original strikes, but between it and the hay meadows, a lot of the forest was still green. After all that wind and smoke roaring back and forth so furiously for so long, it seemed amazing that large patches of unburned forest could still remain. The fire was far from out, however. Wisps of smoke trailed up from green patches as well as the burned areas, and several columns rose from the ridges behind. Farther east, more puffs spiralled. The fire had covered a considerable area, but in only a few places had it got close to the road. I drove past the hay meadows (no cawing ravens now; the creature they had been so desperately trying to get at had been either eaten or consumed by the flames). At the east edge of the fire, extensive fireguards had now been dug on both sides of the highway, one of them wider than the road itself. In some places logs had been piled; these short, skinny Chilcotin trees presumably had some marketable value and would be collected later. One or two pockets of standing browned trees touched the fireguard. No doubt the huge efforts from firefighters as well as the guard itself had prevented the fire from crossing the highway.

Our evacuation order was still in place so I didn't travel farther east. I would have run into the roadblock that had been steadfastly manned at the other end of the fire, at the exact spot, ironically, where I had smelled smoke while driving home in the dark on July 7. Bridges make good spots for roadblocks; no one can sneak around.

So home I went, and opened the windows to the sweet air and birdsong. The garden soil was marvellously wet, the vegetable leaves spangled with water; no extra watering was necessary. It was July 22. Fifteen long days after the fire had started, I was, for the first time, able to feel positive about the whole situation, and had the wonderful anticipation of being able to stay in my own bed for the night.

The next day, I walked onto the north dunes where Miriam and I had gone on day two of the fire. It was still cloudy with not much wind and I could see a considerable distance. The increased elevation revealed one or two more puffers, and there was a haze hovering between the two ridges that bracketed the valley of Colwell Creek. I could hear helicopters constantly, but I could not spot them until a gleam of sun broke through and there was a heliographic flash as a machine turned toward its target. There were two of them, wheeling to a water source, bobbing down behind a ridge then flying back to where they were emptying their buckets. They were probably about twelve kilometres away.

The rufous hummingbirds were thoroughly enjoying their newly filled feeder. The young had now hatched; they would all start tanking up, ready to begin their journey south. They generally left the second week of August. The rain had filled my pond. It was very unusual to see it brimming over in summer. It often dried up completely in hot weather.

The wind stayed quiet, but smoke thickened the air the following day when I went up the south dunes to get a different perspective of the fire. A bald eagle, in the solid brown plumage of its first year, sat on its nest in a dead cottonwood. I wondered if it would survive. Not because of the fire; as long as it wasn't consumed, it would probably weather the smoke. But on the very day the fire started, I found a fresh-killed adult on the highway near downtown Kleena Kleene. It must have been hit by one of the last logging trucks before the ban. Those guys can't afford to stop or swerve for wildlife; it would be too dangerous both for them and for any other human road users. In my hands, the eagle was huge and magnificent—most likely a female. There are scads of these birds in the Bella Coola Valley, but far fewer inland and, due to its proximity to the nest, the dead one was very likely one of the fledgling's parents. Both adults feed the young, but there was now a 50 per cent less chance of it getting a meal.

Despite the reprieve, it was hard to settle to anything. There was all sorts of work I could have done, but I could think of nothing but the fire. My brain could find no room for anything but checking websites, watching the wind and listening to the helicopters and heavy-duty trucks on the highway (it is a kilometre away but I can easily hear them) as they moved equipment. The local loggers might not be hauling any trees but all have found work driving skidders and Cats to fight the fire.

A Helicopter-Crazy Day

PRECIPICE, JULY 22–26

WE HAD TWO MORE MILLIMETRES OF RAIN OVERNIGHT. THE FIRE WAS quiet all day Saturday. The helicopters began arriving at 10:30 a.m. I stood outside as Rob landed by his bucket (each helicopter had a designated spot on our house meadow). Without stopping the propellers he went for one of the cables. "Good," I thought. "He will start bucketing water." But rather than hooking it to the base of the helicopter he threw it onto the back seats. "Oh no—he has to leave the fire and us," I thought. "He must have been called off." He waved and left the bucket. Relief. He would be back. He must have been told to haul some equipment. This was the roller coaster of emotion we were on. Everyone was very reassuring but we never knew how long they would fight our fire, or if they would be called off to go elsewhere.

It was a helicopter-crazy day. The fire was calm and conditions were right so they attacked it with the air of "we can beat this thing." We had come to recognize many of the helicopters by the various throbbings of their rotors. Randy flew a larger version than Rod—a medium. Our toaster on the windowsill would shake and bounce when he began his descent. People were everywhere and there were so many helicopters that some had to land on meadows farther from the house to avoid possible collisions. Their sound was still in the air at 9:00 p.m., though there were fewer of them as the day's battle began winding down.

David P had assumed the role of operations chief and to our relief, he was keeping us as well informed as Arlen had. We learned that he had spotted a new fire, which had puffed up between us and Anahim Lake. It was a sleeper that must have been ignited by a lightning strike from the storm a couple of days before. How dormant they can be, only to flare up once the weather warms under stronger winds! It was Rob who was dispatched with some equipment and an IA crew to deal with it. They put it out before it reached half a hectare in size. When Rob joined us on our porch the next day he described the puffer as the size of a pie plate. This is the fate of most fires in a normal fire season but if it had taken hold it could have been a disaster.

The Precipice Fire had again almost doubled in size and IC began describing it in terms of east and west divisions. The Hotnarko River was the dividing line. This confused Monika and me initially because we always talked in terms of the north or south side of the river. In fact the river flows in an almost direct southwesterly direction. So when they announced they were trying to gain control of the entire western side they were referring to the portion that burned from the Atnarko Trench to the tip of the fire that was closest to us. This was encouraging news and we began expressing optimism that VA0778 would soon be 50 per cent contained. The unit crew from Pemberton was now working at the Atnarko Trench end.

Helicopters dropped water in the area nearest to us to keep the fire on the ground. IC had hoped to put a second unit crew in this area. However, the terrain was very difficult to move around in. Instead, an IA team was dropped in the hills above Stillwater Lake to clear a helipad in preparation for an assault on the east (our "south") front. Here the fire was making a double-pronged attack, like the forked tongue of a snake. One tip of the tongue came against

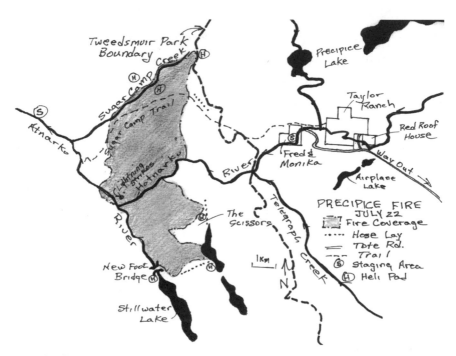

The fire spread out as it moved toward us, creating a complicated front to fight, which the IC called the "scissors." Drawn by Fred Reid.

the shore of an unnamed lake, the other jutted up to the ridges where we had noticed the flames on July 18. The IC described the irregular, jagged perimeter of this portion of the fire as a pair of scissors. David P explained that it was far too dangerous to put ground crews between the blades of the scissors, and they would have to do something about it before they could let anyone in there.

The activity in our yard was hectic, and yet we could hardly see any evidence of the fire itself. However, the fire had become more worrisome because it now had a huge perimeter in difficult terrain. It was smouldering everywhere, waiting for warm weather. They were fighting it on three fronts with five bucketing helicopters and only twenty-five firefighters on the ground. By Monday they hoped to have two unit crews (twenty firefighters each) but the Pemberton crew would be rotating out soon.

Monika and I tried to keep our lives as normal as possible with summer chores of weeding the garden, picking and processing endless strawberries (because we could not get out to sell them, we were putting what we did not give to the firefighters in the freezer), tending the greenhouse, milking cows and training our new calf to a halter.

Two fears plagued me through the course of this drawn-out ordeal: first, that Monika or I might become injured and have to leave the valley; second, that the Hotnarko River level would drop so low that we could no longer direct water onto our meadow where the pressure pump was located. In the morning I noticed the irrigation ditch had run dry. I quickly checked the culverts on a channel of the river we call "the creek." By blocking these culverts with plywood and a plastic bladder we divert water onto the meadow for irrigation. The blocks were holding, but the creek's flow had become too slow to feed the irrigation ditch. I went to where it branched from the main course of the river. It was choked with branches and leaves. I waded, waist deep, into the water and cleared the debris. At once there was a significant increase in the flow. Within an hour our pump had an adequate supply of water again.

Every wildfire fighting organization in Canada was sending people to this province. Eighteen new fires had just been reported in British Columbia, and we were heading into another warming trend. We were about to lose David P the next day with a shift change. There would be two ground crews for one day as they relayed the workload, then back to one. David P mentioned that in a normal year they would have one hundred people on the ground fighting a fire of this size but with the provincial resources stretched to the max they were unavailable. One firefighter transferred from the Riske Creek Fire told me, "It was hell there. The locals did as much as they could as the fire blew by." They were fighting it from inside the fire rather than attacking the perimeter as they were doing here.

Meanwhile, in our little valley we felt very lucky. Our fire was a bumbling fire—creeping here and bubbling there. When the lookouts stationed on Mount Marvin or flying with Helco (helicopter co-ordinator—the one that flies above the other aircraft to direct their movement) spotted flames flaring on the perimeter of the fire, a helicopter was immediately sent to bucket it. Luckily there are lots of lakes in the hills surrounding our valley. The turnaround time from one of these lakes to the fire's edge could be as little as one minute. One pilot did eighty-six turns in two and a half hours, dropping 92,000 litres of water. One of these hot spots needs to be drenched every three minutes or less, just to keep it cool. There was never the illusion that the bucketing would put it out.

That evening I posted: "Everyone we deal with is friendly and accommodating. Pilots and firefighters bring us bread and fresh fruit. They are sensitive to everything we say. When I mentioned in my morning weather report that warming dry weather means haying season and Caleb had started cutting hay in Lee's long meadow, IC was immediately concerned that their helicopters might interfere. I assured them that we would complete the haying in meadows they were not landing in and then switch meadows with the helicopters."

The Chilcotin Warriors

KLEENA KLEENE, JULY 7–27

TATLA LAKE IS FORTY MINUTES' DRIVE FROM MY HOME, BUT IT IS THE focal point of my local community. "Downtown" comprises half a dozen buildings—school, church, hall, clinic, store, motel and restaurant. It is the hub for perhaps three hundred souls scattered over an area that is maybe one and a half hours' drive from end to end. City dwellers cannot imagine referring to people who live so far apart as neighbours, but that is how we perceive ourselves. The more isolated people are, the closer are their emotional ties. Locals are attracted by this combination of physical distance and strong support. There are few of the facilities that most city dwellers take for granted—no cell phone coverage, no firefighting equipment, no close ambulance, no garbage pickup, no sewage system and, for many, no hydro power—but everyone makes their own solutions to these problems. They are independent and resourceful; they look out for their neighbours (even if they are not on speaking terms—yes, it does happen). More importantly, in times of emergency, their many talents are put to good use.

While I had been languishing in the lap of idleness in the Bella Coola Valley, the Tatla Lake community had been getting into gear. Because I was isolated from most of them by the fire itself, I was not aware of these events at the time, but later pieced together the accounts. Some of these stories don't quite mesh; it is like the Indian fable of the six blind men and the elephant. The first falls into the elephant's side and says: "It is a wall." The second touches the tusk and concludes it is a spear. The third encounters the trunk—it is a snake; the fourth the tail—it is a rope; the fifth the ear—it is a fan; and the sixth a leg—he insists it is a tree. Each and every one of us involved with these fires, including distant office workers with their computer models, could amass only a partial picture. Based on this incomplete data, conclusions were made. It was impossible for any-one to see the whole.

Mike King was there at the beginning. He was the pilot of the helicopter that bucketed the little fire north of my place on day two of the fire. He doesn't work for Forestry, but he contracts out to them. On July 7, the day of the strikes, he worked on the blaze by Lee's Corner. The Chilko River was close but in a gully, which made flying into it awkward in the strong wind, and it was also very swift. It is almost impossible to get water from a fast river—the bucket is pulled downstream and doesn't fill properly. A pond was found, but the return time was too far, the wind and the flames were too fierce, so the fire got away from them.

Forestry trains two tiers of personnel to fight fires on the ground. The more elite are those that form an initial attack (IA) crew of three to five (often referred to as the three-, four- or five-pack). They must go through rigorous training and physical tests—carrying hoses full of water, learning to use them and carrying large loads through rough terrain. They are often dropped near the fires by a helicopter.

A second tier of firefighter may work in a twenty-person unit crew (twenty-pack) which is more likely to travel by truck. Unit crews are often First Nations people. Tsi Del Del (Redstone Reserve) had such a team—they used to call themselves the "Fire Injuns" until it became politically incorrect to do so. Some unit crews are government, some are private—the latter being used more and more. One of the best of these was composed of Salish people from the Pemberton area. The younger ones on the unit crew go in first, the older, slower or heavier ones come later. They are used for jobs such as lookouts placed on high points, where they are just as important but do not need to do the heavier work.

Mike's Bell 407 can carry a max of about 825 kilograms. With that it can fly two hours at 120 knots (220 kilometres per hour). An IA crew and all its gear mustn't weigh more than 400 kilograms. The rest of the allowable freight weight is necessary for the pilot, bucket, cable and fuel. To keep the weight manageable and still get a crew of three, no firefighter must weigh more than 77 kilograms.

Usually two IA crews are made ready at the Puntzi tanker base, ten in Williams Lake. Puntzi Mountain Airport, a little bit west of Tsi Del Del, was first operated by Americans in 1951 for the Pinetree Line, part of the Distant Early Warning (DEW) Line. Management was transferred to the Royal Canadian Air Force in 1962, and the place was virtually abandoned by 1988. However, the runway that had been created was one of the longest in the country at the time and it is still the only local one suitable for heavy water bombers (or tankers). Consequently, Forestry maintains a presence; it is also home to an automatic weather station.

On day two Mike worked at Kleena Kleene. The BC Wildfire Service website had pinpointed four fires, but in fact seven strikes had flared up on that fateful day. All were lumped under the number C50744. CIFAC (Cariboo Initial Fire Attack Crew) sent two IA crews in right away.

Three strikes were near Finger Peak. These were the flames Miriam and I had seen in the dark on our way home from Williams Lake. The middle fire, which was above a cliff, was tackled first. The plan was to stop it from spilling down. There was no place to land, so Mike had to hover and drop the crew off. It was already fairly late in the day so though the firefighters managed to build a chopper pad, they had to be taken off and the fire dropped down the cliff anyway.

The westernmost strike had a landing spot close by, but the IA crew soon ran out of water, felt the fire was getting beyond them and asked to be taken off. They never did get to the third fire.

While working up there, Mike noticed more smoke across the Klinaklini River partway to Big Stick Lake. There was a place to land and another IA crew was dropped. A handy pond provided water, and that fire was put out. While working on it, Mike saw the one north of my place. He bucketed several times and then sent an IA crew in and they put it out as well. He was well aware of the danger of this one—all the others were contained by a river and road, whereas this had nothing to stop it travelling a very great way. He carried his first bucket of water from somewhere west of the highway but found ponds, mostly beaver dams, around the fire.

When up there he noticed yet another spiral of smoke north of Big Stick Lake. It was very small and he put that out by bucketing alone. For a while he was doing the rounds of all three fires.

Then the Cariboo Fire Centre near the Williams Lake Airport (not far from the three lightning strikes I had observed from the mechanic's office) was evacuated, and the infrastructure fell apart. All crews, including those based at Puntzi, were deployed on the bigger fires of the east Chilcotin. The only firefighters available in our area were an unofficial group of locals. The West Chilcotin Search and Rescue was getting them organized.

Gerald Kirby is the president, and Selma Padgett the search manager. On July 10, Gerald, Selma and Doug Schuk, Selma's husband and a veteran of forty-five years' firefighting, drove to Kleena Kleene and saw that the fire had expanded considerably, getting dangerously close to the highway.

Selma got out the search and rescue (SAR) satellite phone and started trying to reach the Cariboo Fire Centre. It took several attempts before she managed to get hold of someone who was interested in helping, and then the phone cut out. She kept calling. She was frequently told that someone would phone her back, but they never did. In the meantime, Gerald got in contact with Mike King. Forestry was far too busy elsewhere to offer much assistance at Kleena Kleene. They were well aware of Tatla's efforts to get mobilized and were concerned that so few were trained or had protective clothing. They asked Mike to keep an eye on them and make sure no one killed themselves. (Mike's words.)

Doug and several others loaded heavy machinery onto flat decks and made ready to go—but they had to wait for official permission, as the equipment would not have been covered by insurance. No one could afford to lose a hundred-thousand-dollar bulldozer. Other people were asked to round up whatever tools they had—chainsaws, water tanks, hoses, pumps, pickups, quads. The following morning, July 11, the SAR was issued a fire number—C50744. Kleena Kleene was already under evacuation order, and Tatla Lake was put on evacuation alert. (I was safely ensconced at Stuie at that time.)

Gerald and his wife, Johanna, own the Tatla Lake Manor, and they set up a command centre there. Twenty-nine volunteers, including a couple of teenagers, congregated by the nursing station helipad after lunch. Mike took Doug and three others up in the air to look at the fire and make a plan. While everyone was waiting for them to return, the clinic got a call from Interior Health that the facility had to be closed. This seemed really bizarre, as Tatla was only on evacuation *alert*. One report bandied about was that if anyone was still in the building by 4:30 p.m., they would be arrested. Patrice, our family nurse practitioner, contacted Interior Health and asked if it was OK to move out some of the equipment. (She later told me that the threat of arrest had been unfounded.) Upon being given permission, she and Dr. Rob Coetzee used the waiting firefighters' help to haul every single thing out of the clinic and take it across the road to the community hall. This became the community's clandestine clinic for the next sixteen days.

After making the firefighting plan, two Cats, two excavators and two water tenders on skidders drove to Peter Weiler's property at the south end of the fire. The men with water tanks, pumps and hoses followed them. The fire was very close to the property, but a big field in front of the house could be used for staging. Equipment was sorted and people were organized. Thus ended day one of the Tatla Lake volunteer firefighting effort.

Everyone was back to work at 5:00 a.m. A guard was constructed from a small lake east of staging, up onto the mountain behind Peter Weiler's house, and back down to another small lake next to the hayfields. To be effective, guards need anchor points, that is, places where the fire cannot creep around the ends, and both lakes would answer well. Doug Schuk drove a TD20, just smashing everything down. Earl Schuk followed with a backhoe lifting the trees out of the way. Eric Satre was third with another Cat.

Selma, Gerald, Johanna and Anne Porter, another SAR member, tried to get information from Forestry as to how they should proceed. The lines were down and communications were intermittent so this was not easy. Tatla's end of it was bad enough, but Williams Lake was being evacuated and was barely functioning as well. The power was out for six days; Gerald kept the motel going with a generator and propane, and by various means kept communications flowing. One job was to field calls from people who were frightened about the proximity of the fire—even though they were in fact a good distance away. Most of these were strangers who had vacation cabins and had never experienced a fire situation before. Time had to be found to reassure them.

A couple of local people happened to be qualified first-aid attendants, and Patrice made sure they were comfortable with the equipment in the SAR emergency medical vehicle. It was an old

EMV that had made the rounds of various SAR groups in the Lower Mainland before finding its present home up north, but the locals were very thankful to have it.

On July 12, the first guys from Incident Command flew in by helicopter. They said everyone was doing a great job and to keep on doing what they were doing. On that same day, Doug clocked nineteen hours on the TD20. July 13 saw one of the worst flare-ups during the early part of the fire. That was the first day I had returned home to water the garden and the cop by the bridge had told me they were worried the fire would cross the road. (More of this day's drama later.)

Meanwhile, at the Manor, Johanna and a couple of helpers were scrounging around to find food for the firefighters. The phone lines were operating again by then, and people called to find out what they could do to help. Women started baking bread and cookies and delivering them. One woman had run out of flour, yeast and sugar. No one knew whether the closures of Highway 20 would allow groceries to reach the community. Selma dug in to the supplies from her own household, and the volunteer reciprocated with twenty loaves of bread.

There were now about thirty-five mouths to feed. Some people maintained everyone could bring their own lunches, but others were worried that their home supplies might not last. The Tatla Lake store had closed. Selma contributed all her own bread, cheese, onions and eggs, and the community association donated twelve pork tenderloins. Johanna first depleted the motel's supplies, then bought from Richard at the Nimpo Lake store (an hour west of Tatla). Richard managed to keep his grocery trucks running all through the emergency, even though they had to go through all the fires from Quesnel south to Williams Lake, then west via Riske Creek and Kleena Kleene. It was more expensive for Johanna to buy from Richard, but Williams Lake was evacuated so there was no chance of getting food from there. Johanna knew she would eventually be compensated, but it took a lot of organizing. On top of everything, the power kept going off, sometimes for up to twelve hours at a time.

The firefighters desperately needed hoses and pumps and the fuel for them. The locals used all their private fuel first, then Gerald tried to get stuff from the Puntzi tanker base, but they had none. Tsi Del Del had gas but didn't have an account with Forestry so Gerald bought what he could with his personal credit card.

Selma drove the lunches and dinners to Peter Weiler's staging area. Just after dinner had been delivered at 6:00 p.m. on July 18, she was informed that the fire seemed to be getting pretty close to the road again. So the guys dropped everything and jumped on their machines. Fortunately they were in the process of moving the equipment and were able to get to the new spot very quickly. They worked, as Selma put it, like Chilcotin warriors, and even though the flames came right up to the highway in a couple of places, they managed to stop them from crossing over. That was the day I had arrived home from Bella Coola to water the garden for the second time and had been told that I had to leave.

The same evening, a CIFAC Initial Attack team drove in to Tatla, with five guys from a structural protection unit near Vernon. A representative from the Cariboo Fire Centre was with the IA crew. Doug Schuk had worked with this man on several fires in the past, and he and Selma were very happy to have him as a fire boss. Gerald was now given the title of logistics officer. It was his official job to acquire resources to fight the fire—which he had already been doing anyway.

Eleven days after the fire started, more Forestry workers were turning up, and Forestry said that anyone without an S-100 Fire Suppression Certificate wasn't allowed to work. Many of the volunteers were booted off. There was such a shortage of equipment, however, that all the local stuff was commandeered.

Locals who did not have the certificate had to wait for a course to be offered—and when they passed, it was to find that Forestry had brought in enough outsiders already and would not be employing them. Gerald made a fuss about this and he was able to get many of them reinstated.

Johanna and helpers were feeding an increasing number of firefighters until, by July 25, the number reached eighty-five. Then Forestry announced that they were opening a fire camp at Puntzi. They had their own cooks who would feed the firefighters there. This situation was quite ridiculous. Puntzi was over forty-five minutes east of Tatla and well over an hour from the fire. Some of the firefighters had, in addition, a good part of an hour's drive to reach Tatla in the first place. Gerald got on the phone again with his silver tongue and suggested that the two restaurants, one at Tatla and one at Nimpo, should be given contracts to feed the crews. Both had lost all their summer tourist business; it would give them much needed income. And in the end, this was what was done. Meanwhile, Johanna and Gerald lost their cooking contract, and the income from everyone employed by Forestry who had been staying at the motel as well.

Fighting the fire now took on a whole different flavour. Before Forestry took over, the locals had worked long and hard, and all felt that they had been getting the better of the fire. Now there were long delays at camp and staging before anyone started work. Official Forestry workers are governed by rules. They had to wait for a fire boss to arrive; a safety talk; stretching exercises; then take a long, sedate drive in convoy to the fire. This meant the days were half over before they were allowed to begin. Then the wind would get up and it would be pronounced too dangerous to work. Also, these firefighters were supposed to quit after fourteen days. These restrictions did not apply to independent contractors (like Doug Schuk) and many of these started at crack of dawn and worked 'til dark for more than seventy-five days without a break.

RYLAN WAS ONLY FOURTEEN YEARS OLD WHEN HE VOLUNTEERED TO work on the Kleena Kleene Fire. No one was supposed to be in an evacuation order zone under the age of eighteen, but although Rylan is not a big person, he kept his head down when officials were present, and the other locals were not about to rat on him as they knew he was perfectly competent. I caught up with him at the Tatla Lake School, after the fire was over. He is not much good at putting pen to paper, but his mind processes tiny details in a very orderly way. Here is his story pretty much in his own words.

"I got a ride from home with a neighbour on July 11 and we arrived at Tatla just in time to help move all the equipment out of the clinic and into the community hall. Then we went to staging in Peter Weiler's field. We spent most of the rest of that day sorting equipment and giving it out to various people. It was mostly private stuff—pumps, hoses, water tanks on the backs of pickups, quads, shovels, chainsaws, hard hats, Icom handheld radios and the like.

"The next day I left home at 3:00 a.m. and we signed on at staging at four. While the Cats began to make a fireguard behind Peter Weiler's house I went with Darryl down Colwell Road, which was not far from staging, but on the opposite side of the highway. Darryl had a pickup with a thousand-litre water tank on the back. The road is only about a kilometre long and it ends by the creek that runs out of One Eye Lake. There are four or five buildings there, most of which are not occupied full-time, and all of which had been evacuated as they were in the direct path of the fire. I spent four days there helping to cut trees down around the buildings, and watering them and the surrounding ground.

"After that we worked the fire lines where the Cats had gone behind Peter Weiler's house. The fire was pretty close and we had to douse the hot spots along the guard to prevent the fire from jumping it. Darryl drove his pickup and I stood in the back, operating the hose. When the water tank was empty, we had to go back to the creek to fill it up again.

"One time there were three five-packs [teams of five people] working there and the wind got up to twenty-seven kilometres per hour. We had to get out of there—we all jumped onto a single side-by-side and got back to staging, abandoning all the other equipment. But in a couple of hours the wind died down and we were able to resume work. All the equipment was OK.

"July 13 was when the fire got really close to the highway. I was on the back of John's water truck that time and we were the closest, so were the first responders. We drove up and down the highway watering what we could. I was operating the hose from the back of the truck, but John said we weren't doing any good so he told me to get in there. The hose was sixty metres long, and I went into the forest as far as it would stretch. It looked like the flames were sixty metres high! The worst thing was the noise. There was an incredible roar, like an express train and a jet engine all in one. The smoke was terrible and after a while I started getting a really bad headache and feeling dizzy, and I had to go to the EMV to get a dose of oxygen. Then I went back into the fire and worked two more hours. Two other guys had to be given oxygen after me. Pretty late in the evening, the wind died down and we felt that the fire was under control and we could go home to bed. I had worked seventeen hours that day. I was wearing a hoodie to try and protect myself from the flying sparks, but the synthetic fabric just melted when the sparks landed, and I counted thirty-six burns on my arms.

"A few days later, Forestry came in and started laying down rules. At fourteen years old I was not even supposed to be there but I guess they were so short-handed they would use anyone. They did make me back off from the fire line, but they gave me a job as staging area manager. I was kept very busy organizing parking (the helicopters were also landing and taking off from there, so space had to be kept for them) and collecting and doling out equipment. I even spent time trying to fix pumps. A four-wheeler was assigned to me and I was supposed to map all the fireguards with a GPS and write down when they were made. This was quite hard as few people could remember the actual dates because they were all working so hard. I also used the quad to make deliveries of small equipment back and forth along the highway, pumps mostly. Sometimes I had such a big load I had to stand, as I couldn't see over the top. One time I was taking stuff to the Cat guard that comes down to the lake beside the hayfields. It's pretty steep and I had a real hard time getting up there. Another time I had to make way for a Cat coming toward me. The guard was so narrow, the quad began to tip over the edge, but before it could roll the nearest five-pack ran and caught it and turned me upright again.

"On July 25, Forestry moved command to Puntzi and most people were booted off. I already had an s-100 and stayed a day or two longer, but when they found out how young I was, I was booted off as well, as Forestry didn't want the insurance hassle.

"When we started, we didn't know if we were going to get paid, we just wanted to help. But they did pay us in the end. I worked seventeen long days and got fifteen dollars an hour. I was quite happy with that!"

FOR ME, THE MOST PUZZLING ASPECT OF THE WHOLE SITUATION WAS the closing of the Tatla Lake clinic. There are eight clinics in the Chilcotin, with a seven-hour drive between the ones at either end. All of them were affected in one way or another by the fires. Not only were roads closed, but the hospital at Williams Lake, the usual place to refer all but the most serious of cases, was abandoned when the town was evacuated.

The Tsi Del Del and Ulkatcho (at Anahim Lake) clinics could keep functioning, but the Tatla clinic is not band affiliated and

Interior Health has much stricter legal issues. So on July 11, the Tatla clinic was officially closed.

Our tiny community is very fortunate to have a very strong medical presence. Ruth has been our local nurse for donkey's years, and she knows everything there is to know about running a medical presence in an isolated area. However, she happened to be out of the area when the fires started. Her temporary replacements were immediately moved out by Interior Health and deployed elsewhere. Patrice Gordon, our family nurse practitioner, has also served the Chilcotin for many years. She travels to all eight clinics, some of which are a four-hour drive from her home. Dr. Rob Coetzee, her husband and the newest member of our team, would normally spend two days at the Tatla clinic, two days at the Ulkatcho clinic at Anahim Lake, and the rest at the Tsi Del Del and Xeni Gwet'in (Nemiah Reserve) clinics. Both Patrice and Doctor Rob have worked in extreme situations— refugee camps, ebola centres, Antarctica, etc.—so are fully qualified to deal with emergencies. Patrice even belongs to the International sos, which means she keeps a bag packed ready to travel instantly to a world disaster. Surely these people were well qualified to deal with our little fire situation.

Patrice and Doctor Rob travelled to the Tsi Del Del and Ulkatcho clinics on schedule, possessing full-time permits to go through the fire zones. But Interior Health could not allow them to operate in the Tatla clinic; hence the move to the do-it-yourself facility in the hall across the road. Interior Health did not endorse this decision but nonetheless had nothing but admiration for our medical duo.

Patrice took on the task of managing all eight of the clinics on the Chilcotin. It was very difficult at first when there was no power, phone or internet. The Interior Health incident commander at Williams Lake could call her by satellite phone but Patrice could receive the calls only when her own aerial was set up, and this could happen only while she was driving. Fortunately, the internet was back up again in a couple of days and the land phone in a week.

Right from the start, even before anyone knew how huge the whole situation was going to be, medical personnel made lists of all the fragile patients in the huge area involved, particularly those with respiratory problems. They sorted out where they would go and how they would be moved if it became necessary. There were a few emergencies. A child with suspected appendicitis had to be medivaced from one community to Kamloops by helicopter. (He was OK.) Two imminent births needed attention. The place where one woman had booked was unavailable; she had family near Langley, so Patrice called the Langley Memorial Hospital, spoke with an obstetrician and asked whether they could take the patient at short notice. "But of course!" The obstetrician exclaimed. The patient was given a permit to go through Kleena Kleene to the Anahim Lake Airport, and then flown south. She said she was treated like royalty.

Another pregnant woman had already moved to Williams Lake to have her baby just before the fires started. She decided to return home to fetch some items—however, the Riske Creek Fire blew up and closed the highway behind her. Patrice was well aware that the patient had started labour pains two weeks earlier than expected, and also that she was known to have fast deliveries. Patrice tried to arrange a helicopter. A couple of hours later the helicopter still hadn't come, so Patrice phoned again and was told that Williams Lake Airport was on fire and it was too smoky to fly anyway. In the end, an RCMP escort was arranged so that she could travel through the fire.

On July 27, after the Tatla Lake alert was lifted due to the welcome rain, Patrice and Doctor Rob moved everything back into the clinic.

One of the biggest challenges throughout the emergency was organizing medication. People were running out, as they could not get to the stores or clinics that they would normally attend. Doctor Rob and Patrice had to sort out who needed what, where they could find the medications, and how they could get them to the people who needed them. Patrice would phone the health director of the patient's clinic—the nurse if there was one, or just anyone suitable at the various communities. Some people would send their requests through the community's spokesperson and some would contact her privately. A lot of her patients were not great internet users, though many of them checked Facebook, so she even got requests that way. Then Patrice would phone pharmacies in Prince George, Kamloops and the Vancouver area. On two occasions, packages were put together in Prince George: prescriptions, dressings, baby formula and so on. A military helicopter made these drops in Xeni Gwet'in and Tsi Del Del. In the Lower Mainland, Patrice found a pharmacist in Tsawwassen who was very helpful. She would deliver what was needed to Pacific Coastal Airlines in Vancouver, who would fly it to Anahim Lake three times a week. The Ulkatcho clinic would take what they needed, and the RCMP would head south with the rest. Patrice would meet them on the highway, and she would then drive partway to Tsi Del Del whose nurse would have driven north. Tsi Del Del's nurse would then arrange to meet her colleague from Alexis Creek. Patrice was thrilled at the way everyone worked together in this time of great difficulty.

Part Two

A Second Back Burn

PRECIPICE, JULY 24–29

ON JULY 24, KATE M, THE CURRENT INCIDENT COMMANDER, AN-
nounced they were going to do another back burn, this time to help
make the "scissors" area safer. IC had been working on the plans for
days. A unit crew and danger tree fallers had cut a fuel-free guard
between the points of the scissors. They had cleared a four-metre-
wide swath, throwing all the fuel onto the green side of the guard.
They had then hand-ignited the forest, pushing the fire into the black
side to make a hundred-metre-wide fuel-free barrier. It was a phe-
nomenal effort for so few people over such rough terrain in just a
few days. They were now preparing to back burn the whole area between the scissors. This would greatly shorten the perimeter of the
fire, making it less dangerous for everyone concerned.

As part of the preparation for the back burn, they brought in a
"bird-dog" and three air tankers to drop fire retardant on the fuel-
free guard—"to harden it." All helicopters were grounded while the
planes were in the air. We watched the aerial ballet from our meadows. The small bird-dog aircraft circled and marked the path for the
larger planes that flew in wider arcs over our house before coming
into line and dropping the bright red retardant.

We had to say goodbye to helicopter pilots Rob and Jim, and Operations Chief David P. They were very special, kind and generous to us. We began to marvel at how seamlessly the personnel can change: people apparently switching jobs within the Incident Command without a hitch. Brett, an Australian ignition specialist, was to be in charge of the back burn.

In the late afternoon of July 25, Kate M asked me if Caleb was still around. He had come over that morning to discuss plans for haying. When he grew bored with all the activity in our yard and could see no more obvious fire drama, he got on his ATV to go home. It would not start with the key and when he went to pull the cord, it ripped from the machine. I offered my ATV, which had been sputtering unreliably all summer. After a few futile attempts at starting that one, Caleb announced that he would walk. I told Kate that he had just left. She asked if I could fetch him. I rushed to the car, hoping that *it* would start because it had not been moved for almost three weeks. Caleb was at the edge of our meadows when I caught up with him. He grumbled but agreed to come.

Kate asked us all to meet in the house. She stood behind our couch as if it were a lectern and told us they were planning on doing the "scissors" back burn on the following day. She iterated what we already knew—that if the dreaded southwest winds got up and the burn got out of control, we would be directly in its path. The alternative to the burn would be many expensive hours of helicopter bucketing and a much longer time under an evacuation order. She gave us the "you are under order and are advised to leave" speech. I was tired, a bit sad, also anxious, with a sense of déjà vu. I had felt a strong connectedness to those fighting the fire. Now I was just an ordinary citizen who was expected to move out. None of us went, needless to say.

After all the preparation, the back burn did not take place as planned. We were unsure whether it was because the winds were wrong or whether there was a poor humidity and temperature balance. As I left on my tractor for Lee's long meadow to begin raking the hay Caleb had cut two days earlier, I watched Kate M and Brett walking between helicopters, heads down in a deep discussion. It pained me not to be involved with these discussions but it was best not to interfere with their work. They had a job to do and so did I. Theirs was fighting the fire—and mine was haying.

After cutting the Taylor Ranch's long meadow, Caleb moved the machinery to our place to mow our island and west meadows. By Wednesday afternoon on July 26, haying was in full swing and I briefly ignored the fire. It was a hectic start. I am notorious for misplacing tools and the fire highlighted this fault. Equipment had been moved during the structural protection work. As I scrambled to relocate what I needed for haying, I had to abandon our ATV in our big meadow after forgetting to refuel it. There were other glitches. While moving to our west meadow, Caleb high-centred his tractor on a rock that had slid from the trail's cutbank and lay beneath tall grass. It took us over an hour to pack enough stones and soil around the rock so he was able to back away. There was no damage to the oil pan but I had to create new access to the meadow by pushing aside large rocks and young trees with my tractor. A large Douglas fir had fallen onto the meadow and had to be moved to the side.

The fire was still out there, of course, and IC continued to pound it with water by helicopter. Monika maintained the home front—keeping pilots and other firefighters supplied with strawberries and coffee. The weather was perfect for the haying—warm temperatures, no rain or heavy dew, and dry winds—but my worry increased as such conditions were also likely to waken the fire. The grass in the meadows beyond our house had grown tall and lanky. It was rapidly drying and would present a severe fire hazard should an ember land in it. Haying was a race both against time and the fire. It needed to be done, not just because the crop had to be harvested, but also so the medium-sized helicopters could be moved from the south meadow to the west meadow. The grass in these staging areas had grown and we could not get rid of that fire hazard until the machines were out of the way.

We continued to have many aggravating glitches. All the machinery was old and unreliable. One baler had to be abandoned and the second was not cutting the string that tied the bales. After fiddling with the mechanism for a few hours we decided to cut the string by hand. Caleb lost his knife and I had to walk next to the baler to cut the bales free. When I felt I had an opportunity to move the bales to the side of the meadow, I would jump on my tractor to do so, but was very hesitant to keep Caleb waiting. Once the bales had been relocated to the edges of the meadow there was plenty of room for the helicopters to land.

On July 27, we were told that Kate M and Brett were planning two back burns. As well as the one between the scissor points, they wanted to tackle a green area well inside the fire's perimeter on the north side of the Hotnarko River. This type of burn is also called an "inside" or "controlled" burn. The reasoning was that if these green islands were ignored and the fire crept into them, as was very likely to happen, there would create a lot of heat and dangerous flying embers. Inside burning is the least dangerous type of back burn for the firefighters because it is far behind the perimeter of the fire. While it might seem a shame to burn green timber, the BC Wildfire Service maintained it would make the fire easier to control.

The experienced grey-haired pilot was brought in again and the cycle of helicopters dropping fuel began. They tackled the green area first. There was less to see this time because the ignition was farther from the ridges surrounding our meadows. By the time they completed the green area, it was too cool and damp to start the one between the tongues of the scissors.

In the evening, Monika wrote: "Only a short post today, Fred is tired from haying and not much has happened. The ground crew is extending a second four-metre-wide fire-break from the southern point of the 'scissor' points toward the Atnarko Canyon near Stillwater Lake. They will lay hoses and sprinklers along the guard. They plan on widening the line by hand-burning section after section along the line to make a forty-metre-wide fire break. Slow, methodical and safe. Main priority is still to keep the north flank quiet by bucketing it whenever something stirs. We are sooooo grateful for all the efforts that are made!"

I tried to report the weather at the same time each day but by Friday, July 28, I was beginning to tire: "To Kate M—Precipice Morning Weather Report—I slept in a bit today. Must be because these reports are so repetitive. The barometer has not moved in four days. 9.4 degrees Celsius, moderate dew. No rain and no wind. A good day for both firefighting and haying."

Her response: "Everybody will be productive today. Thanks Fred."

I was on the tractor every day now—starting when the dew had evaporated from the windrows and ending once all cut hay had been turned, always conscious of the sounds of the tractor and rake—listening for the possibility of something going wrong. Occasionally I got confused by a strange, muffled throbbing sound. When I slowed the tractor to look back at the rake, I realized there was a helicopter passing overhead. My nerves had become frayed by the fire.

The Precipice Fire was becoming a long, drawn-out ordeal but we had many friends affected by other fires. Nicola and Jerry evacuated at 108 Mile. Dominique and Ben were surrounded by the Chezacut Fire. Clint and Karen were plagued by roadblocks and on-again, off-again evacuation orders near Williams Lake. Jade and Ryan with their two young children were isolated from their Red Roof House, and Chris was also under order but staying put at Kleena Kleene.

Lee Taylor had finally secured a rancher's pass so he and Pat could pass through roadblocks between Vancouver and Anahim Lake. Pat briefly posted: "Highway 20 is open to east *and* west traffic with understanding that residents must be on alert. As far as I know our valley is still on evacuation order. But we hope to head home to the ranch on Sunday/Monday. I am anxious about going into the fire zone but Lee is not."

In my July 29 weather report, I included: "The fire is the most active we have seen it for a while. This is probably due to a gradual drop in the relative humidity since the rain." I was very pleased to find that Mark had come back.

Our little conflagration seemed rather unexciting compared to all the other fires in British Columbia. I was still at odds with how other people criticized the way "their" fires were fought. I received an email from a friend in Tatla. It was written in the haste and anxiousness that people were feeling those days. "We've had one food drop in 3 wks; KD, crackers, beans, soup, baby food, diapers... some food/fuel trucked in earlier but gone now... useful but not enough... we're OK but there's lots of folks who aren't... No mail since July 7... power/phones on, happy for that." She was disappointed with information that she received... "Very superficial" were the words she used.

We received a steady stream of well wishes that gave us support and encouragement to carry on. I felt sheepish about our Precipice Fire and all the help we were receiving. When we were short of chicken feed a pilot delivered some directly to our door. We were continually supplied with bread, fruit and peanut butter. We could repay only with strawberries and coffee.

The fire's activity had increased during the few days of dry weather but on July 30 we had a couple of showers, so haying had to be put on hold. This was, however, advantageous to the firefighters. Bucketing by four or five helicopters returned the fire to a cool state and the ground crew made good progress along the fire-break above Stillwater Lake. They hoped to finish in one more day and Brett would be able to complete controlled burns in that area. They would first burn the pine, which doesn't burn as hot as the spruce. All very interesting and a bit nerve-wracking, especially as we had just heard that a back burn on the Elephant Hill Fire near Clinton went wrong. The fire raged up a mountain, forcing the evacuation of the town. This fuelled the outrage against back burning, and the media had a field day. That fire closed Highway 97 again so Pat and Lee had to figure out another route for their return to the Precipice.

Mark returned as incident commander; Kate M transitioned out and moved to Helco where she would fly with the helicopter, monitoring air traffic and looking for hot spots in the fire. There were now two "heavies" (Russian-built Kamov helicopters) and three "mediums" bucketing water, and a couple of smaller helicopters moving personnel and equipment. Demitri Vaisius was now operations chief.

The precipitation (which had been a lot less than at Kleena Kleene) didn't slow down haying significantly and we were able to finish baling our west meadow so the pilots could land there, and Caleb cut the dry grass in the south meadow behind the house.

The personnel within the Comox structural protection unit were transitioning also. New people were coming into the valley almost every day. They installed sprinklers around the Range Cabin and reconfigured the pumps and hoses at the Taylor Ranch and Red Roof House. They enhanced the protection at our place until all of our buildings had sprinklers around or above them. We had nearly half a kilometre of mainline hose with twenty-two two-centimetre hoses branching off it feeding sprinklers.

Our concern about the rapidly dropping Hotnarko River intensified. The flow onto the meadow was becoming a trickle. Monika and I ran the pump for only half an hour in the evening to wet the ground and ensure that the system was working. The structural protection people were surprised at how little fuel we used.

Monika waded into the river and cleared more debris from the inlet to the creek. We discussed with the Comox crew the possibility that we might have to move the two pumps from the irrigation ditch to the creek or the river. The creek's flow was also dropping rapidly. The river had much more water, but using it would mean laying a hundred to a hundred fifty metres of new hose, and it would take us much longer to get to the pump in an emergency. We elected to wait.

Caleb's frustration with the structural protection people intensified. Whenever they came into the valley, they would run the pumps at the Taylor house and Red Roof House, and leave them on when they left. This drained the bladder at the Taylor house, which Caleb had to refill. The bladder at the Red Roof House had been abandoned because of leaks. A Wajax pump was placed by the river far below the house. This powerful pump easily pushed the water up a hundred metres to the sprinklers. Caleb was also concerned about the depletion of fuel when the pumps were left running.

Although Highway 97 was closed at Clinton, an alternative route via the Coquihalla and Highway 24 allowed Pat and Lee to head north. They stayed overnight with Clint and Karen Thompson, whose home is half an hour south of Williams Lake, and with whom all of us Precipice people stay when travelling to and from the coast. Their place was shrouded in smoke from the many fires burning around the city. It had been a struggle for them juggling power outages and evacuation orders. They managed to keep water and minimal power going by running a generator. A large water tank and many buckets full of water and rags had been placed near their old log house in case of falling embers. Clint recounted how he had watched the lightning strikes and instant fires that broke out on July 7. By dusk the smoky grey skies cloaked a fiery orange sun descending among the pines on the hills to the west. It was a harbinger to the devastation Pat and Lee would drive through the following day.

South of Williams Lake, the fires had been quick and destructive, but by now many were under control and most of the life there had returned to normal. But along Highway 20, Pat and Lee witnessed kilometres of burnt forest and rangeland. It was sobering to see the complete absence of the restaurant at Lee's Corner, which had been a stopping place for all of us. Smoke dogged them for most of the trip, and at the Kleena Kleene Fire, flames could still be seen. They arrived safely in the Precipice that evening.

Meanwhile Monika and I were becoming resigned to the fire. It had been unable to move for a while, but it was resilient against the constant pounding with water. The unit crew was still working on the fuel-free guard in an attempt to contain the corner above Stillwater Lake, and helicopters were flying everywhere to put out any hot spot near its perimeter.

My frustration with this stalemate appeared in my evening post: "Our boring fire, our persistent fire, our annoying fire. It remains our captor. Each day they dump a lake-load of water on it and each morning it shows us new puffs of smoke. Our benevolent fire. Every day we are exposed to the devastation of the fires in this province yet we waken to clear sky and nice air. Sometimes I feel a bit of the Stockholm syndrome. Our captor shows us mercy, it shows us how nice it can be compared to other fires, yet it persists three kilometres from our home—not allowing our volunteers back, not allowing us to leave. Of course we could leave. But we would not be allowed home again. That would be giving in to the fire."

Precipice Morning Weather Report, Tuesday, August 1. "Hazy and calm. Must be a fire somewhere... The barometer is still rising."

Our fire had an aggravating, persistent, yet capricious nature. One day the skies would be clear and you would hardly know it was out there, and the next, we would be smoked right in. We occasionally saw grey plumes from a hot spot but it mostly remained quiet under the relentless pounding from the helicopters.

We were all happy to have Lee back in the valley. We had been struggling with the balers for the last three days. Lee threw himself at them immediately as he and Pat settled in. Caleb had been reluctant to cut more hay until he was certain that the balers would be working properly, so I had a day off from raking.

I was becoming complacent with the fire, which hadn't grown beyond twenty-five hundred hectares for days. But Monika was always vigilant and anxious. Mark and ic intently monitored all available weather information including my morning reports. They were looking for indicators that would increase fire activity. The continued drying trend was a major concern, as was the poor overnight recovery of humidity. I began to pay more attention to how much moisture settled during the dark hours. Every morning I dragged my feet through the grass where it was short to feel how wet it was, and drew a diagonal line across the dew on the window of our truck parked in the meadow to see how large a drop would collect at the bottom.

On Facebook, Pat related her first impressions after coming home: "Wednesday, August 2, 7:45 a.m. Woke up to low-lying smoke this morning, nine degrees Celsius. The quiet is loud. Breathing is fine. Eerie orange light, our own little rock-'n'-roll light show introduces us to another day of watching and waiting. Lee is fixing mowers and balers. Mama Fox welcoming us back into the valley." (Pat had been sharing posts of a fox that visited her home over the past year and people always inquired after the fox).

Although the fire was not showing much activity, the fight against it remained intense. On that same day, after almost a week of preparation, they were able to complete the back burn within the scissors' arms. The intensity of the fight against the fire gave us a lot of confidence and I boldly predicted that they would soon have it 30 to 50 per cent contained.

But we were once again shrouded by very dense smoke. Helicopters could not fly. It would have been a quiet day but for the rattle of haying machinery. We had two more days' work then we would move the equipment to the Taylor Ranch.

When the helicopters could not fly to keep the fire calm, our anxiety increased. Where it was closest to us, the fire kicked up. We couldn't see anything to the southwest because of the thick smoke but we were certain it was active. We prayed that the fireguards would hold. We had been living with this fire for four weeks now. Enough was enough.

IC was increasingly concerned that the fire would get past the Precipice on the north side. The valley used to have a phone line, but it was so difficult to maintain that in 2000 a tower was installed on top of the basalt cliff to receive a microwave signal from a tower at Nimpo Lake. The signal is beamed down to our houses, connecting us to the provincial phone system. Because of the microwave radio links we were the only area in the West Chilcotin that never had our phone service interrupted throughout the fires, allowing Lee to have daily contact with Caleb at the ranch.

Part of a unit crew was deployed to protect this radio tower. These firefighters falled trees and hand-dug a fuel-free ring just outside the cables that supported the tower so that a ground fire could not creep to the instruments at the tower's base. A Caterpillar was contracted to construct a guard from the rimrock just east of our phone tower to the west end of Hotnarko Lake. When heavy equipment is used to build a fire-break, it is called a "machine guard." This machine guard was contracted to prevent the fire from passing the Precipice and advancing to Anahim Lake.

We got word that Arlen would be coming back. "Hi Arlen," I wrote. "We welcome your return. Lee and Pat are back for the haying season so there are more souls to look out for. Our social life has increased considerably."

Smoke blanketed our world, reducing it to an ominous gloom. It also covered the southern half of the province. Son-in-law Barry commented from Nanaimo: "You don't smell it here, but you definitely see it. At least it tempers the sun a bit in this insane heat."

Chris at Kleena Kleene: "The heavy greyness everywhere is depressing. It is eerily silent. No helicopters or wind here, either. Even the birds have quit singing."

Susan from the Sunshine Coast: "We have had smoky grey skies here now for two days—I just can't imagine how you are keeping sane out there. It is oppressive. I hope it helps to know friends are thinking of you and following your summer as it unfolds, and hoping for it to get better every day."

My sister visiting in the Kootenays: "We can barely see the mountains across the valley."

I responded. "What? You can see the mountains?! The ridges just next to our meadows are as far as we can see." Less than half a kilometre.

A Short Reprieve

KLEENA KLEENE, JULY 26—AUGUST 3

ON JULY 26 I PICKED UP TWO FRIENDS WHO HAD BEEN VOLUNTEERING at my old mountain resort, Nuk Tessli, and took them to the Anahim Lake Airport. Living in an area under evacuation order, I was not supposed to leave my property, so I felt sneaky driving there. Anahim Lake was not even on alert; there were still no barriers between me and that community so I hoped I could get away with it.

My visitors were going to Vancouver, but the schedule dictated that the plane was to fly to Bella Coola, as it usually did, en route. However, when the plane landed at Anahim, the two pilots were in no hurry to move. They came into the office and got themselves coffees. Eventually a spokesperson came and said they were waiting for word that it was clear enough to fly into Bella Coola. Although there was the ubiquitous smoke in the atmosphere, this was not the problem. In the Bella Coola Valley, it was raining. We could see black clouds and the occasional dragging shower in that direction. Usually, if the weather is bad, a minibus is laid on. Passengers from Bella Coola would have to be driven up the Hill to catch the plane at Anahim. Anahim passengers would have to wait for over two hours until the rest of the fares arrived. But today it was announced that there would be no bus. If the weather didn't clear, the plane would simply go back to Vancouver. This was no problem for my friends, but four guys were anxious to get to Bella Coola to go fishing. No such thing as a car hire in this part of the world; the only option open to them was to charter a helicopter. They were seriously considering it. It would not be cheap. And it might be difficult to find one.

The little waiting room was full of passengers and bored kids. This is a new airport building and it is small but very fancy. It was quiet and air-conditioned inside; outside, it was not only very hot and smoky, it was also incredibly noisy. Helicopters rattled in constantly to fuel up and give the pilots some downtime. These machines were working on the Precipice Fire. Most of the choppers were the big ones with double rotors on top and a tail like an airplane. The effect of smoke and helicopters in a fire area has often been compared to that of a war zone, but my companions were Israeli and I realized that there was one big difference. Our helicopters were friendly.

Most of us were royally entertained by all the goings-on. One little boy of about seven, however, had his back to the window, and he stared at a phone, playing a computer game. The only time I saw him lift his eyes from his device was when his dad gave him a chocolate bar. There was this ultra-dramatic real-life drama going on out the window, and all he wanted was his screen.

A squally shower blew furious horizontal rain for about five minutes, but that was the only precipitation we got on the plateau. The helicopters came and went. As each battered its way into the squalls, buckets trailing, I sent my thoughts with it, imagining its journey to the Precipice.

David J was finishing up his work in the Precipice and was going to transfer to the Cariboo Fire District. He lived at Nimpo Lake. I buy strawberries from Fred and Monika every summer—I was wondering if I was going to be able to get them this year. I phoned Monika—yes, David J was there and yes they could ship twenty kilos out with him! So the following morning I nipped back into Nimpo

Lake early and picked up the strawberries from David's home. It takes me all day to process that many. I couldn't imagine how much tedium Fred and Monika were going through picking mounds of strawberries every day and putting them in their freezers (for pies or the firefighters).

As the fires settled down in this cooler, damper weather, Highway 97, both north and south of Williams Lake, was reopened, and quite a few residents were allowed home. The power had been on and off so much that most people had lost their freezers. It would be impossible to clean them properly once rotten meat and fish had been sitting in them for all that time. There was also the danger of coming home to frozen contents, but not knowing whether they had been thawed and frozen again. A useful trick flew around cyberspace. If you know you are going away, fill a small container with water, then freeze it. Place a penny on top. If the penny is still there when you get home, your freezer never thawed. If it is at the bottom of the container, thawing and refreezing has taken place.

On July 29, I perused the usual round of websites and was puzzled to see no closures listed for Highway 20 on DriveBC's website. Was this accurate? The information on the BC Wildfires Service site was days old and gave no clue. But then I got an email from a friend. "Hooray, you're on alert!" *What?* I was directed to the Cariboo Regional District's Emergency Operation Centre. This was a new website to add to my browser list. Sure enough, the Kleena Kleene area along the highway (but not in the bush) had now been downgraded from "order" to "alert." Residents could legally travel or come home. All my immediate neighbours were home anyway, but it gave us a sudden sense of freedom. No longer could we be chastised for driving around without a permit. I was very skeptical as to how long this situation would last, however. We were now approaching what was normally the most dangerous part of the fire season. Both the times I had been evacuated in the past were because of fires that had started on July 31. The soaker that had dumped so much rain at Tatla had happened five days before. Already the land was drying—I was watering the garden again—and the fire activity had increased.

Being downgraded to "alert" meant that all kinds of things could happen. The mail truck normally comes along Highway 20 all the way from Williams Lake to Bella Coola three days a week. There had been no delivery since the start of the fire. Anahim Lake and Bella Coola had received mail, but it had arrived by air. Because the Kleena Kleene post office had been in the evacuation order zone, we'd had none. We had been informed that it was being held for us in Williams Lake and we could go and pick it up if we wanted—but no one was going to be stupid enough to do that while our order was in force. Now that the area had been downgraded to "alert," the first mail truck in three weeks came through on July 31. I do most of my business online, but it was nice to have that tangible contact with the outside world. One surprise item I received was a box of books from Harbour Publishing. My twelfth book, *Harry: A Wilderness Dog Saga* was just out, and the box contained the ten freebies the publisher sends to its authors. It is always exciting to see a new book when it is first in print. It was a double pleasure this time, as it was a little reminder that, in the world outside our rigid boundaries of fire and smoke, a parallel, more "normal" world existed.

When I was last in Williams Lake (the day the fires started), I was told by my mechanic that the next time I came to town I should arrange to have new shoes and calipers for the front brakes. Not only had that "next time" not happened, but in the meantime I had also driven several times up and down the infamous Bella Coola Hill. Not that I use the brakes much there; the van gears right down and it is only on the hairpins that they are needed. Theoretically, now that we were on evacuation alert, I could go to Williams Lake to get this work done. But all those fires back on the East Chilcotin were still very active. They could flare up in a heartbeat. The last thing I wanted was to be stranded on the wrong side of the fires if the road was closed again.

There were a couple of mechanics to choose from in the Bella Coola Valley, but would they have parts? Ninety-nine per cent of all freight—groceries, gas, parts, etc.—is driven in by road. Tankers and sixteen-wheelers must all manoeuvre their monstrous vehicles up and down the hairpin bends of the Hill. Had the freight trucks kept running throughout all the closures? It appeared they had. It couldn't have been very comfortable for some of the drivers, particularly those hauling gas and propane, to rattle along between bands of forests that were flaming on both sides of the road. A driver delivering liquid methane to the Anahim Lake power station later told me that he was advised not to exceed thirty kilometres per hour within the actively burning areas, in case he created turbulence that could fan the flames.

I phoned a garage down in the valley and asked them if they could get the parts and when. "About five days, probably," was the reply. So back down the Hill I went. But this time I decided I could enjoy the journey. At the top of the Hill were trails heading into the volcanic Rainbow Range. All backcountry access was denied—it was still very hot and dry everywhere—but one of the trails barely left the road. It ran along a creek and at this time of year there was generally a good show of alpine flowers. I ignored the *Area Closed Due to Wildfire Activity* notice and hopped over the chain. The surroundings had been burned over a decade ago. Although no new trees had started on the steep, rocky ground, herbage covered most of the space between the blackened trunks, many of which now sported scrofulous pale patches where charred bark had fallen off. Away from the creek everything was brittle and dry, and few flowers were blooming. It was a colour scheme of three. Black branches, tawny grass and deep blue sky. But close to the water, agoseris, both yellow and orange, mauve wandering fleabanes, purple asters, white valerian, and red paintbrush made bold splashes of colour against the charcoal of the fallen trees. Lupins were present but their ultra-marine blossoms had finished.

The temperature was in the thirties, even at that altitude (1,600 metres), and as I dropped down into the valley the heat increased, though the heavy tree shade at the bottom made it more tolerable. I made myself at home in my designated cabin, and went down to the garage early the following morning. Nearby was an organic pick-your-own blueberry farm, another place I had been hoping to harvest from but hadn't been sure whether the fires would let me. Even at 8:00 a.m., it was extremely hot. I worked as much as possible on the shady sides of the rows. Robins cackled their warning cries constantly—they must have made off with a ton of berries. The farm owner said she'd never seen so many robins. The usual predatory hawks were not around. Not only had humans' lives been disrupted because of these fires—wildlife patterns had also been changed.

As I worked, the valley slowly filled with smoke. The sun glared through it and it became a white haze. This was primarily a result of back burning at the Precipice. The gentle east wind was perfect for the job—but not so pleasant for the residents downwind. Katie's asthma made the smoke a serious cause for concern.

With happy brakes I approached the Hill, anxious to get the berries into the freezer as soon as possible. I got a fright at the bottom, as a temporary Highways sign was flashing a warning. "Oh no," I thought. "They've closed the road." But in fact it was to say the road was open! And going up, I met a tourist. You can always tell a tourist on the Hill. Locals wave; tourists ignore other drivers and often have grim faces as they negotiate the twists and turns. This one was towing a boat. "He's brave," I thought. "He could very well get stuck down in the valley if the road closes again."

The air was clear and sunny going up, but at the top my heart sank. Ahead of me, a broad swath of smoke lay across the Chilcotin.

"Perhaps it's from the Precipice Fire," I hoped. But no, it was from Kleena Kleene. They were back burning there, too, and my home was exactly downwind of their efforts. The smoke grew thicker as I drove into my yard, and from the house I could barely see the cottonwoods beside the river half a kilometre away, let alone Internet Hill. It was the thickest smoke I had yet experienced. It was harsh on the throat and the brown gloom robbed the world of colour. But I really couldn't face leaving again. I was home and I was, for the moment, safe: I was just going to have to put up with it.

FIRE IS LIKE A DRAGON. IT USUALLY GOES TO SLEEP AT NIGHT AND IS often lazy about getting up in the morning. But when the wind starts to puff and lick among the trees, the fire dragon rears its scaly snout and breathes out smoke and flame again.

At the beginning of August, Google Earth's wildfire overlay showed that our fire had travelled a fair distance west from the original strikes. It had now surrounded Finger Peak and was beginning to drop down into the Klinaklini River, which runs immediately below the peak's dramatic western cliff. If you zoom right in to the wildfire overlay site, the dots turn into squares that overlap like a kind of crazy quilt, and these became monstrously distorted over rugged topography.

The great increase in heat and dryness made me think the evacuation alert would soon be ending, but it was still legal for me to drive, and the air was clear enough to make it worthwhile to climb to the top of Internet Hill. Trees hide a lot of the view from there, but it is possible to see a little farther down into the Klinaklini Valley than is visible from my house. Although there wasn't a great deal of smoke, heat waves and the faint blue haze showed that a well-established fire was down there. I knew that part of the valley to be narrow and steep sided, and full of quite good timber. It was a place where a fire dragon could be very happy. This location was exactly southwest

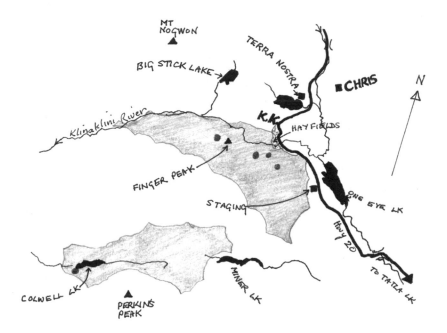

= Fire Information. From Interactive Map, Natural Resources, Canada
August 4 2017

This shows the Kleena Kleene Fire's perimeters on August 4, as
represented by Natural Resources Canada's Interactive Maps.
Drawn by Chris Czajkowski.

of my place and if the wind got behind it, it would shoot straight
toward me.

I was a bit puzzled as to why no one seemed to be working it. The
location was close enough that I could not fail to hear any aircraft
going in that direction and as far as I could make out, no one had
even been to look at it. The other end of the fire was receiving constant attention. Helicopters were bucketing, and now I could hear
the heavy drone of water bombers as they circled and swooped.
There was enough smoke to prevent me from seeing them, but the

sound was unmistakable. All this very audible activity was twice the distance away from the fire that was southwest of me.

The Precipice Wildfire of Note information, put out by the Coastal Wildfire Service, had been dropped almost daily into my mailbox; right from the beginning, all the firefighting resources had been listed. Now, for the first time, a month after the fire had started, the Cariboo Wildfire Service finally got their act together, and these figures appeared on the Kleena Kleene page. Seventy-two firefighters, eight helicopters and ten pieces of heavy equipment. All of them apparently concentrated at the south end.

Environment Canada weather forecast showed a cold front was coming in. Nothing was mentioned about winds on that website, but they can be quite wild ahead of these fronts. On the afternoon of August 3, the fire dragon began to stir.

A suddenly gusty wind cleared the air around my place, but angry-looking clouds of smoke topped by pyrocumuli reared up from Colwell Creek. They gave me the usual visceral feeling of dread, but they were several kilometres south and I instructed my nervous brain to calm down as they were being carried still farther away.

More alarmingly, a great fan of smoke began spreading from the Precipice area. It was blowing my way. I had not seen smoke climbing out of their valley like that before. At once to the websites. The crazy quilt on the Google Earth wildfire overlay showed that the fire had now engulfed Fred and Monika's buildings. They seemed to me to be in sudden and very serious danger. I went straight to their Facebook page. People commenting sent the usual good wishes—"pink fire protection bubbles" and the like. But I was in terror for them. I didn't post, but emailed them and said: "I am not going to say anything about the fire. There is nothing that I can say. You know how I feel."

Rank Five

PRECIPICE, AUGUST 3

"PRECIPICE MORNING WEATHER REPORT—THURSDAY, AUGUST 3. THE barometer dropped slightly. Moderate dew, no rain and no night wind. The haze has lifted marginally and the fire is active on the north flank. 8.4 degrees Celsius."

"Thanks Fred, we have good ceiling this morning and you will see us bucketing shortly. Today we have a number of new staff/fallers coming in, so there will be some fresh faces around your place. Pascal has taken over from Rick (structure protection unit) and I have a new operations chief (Lonny) that will be transitioning in also. Cheers. Mark."

Little did I realize how important my comment about "no night wind" was. Our strongest winds are out of the west or southwest. They are the ones that drive the fire toward us. But the quiet zephyrs at night come out of the east as the cooling air drains toward the Pacific. It is these winds that push the fire back on itself and deplete it of momentum. We had not had night winds for a few days.

We were so naive about fires. We could not read the signs that would allow the fire to rage. We had seen it do so only a couple of times in the whole month that we had been affected by it. The fire had not moved rapidly in a number of days; however, IC was anxious.

The cover of the Incident Action Plan for August 3 read, "Be continually aware of the increase in fire activity and potential for high rates of spread. The fire has been sleeping for several days and is ready to 'pop' at any moment. Be sure you are in constant communication with your supervisor and be prepared to use your escape routes and safety zones."

Ravens had been gathering around our big meadow and the smell of death mixed with smoke hung most heavily in the morning. After two days of passing through the stench on my way to the Taylor Ranch for haying, I suspected that we had lost Cactus, our old "dude horse."

After a brief search we found his body. Cactus was as tranquil and pleasant as any old horse could be, although he would temporarily move away when we came with a halter. He had been broken almost thirty years before. He had been trained to be a bucking bronco for the rodeo circuit, but like Ferdinand the bull, he was just too nice.

His teeth had been "floated" (filed to make them more even so he could better chew hay) last fall but he still struggled to get through the winter, even with the supplements we had fed him. He had been wandering between the Taylor Ranch and our home looking for the tenderest grass. Hard of hearing and maybe a little blind, we had barred him from the yard when he became a risk for the helicopters. As the grass grew taller and less succulent he was probably having a hard time getting it down. We last saw him over a week ago but assumed he was puttering away happily on his own—he shunned other horses and cattle. We found him half sunken into the Hotnarko River. He must have slipped in and was too weak to crawl out. Monika last rode him on the spring cattle drive of this year. We decided to leave him there—mother nature would take care of his funeral.

One day of not being able to bucket the Precipice Fire was all it needed. It had enough energy and fuel to finally make a run at us.

Mark was quick to recognize that the fire would not be denied on this day. Even before noon it was building a huge plume two to three kilometres to our northwest. The helicopters were called out of the sky and the bird-dog, with two bombers, were brought in to drop retardant between our home and the rapidly escalating fire. Lee and Pat visited just before noon to get some vegetables and move haying equipment to their ranch; perfect timing to watch the airshow. We gazed in awe as the towering column of angry smoke grew behind the circling bird-dog and its two large companions. They dropped a solid line of red retardant just beyond the crest of our valley's north ridge. I will never be quite sure why we remained so calm as we watched the smoke plume. But when Lee and Pat left, we felt edgy and unsure that we would be protected against the growing menace.

After another hour the massive column had become a wall of boiling smoke and the fire was too hot for helicopters to bucket it. The smoke had morphed from a mix of orange, grey and white to a more threatening black curtain gradually closing across our northwestern horizon. It was so massive that it became difficult to photograph—all you could see was a wall of black. Its forward edge highlighted its surreal nature. The sky next to it was a brilliant blue, indicative of a normal hot summer day. But this day was far from normal.

We were so mesmerized by the smoke that we hardly paid attention to what the helicopters were doing. After the planes flew away, the mediums were called back to base. The smaller two were busy removing all equipment—the remaining fuel barrels, nets and buckets— from our meadows. They were pulling out. The BC Wildfire Service ranks fires from one to six. Rank one being a smouldering ground fire. Rank six, the most dangerous, is a blow-up or conflagration when the forest literally explodes. We were now suddenly faced with a rapidly moving rank five, an extremely vigorous surface fire with an active crown fire. The raging flames were so close that one pilot refused to land on our meadows.

A curtain of black smoke from the rank-five blaze draws across our northeast horizon, drawing the brilliant sunny day to a close on August 3. Photo by Fred Reid.

VA0778 was also active elsewhere. Winds were fanning the fire to our southwest, pushing it toward us directly up the Hotnarko Canyon. The entire western horizon danced with yellow, orange, white and grey smoke but the most terrifying was the advancing wall of very black smoke to our northwest. We could hardly take our eyes off it.

The structural protection team had just undergone a shift change, and new personnel were brought by helicopter to our meadow where their truck had been parked for the last two weeks. They were tasked with securing the safety of all buildings in the Precipice—ensuring that there was enough fuel and water to keep sprinklers running at five sites. Pascal, the new unit head, had been at our place for the initial installation and was familiar with the layout. He was young but held a quiet confidence behind icy light-blue eyes. In a last-minute decision it was decided to move the pumps from the irrigation ditch to the creek. When the system was fired up the powerful pump sucked sand from the creek bed into the lines of hose and plugged almost all of the sprinklers. Faced with the tedious process of unclogging them, Pascal divided his unit into two groups. He left with some to check the fuel and water supply at the other sites and to turn on their sprinklers. At our place three crew members went from one sprinkler to the next to unclog the nozzles. The tedious process gobbled up valuable time. The fire was advancing rapidly. We were constantly looking over our shoulders at the growing menace, but panic did not set in.

Finally the sprinklers were cleared and a young member of the structural protection crew came to me for a funnel. They needed to mix two-stroke oil with gas and ensure the gas cans were full. I had two fuel funnels, and asked him to come with me to where I had positioned an irrigation pump. But there was no funnel by the pump nor at the next possible site where I might have left it. Embarrassed, I asked him to return to the creek until I found one.

All members of firefighting crews have two-way radios. While I was looking for the funnel, the call came out from ic that all structural protection people were to leave the valley immediately. The conflagration was "spotting" (throwing embers that ignite new fires) as much as half a kilometre ahead of the main burn, and flames could be seen licking at the edge of the ridge—its angry core just beyond. I finally found a funnel and reached the creek where the pumps were installed. I stopped, speechless, as one might do having walked into a domestic dispute. Two structural protection people were next to the pumps standing in a mixture of oil, gas, water and muck at the other side of the creek. They had managed to get oil and gas into a can using a cut-off plastic oil carton as a funnel, but had spilled some in the process. The older man was panicking as a result of the radio call and was frantically pulling on the cord to start the pump. It was not even sputtering.

He yelled, "It has something to do with the prime," still pulling rapidly on the cord.

The younger thought he meant the priming of water in the intake line and went to disconnect the intake hose.

"Don't touch that," screamed the older. I nodded in dumb silence knowing that was not the issue but not wanting to add to the confusion.

"You have to calm down," demanded the younger. I again wordlessly nodded.

The older kept ripping at the cord and adjusting the throttle and choke levers.

The younger beseeched him to calm down again, only to have him yell out in tearful panic, "*We are in wildfire mode.*"

I was still motionless when Pascal nudged me aside and crossed the creek. He asked what they had done and bent over the pump, checking the hose connections. Everything seemed fine and he explained that if the gas line was removed from the can you had to constantly pump a bulb in the line until the fuel reached the pump (being careful not to flood it). After a few times alternately pumping the bulb and casually pulling the cord, the pump began to sputter.

He turned to the two. "Now *you* go to the truck and *don't move.*" He continued nursing the pump until it ran smoothly and the sprinklers sprang to life over the greenhouse and Monika's cabin. As he got up to leave I asked him to relate the issues to me once again. He calmly explained the importance of not letting the gas line drain, and if it did, it was essential to keep pumping the bulb until it was completely refilled.

Since their first day at our place, Comox Fire Rescue had left a truck in our meadow. They would fly in by helicopter and drive back and forth between all the structures in the valley. Faced with the possibility of our place being overrun by the fire, they took the truck out to Anahim Lake.

Mark was not pleased to hear that Lee and Pat had come into the valley. He went at once to the Taylors' and strongly advised them to evacuate. Lee's knee was not 100 per cent. He still limped badly and had promised Pat that in an emergency they would leave, so this is what they did. They followed the structural protection people out. Fortunately, the tote road ran away from the fire. The smaller helicopters had cleared our meadows of their equipment. At the onset of the fire, weeks before, I had joked with Monika that when they started moving out the equipment we would know we were in danger. That day had finally come. Mark returned with Dan, from IC, and said we should really leave. They had reserved two places for us in the helicopter. Monika and I sat on the back of our old pickup parked in the meadow. We stared at the northern horizon now covered with the boiling smoke and shook our heads.

"It looks like a scene from *Ghostbusters II*," I muttered.

"We will watch it from the air as long as we can but we have to go now," Mark added as he returned to the helicopter.

I wandered out to the barn and sprayed water on the walls one more time. The action felt pathetic but I had to do something. Monika joined me and we again stood mesmerized by the fire—flames were now licking at the top of the ridge above the greenhouse. Then we noticed plumes of smoke rising from the slopes between our place and the Taylors'. The fire was passing us, throwing embers with ease over our largest meadow, starting new blazes, surrounding us and advancing toward the ranch. Embers must have fallen on our meadows as well but they were cut and still moist after our extended irrigation in preparation for this event.

Mark spotted the new plumes from his helicopter and called for the two heavies to bucket them. They were far enough from the

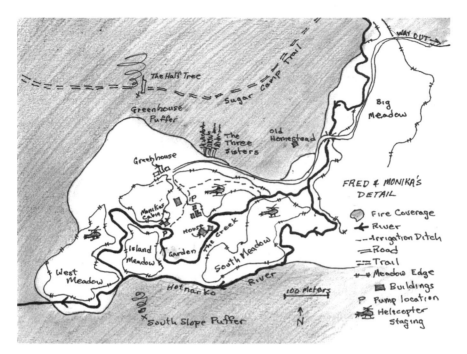

After the rank-five blaze on August 3, the fire continued to creep into our property—but our structures and lives were protected by the green meadow, which it could not penetrate. Drawn by Fred Reid.

rank-five inferno to be safe. They could not bucket for long, however, as darkness quickly encroached. We now had flames on three sides and understood why you should not leave at the last minute in front of a raging fire.

As darkness fell, a red glow etched the sky above our northern ridge. Embers had fallen onto the slope above the greenhouse and there were several spot fires under the pines but none that were close enough to cause major concern. Monika and I had become accustomed to the habits of fire so when we sensed it settling beyond the ridge we knew the threat of thrown embers had passed and we became a bit giddy.

When the phone rang I thought it would be Lee or Pat checking in, but the voice on the other end identified himself as Dennis from the RCMP. I assumed he was from the Anahim Lake detachment.

"We heard that the fire is threatening your place. How close is it?"

"Just above the ridge. Within a couple of hundred metres."

"Can we send in a helicopter tomorrow to get you out?"

"It will probably be very smoky, and we do not want to go."

"Why don't you want to go?"

I tried to be light. "Because the world out there is crazier than here—even with the fire."

He was absolutely humourless and began repeatedly asking me who was in the house and how our names were spelled and why we would not leave, and again wanting our names. When he asked me when was the last time an RCMP officer had visited and who he was I realized that he must not be from Anahim Lake.

"Where are you calling from?"

"Williams Lake."

"Why!" I said. "I shouldn't even be talking to you. This is a Coastal fire, not a Cariboo fire."

He didn't get the joke.

Pat and Lee drove to Anahim Lake to register their evacuation and then to Clint and Karen's south of Williams Lake. Close to midnight Pat posted: "Thursday, August 3, 11:20 p.m. The fire got too close for my comfort today so Lee and I left the valley. Caleb and Fred and Monika chose to stay. Their buildings and our ranch structures are well sprinkled but our house is too far from the river so our sprinkler system will run out after three hours if it is not attended. We drove through dense smoke and falling ash along Highway 20 to get here. Lee was exhausted and slept a lot of the way. Thirty minutes before we left he had to start up the bulldozer to get to a new water supply down at the ranch buildings. Yesterday, he fixed a baler and moved haying equipment back up to our place. So our short three-day visit was busy. Feeling anxious for our friends but know they are making informed decision to stay. They have been living through this for four weeks, but it is all new and very scary for me."

Pat shared a photo she took of Mark and his fellow firefighters at the Anahim Lake Airport. Seeing the picture, I was struck with an overwhelming feeling of loss. The feeling surprised me and neither Monika nor I could explain it. I felt it might have been brought on by the dramatic advance of the fire. We had lost the battle; it was now upon us. Our meadows could no longer be used as a staging area, which meant we were also going to lose the energy and excitement involved in fighting the fire over the last month. We had come to rely so much on these people and felt the comradeship one gets when thrown together under a crisis. Monika, who was more frightened of the fire than I, explained it as a loss of security like a young child might feel when their parent leaves them suddenly alone in a room. The parent could have just gone to the next room but the child's feeling of vulnerability is strongly felt. Like the child, we were suddenly alone.

Unable to sleep, Monika and I went outside and studied the aftermath of the rank-five blaze. Our north ridge was silhouetted against its yellow/orange glow—still very hot. At times it would flare above the ridge but it seemed distant and less threatening. The five or six spot fires on the slope next to the greenhouse were all less than twenty square metres, and entirely on the ground. The largest was directly above a knoll on which three large Douglas fir that we called the "Three Sisters" stood. We shut down the sprinklers, set the alarm to go off every two hours so that we could check on the fire, and went to bed.

The Fire Is Guided Past Us

PRECIPICE, AUGUST 4–5

WE HAD A RESTLESS NIGHT. A RED GLOW PERSISTED BEYOND THE trees in both the western and northern horizons. Our sleep was often broken by the barking of Buster, our remaining dog. He seemed to be disturbed by the fire and I guess he was—reacting to the occasional flare as trees candled or crashed as they fell just beyond our meadow. The fire was still very intense (now a rank four) as it consumed the fuel on our valley's edge.

Night was just beginning to turn into day as I went to the outhouse at 4:00 a.m. The glow behind the ridge was not as evident now but the spot fires on the greenhouse slope seemed already to be heating up. I could hear them crackling as they searched for more fuel. The one above the Three Sisters had expanded by several square metres. I anxiously looked up—I could see stars. I hoped that the smoke would not settle and prevent the helicopters from coming in.

My weather report on the morning of August 4 was more personal than usual. "It was an anxious night. The smoke settled at about 5:30 a.m. There is still a wall of smoke to the west but it's a bit thinner to the east. The fire spotted on the hill above the greenhouse. One blaze is now roughly ten by twenty metres in size. I have attached a picture. 8.6 degrees, little dew, no rain and no wind. It promises to be a very hot day. The sun is breaking through in the southeast and the smoke seems to be lifting in that direction."

Later in the morning I added, "Still very socked in to the west. Seventeen degrees and a breeze has just started—seems to be out of the south."

Mark responded, "Thank you for the update, Fred. Please keep these coming. We have Structure Protection heading your way, along with some IA crews to assist them. We are attempting to get in by helicopter to assess the fire growth, but the smoke is still hampering our ability to do so. I am going to make another try shortly."

Ken from IC also responded. "Thank you for checking back. We were all so relieved to hear that you got through that terrible night. The crews are just getting ready to head out to your place this morning. Hopefully, you will all have another good day. Take care and don't hesitate to call or email anytime."

Arlen chipped in. "Sounds like you guys had an interesting time. I am now sitting across from Mark and saw the email you sent him. They gave me fifteen minutes notice at around 4:30 yesterday to head back to Bella Coola. Look forward to seeing you guys—unfortunately not the best circumstances. I am glad that you guys are doing OK."

VA0778, it appeared, had exploded. It had grown from twenty-five hundred to thirty-six hundred hectares in a single day.

The fire now smouldered as a rank-two fire on the slopes just above our greenhouse. We had been the first line of defence against the fire's onslaught, but now we were surrounded by it. Many things would change. Anahim Lake was put under evacuation alert. IC contracted heavy equipment to construct more fire-breaks between us and Anahim Lake. The Taylor Ranch would now become the staging area.

The smoke continued to settle all morning. With the thick shroud back in place, feelings of hopelessness increased. We had now experienced the advance of the fire twice. Both times it had hidden below its veil of smoke where it could not be fought with helicopters. "I am a little sorry for all these gloomy posts," I wrote. "I am drawn to the fire constantly now. I have little enthusiasm for anything else. I was in our south meadow cutting hay with the scythe when the fire took off yesterday. Now I wonder why I do any of these chores, yet today the strawberries have to be picked and the greenhouse watered. But first we will check all our pumps."

Pat replied: "Friday, August 4, noon: Thank you Fred and Monika for the continued updates. It is the only way people know you are alive and functioning. We brought the strawberries you gave us out with us—odd what one packs at the last moment. Their ripe fresh juiciness sustained us on our long smoky drive to WL and supplied a delicious contribution to our morning breakfast.

"As we drove through the ash-falling darkness last night, I wondered if we had just leaped from the frying pan into the fire. What if we had hit a deer or other wildlife on our way? Interesting to me how 'living life in a crisis zone' reveals the oddities and the beauty of this precious life we live.

"Lots of people sending you good wishes, affirmations and love—a whirlwind of strong powerful energy coming your way—although more wind is not what you need. Ha! Be well! Much love!"

As soon as he could, Mark came in to see how we were doing. With him were the pilot, a new one this time (from Australia); Kelly, a new ignition specialist—friendly and open; Lonny—a bit stand-offish; and Arlen, now bearded like a hockey player in the playoffs. I did not recognize him at first—until he spoke and his shy smile shone through the beard. I stumbled to give him a hug. He introduced Lonny as the "equipment guy." I thought Lonny must be a Caterpillar driver because he stood back but he had the classic red shirt of a provincial firefighter. It would be another change of command. How could I remember all the names of the people I would be so grateful to?

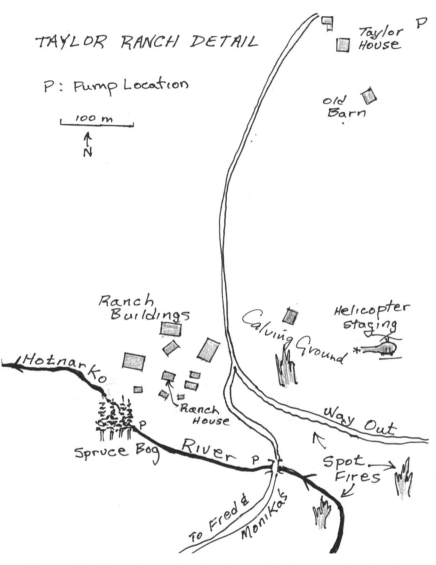

TAYLOR RANCH DETAIL

P: Pump Location

100 m

N

Taylor House — P

Old Barn

Ranch Buildings

Calving Ground

Helicopter staging

Hotnarko

Spruce Bog

Ranch House

River — P

Way Out

Spot Fires

To Fred & Monika's

The ranch buildings close to the river were easier to protect than the house, which had only a limited water supply. Spot fires were the biggest concern. Drawn by Fred Reid.

Caleb struggled to improve the fire protection at the Taylor Ranch. It was now directly in line of the advancing flames. That ever resourceful man had designed a better way to bring water to the bladder at the Taylor house, and the structural protection crew brought in a second pump, which would increase the effectiveness as long as there was water available.

The heavies were called in and they began dumping water between our home and the Taylor place. It seemed a bit hopeless because the fires were growing so rapidly. The helicopters would occasionally swing by to drop a bucketload on the spot fire near our greenhouse—not to put it out but rather move it gradually down to the meadow's edge. Allowing it to continue to burn slowly takes away the fuel and protects our buildings from future flare-ups. The Douglas fir and aspen will survive this slow burning process but many of the pines go up as fiery candles. The juniper growing close to the ground sizzled and crackled angrily as the fire crept under it. Suddenly there was smoke and steam as the bushes were consumed.

I had been oblivious to the stress I had been under until the end of the day, when I suddenly felt much lighter. I wrote: "You are all spared a long post. I had written one only to have it gobbled up because I hit the wrong key or something. We slept in the middle of the day."

Monika and I actually nodded off with the reassuring sound of the heavies' propellers pounding away. When we got up, we started the sprinklers around the house, then walked to the greenhouse. We questioned why the fire above it did not seem so threatening. "Is this," we thought, "the new normal?"

The following morning, Mark informed me: "We have crews rolling in this morning to address that spot fire. Our weather forecaster advised me yesterday that smoke will be worse… So crews will be accessing by vehicle. I have other wheels turning including dozer lines going in to the west, and some additional dozer lines to strengthen the Beef Trail around Anahim. So please keep me posted if you observe any changes in wind or fire behaviour."

A little later I emailed. "Fucking computer is so slow this morning. The wind has picked up and swung. It is coming from the northeast. Visibility is good from the east. You would be able to get in if you can get out of Bella Coola and swing around the smoke."

"Roger, thanks Fred... I'll try it."

With the fire now burning between our two properties, Caleb realized he might not be able to rely on us for help if the farm road between us were cut off. The Taylor Ranch was much more difficult to protect than our place—more treed, and with deep organic material in the form of uneaten hay and manure close to the buildings.

Caleb invited Clemens, a friend of his from Anahim Lake, to come into the valley. Clemens, a middle-aged European, had never experienced wildfires but he had helped set up the initial sprinkler system at the ranch. Lee began to worry about his cows up on their summer range. They would be directly in the fire's path should it take off for Anahim Lake.

Being within the fire brought many new emotions. We were now prisoners more than ever, but it did not feel the same. Instead of feeling *captured* by it, we actually became *captivated* by it. We were fascinated, wanting to know it more intimately. We were excited to see where it might flare up or if it would just creep and crawl. We lamented losses as well. We were familiar with trees that would catch our eye depending on season and light. The forest on the upper edge of the ridge to our north had burned. Certain trees on that ridge had always drawn my attention whenever I walked to the greenhouse. Some of them were now skeletons.

The list of people interested in our posts grew. We craved and sought their contributions. We missed our constant contact with helicopters and their crews, but now we had this growing new support. There were old friends and new friends. People as close as our neighbours in Stuie. "So glad we've connected with you now on FB to see so clearly what's happening uphill of us. All we get is the smoke, ash and choppers overhead. When they go back and forth, we try to imagine what's happening. You have lots of amazing support, though it appears a never-ending battle. We're feeling the stress here, eighteen kilometres away. I can only imagine how weary you must be. Stay safe. And know that there's always a cabin for you here! Hugs, from your Stuie neighbours Katie & Dennis."

Mark and Arlen would continue to come to our place as much as they could and were very keen on keeping us updated. But Mark flashed a rare show of anger when I told him that Clemens had come into the valley.

The fire still burned on the ground along the entire north slope and was dangerously close to the greenhouse and the Three Sisters. As the day's temperature climbed I began to get nervous. At 1:00 p.m. I turned on the sprinklers above the greenhouse. I felt it was not necessary to run the line that covered the house and the other buildings as they were not close to the fire. A unit crew had spent the morning establishing a cache of equipment on our big meadow, and a pump next to the river. They had laid over a kilometre of hose on the road between our place and the Taylors'. The road had acted as an effective fire-break, and they were watering the edge of it.

By 2:30 it was eerily quiet. They pulled the helicopters out because it was too smoky. The fire had gone into hiding again. This was good news for Anahim Lake but was always a little scary for us.

Only 6:30 p.m., but the colours and aura of this place made it look like the same time in early winter. There was still an hour or two of daylight ahead of us, but the sun was blocked by the thick blanket of smoke. Ash fell like that first early winter snowfall on the prairie. Lazy, lonely flakes drifting slowly to the frozen ground. These flakes, however, were not the geometric and elaborate shapes created by ice, but parched, hollowed-out alder or birch leaves. The temperature also belied this winter look; it was hot and humid, the ground was not frozen and our meadows were very green. The fire gently crawled through the valley bottom to the west of us sending up columns of smoke barely visible through the thick haze. There was very little wind—also like winter days on the prairie. Oh yeah! The bugs were too bad for it to be winter.

The Taylor Ranch did not have a view down the valley like we did, and each day Caleb grew more concerned as he could not see anything but smoke. He phoned frequently to find out what was going on. Now he asked why the ash was falling.

I explained, "It is just the fire in the Hotnarko Canyon settling down for the night. It is nothing to worry about. The more serious fire is the one above us. It's much hotter and may carry tips of spruce or pine branches. If they fly about, they will not drop as snowflakes but as small embers. But I don't think that will happen right now as the wind is not strong enough."

The fire had grown to 4,330 hectares.

Evacuation Order Again

KLEENA KLEENE, AUGUST 4–10

AUGUST 4, FOUR WEEKS TO THE DAY AFTER THE FIRST LIGHTNING storms and six days after we were downgraded to "alert," I received a phone call from Gerald at the Tatla Lake Manor. He was speaking with his Search and Rescue hat on. He told me that we were under evacuation order again. Gerald spouted the dogma that I was not to go to Bella Coola this time, but had to go east to Williams Lake. "I know," he said when I expostulated. "Total BS but this is what I have been told to say. I'm just giving you a heads-up." The police, he informed me, would be around to enforce the order.

I had not unpacked very much from the van, only food that might be compromised by heat. One item was the tote full of organic seeds and grains. This food would be impossible to replace locally. I am used to shopping for weeks or even months at a time, but on July 7 I had not anticipated being away from town so long. I was far from starving, but I might have to start rationing some of the items. At least I had the garden. I was eating a ton of greens by now, and the very first carrots.

The tote had been too heavy to lift and I was too lazy to unpack it, so I had backed the van to the loading bay and dragged the tote into the comparative cool of my outer room. I did not want to return the food into the van if I didn't have to, but in view of the upsurge in fire activity, I placed the van by the loading bay again so that the tote could be slid back in without delay.

A short time later, a cop drove into the yard. He asked for my address. I gave the property number and followed it with Highway 20. He did not know where Highway 20 was. "You've just been driving on it!" I exclaimed. He was from Alberta and had arrived only the day before. Large quantities of personnel were now swarming into the area, all coming for a two-week stint before being relieved by the next batch. It seems to be an ongoing frustration with this cumbersome firefighting machinery that the outsiders come in totally unprepared. They don't have the faintest idea of the geography of the country; they don't seem to be provided with maps or any other information from their predecessors—and they never think to enlist the help of locals. Each new batch of workers—and this appears to happen in all levels of firefighting from administration down to the lowliest shoveller—has to start from scratch. This seems to be in total contrast to Fred's accounts of what is going on in the Precipice. It was evident that the Coastal Division of the BC Wildfire Service was prepared to inform the public better—even I obtained far more information from them than I did from the Cariboo Division—but I wonder how frustrated Fred and Monika would feel if they were not in daily, face-to-face contact with the firefighting personnel?

The police officer repeated what Gerald had said, but this time I replied that I was not even going down to Bella Coola—I had assessed my risk factor, and I was staying. None of my immediate neighbours had left all the time the fire had been burning.

The cop did not look happy. He fished out a form. He needed to know the address of my next of kin in case I died. (They actually say this: it is obviously supposed to make people fearful and therefore more compliant.) I told him my next of kin was a brother who lived in England. I gave him my brother's name—spelled it slowly while he laboriously wrote it. *Czajkowski* bamboozles most North Americans when they first encounter it. My brother's address was also very difficult for him to process. "Ninety-six, capital *T*, small *o*, small *r*. Space. Small *o*, apostrophe. Space. Capital *M*, *o*, *o*, *r* Road." I named a small town in England that also needed spelling out. All this had to be repeated. He was a nice man but obviously not the sharpest sliver in the woodpile. Next he asked for my dentist. (This was also standard practice, so that if bodies were found they could be identified by their teeth.) "The last one I went to," I said, "was a travelling dentist who came to Anahim Lake a couple of years ago." You could see the poor man's shoulders slump as he struggled to write *travelling dentist* in the space provided. After that he gave up on me. I did not fit into the form's neat little boxes. Nor would anyone else around here. The officer must have had a really bad day.

I maintain a blog and throughout the fire I sometimes received criticism about my decision to stay. "It is putting fire personnel in danger if you don't get out," was the main complaint. Fair enough. But this is not a city. City people have to go. It would be a disaster if hundreds decided to flee all at once at the last minute. Also, city life would grind to a halt without electric power. No one could buy anything; gas pumps wouldn't work; people couldn't even flush their toilets. Out here, we are not reliant on hydroelectricity. Even those who are hooked up to the system have alternative ways of dealing with power outages. Everyone has bulk supplies of food and fuel, and we have tools to get ourselves out of difficulties such as blocked roads. We know where our neighbours are, even the ones more than an hour's drive away. We rely on each other. It's true that I probably would not have been as cavalier about staying if it wasn't for the internet. I figured I had as good a take on what was happening as most office personnel. I also had a lot of experience dodging fires—though none as serious for me as this one. I knew the country. I had a very good idea of how to read the sky and interpret the online

weather forecasts to determine what to expect in my area. I understood how the fire would be affected.

At the beginning, we kept in touch with the Tatla Command
Centre—they knew where everyone was. But when Forestry took
over and moved the command centre to Puntzi, we became nothing
but nuisance statistics. Sure, our staying, under those circumstances,
was a logistical nightmare. Why didn't Forestry keep the Tatla
Command Centre going? It would have helped them greatly.

WHAT, I WONDERED, HAD HAPPENED TO THE PEOPLE WHO LIVED CLOSE
to where the fire had almost crossed the road on July 13? Jaden was
the only year-round resident; his place was about eight kilometres
from mine as the helicopter flies, though much farther by road.
Jaden came into this country five years ago and lived in a tent while
he built himself a house. Now that the fire was flexing its muscles
again, would his place be in danger? The fire maps were indicating
that the new spread of flames was quite a bit south of his home
this time.

I sent him an email: "Where are you?"

"At home right now," he replied. "I evacuated the first time but
I'm not leaving now unless I absolutely have to."

And this was the story he told me.

On July 7, he had been at his cabin, counting the lightning strikes
on the ridges behind the hayfields at downtown Kleena Kleene. The
flames were a kilometre away. Like me, he watched and evaluated. On
July 9 the wind started to get up. Jaden had previously hand-dug a
small pond near his house to use for watering his garden. One of his
neighbours came around with a hose and a pump and they wet the
ground around Jaden's house as best as they could, but the little pond
soon ran dry. Jaden started putting things into his car; the smoke
increased, and in the gloom, he started racking up a good dose of panic.
He took the depressing decision to cut down all the trees around his

place. They weren't very big, but they had added an attractive and shady frame to his house. Now he was creating a yard of stumps.

He went over to the neighbour's to eat. Both men were in a high state of anxiety. That night, Jaden didn't get much sleep. Every couple of hours he got up to watch the progress of the fires.

The two of them were sitting down to dinner again at the neighbour's house on July 10 when the cops came. A man and a woman, so not the same ones who visited me.

"They were highly nervous," Jaden told me. "I thought cops were supposed to show how calm they were and in control of the situation, but these ones were going crazy.

"'You've gotta get out of here!' They spoke with panicky raised voices. And they made a big point of *at once*. Meaning, like, 'drop all your things and run, you're not allowed to take your time and pack.'"

Jaden told them he was going home to get some last-minute stuff.

"'No you're not!'

"'Yes I am!'

"'No you're not! You must LEAVE. RIGHT. NOW!'"

The neighbour insisted he was staying, and he tried to persuade Jaden to do the same and help him fight the fire. But Jaden's property was closer to the blaze and he felt that his life and the lives of his two dogs were more important than anything else, so he went back home, finished packing and at 10:00 p.m. looked back at his house and said goodbye.

There was very little traffic on the road. After Alexis Creek, he was bracketed by flames as he drove. The smoke was so thick he couldn't go more than fifty kilometres per hour. It was end-of-the-world eerie.

Half an hour from Williams Lake he encountered the first police barrier—the only one at that time. They were not preventing him from going east; they were only there to stop unauthorized westbound traffic. Jaden had friends in Vancouver and this was where he was aiming for, but the cops told him he wouldn't be able to go south because the 108 Mile Fire had closed Highway 97. He would have to first go north to Prince George. Jaden figured Prince George, densely surrounded by dry forest, had the potential to be another major fire hazard; at least Vancouver's wet climate and population density meant that most fires down there were kept under control. He could not believe that there wasn't an alternative way south even if the regular highways were closed.

Williams Lake was not yet evacuated and Jaden was able to get a coffee at Tim Hortons. The first barrier was at 150 Mile, not far from Williams Lake. The cop wasn't local and though he was pleasant about it, he was adamant that there was no alternative way to go. A kilometre farther back, however, Jaden had noted a side road blocked by another barrier. This proved to be manned by local cops, and they told him about a series of logging roads that might get him round the 108 Fire. It was now 2:00 a.m. Jaden knew the country fairly well and he was familiar enough with the start of the route so at first he had no problem. The roads were little used, rough and dusty. After a couple of hours' driving he needed to refer to his maps and GPS. Unfortunately he had packed in such a hurry that they were at the bottom of his stuff. It was just starting to get light at 4:30 a.m. when he unloaded the car to look for them. Naturally, they were in the very last container that he unearthed.

It was 7:00 a.m. when he arrived at Lillooet. It was the first time for days that he had been in an area free from all the signs of fires. Smoke, flames, road barriers—"It was like Armageddon," he described. Everyone he'd met up to now had been tense and serious. Now he could relax a little. But he did not stop. He knocked on the door of his friends' apartment in Vancouver at 11:00 a.m. He was so exhausted he could hardly speak. His friends welcomed him with open arms, but no one at that moment realized Jaden would be staying there for nearly a month.

It was a different kind of hell for Jaden. Like me, he needs space around him and was totally stifled in a city environment. He also felt very awkward imposing on his friends' hospitality. The apartment didn't allow dogs, but they broke the rules and smuggled them in anyway. (They were just little guys.)

Finally he heard that Highway 20 was open again and all the Chilcotin fires (except the Precipice) were upgraded to evacuation alert. He made haste to head north. But that very same day, Highway 97 was closed again due to the Elephant Hill Fire. (It was this flare-up that had prevented Pat and Lee from heading to the ranch at the same time.) His original route was still open, though, so he returned via the logging roads. His little car was old, and it had taken a good beating the first time; it received another battering on the drive north.

He drove into his yard to find he had acquired a new piece of furniture. An orange bladder full of water sat in the middle of his parking lot. It had been set up early on, when the flames had come very close to his house. Hoses and sprinklers snaked around his yard. That part of the fire, however, now seemed to be under control.

Now that Jaden was home, we were able to check up on each other and trade information. It was comforting to have another pair of eyes on the fire.

WE WERE NOW PRISONERS OF THE FIRE DRAGON. HE WAS HOLDING US in thrall with his smoke. Not the occasional thick blanket that is blown away in a few hours, or the tower-block columns rolling up from newly consumed material, but a solid bronze twilight. It had been going on for over a week. Days were brown, nights were thick and black. The smoke settled even deeper then; I sometimes slept with a scarf over my nose and mouth. When I stood on my deck in the daytime, I could just make out the far side of my property; I calculated, therefore, that visibility was about three hundred metres. Looking toward the mountains, I could not even distinguish the cottonwoods that line the river. They are half a kilometre away. I worried about the effect of the smoke on my lungs. I would have loved to have been able to leave and breathe clean air, but as people were now saying that the authorities were threatening to "forcibly" (in handcuffs?) escort residents out of the fire zone if they found us off our properties, and wouldn't let us return, I dared not go.

I reminded myself that in many cities of the world, this atmosphere was normal. Even Williams Lake used to be like this when the mills still operated the old beehive burners. Moreover, the air in some of these cities is not just full of particles, but toxic chemicals as well.

Environment Canada's satellite photos showed a huge area over most of British Columbia free of water vapour. Thirty-degree temperatures seemed to be the norm. But this vast area was far from clear. It was covered by a static brown blanket of smoke. At its southwestern end there must have been a wind, for it flowed over Vancouver and Seattle, and swept way out into the Pacific Ocean. News items issued warnings to city folk about their terrible air-quality index; the slant of the articles was almost accusatory, as if they blamed us for their inconvenience. Friends emailed me with their air-quality figures, but there were no measurements for this area. A Vancouver friend excitedly told me about the weird orange light in that city. We got orange light sometimes, and it was eerie and beautiful at the same time. But it happened only when the smoke was not all that thick. In this solid gloom, everything was brown. I did not even hear helicopters much. The smoke was likely too dense for them to work.

Even when there were no shadows on the ground, the sun in the sky in the middle of the day was too bright to look at, and this kept my solar panels charged so that, at least, was something. The previous weekend, the promise of showers had appeared briefly on the weather forecast. It was so dark that morning that I wondered whether clouds were building up behind the smoke. But the sun, which could not penetrate smoke close to the ground, eventually manifested itself dimly when it was higher in the sky. There was not even a hint of rain. As the sun lowered, it turned red and finally a peculiar brownish pink before it dissolved into the murk. It was an alien colour scheme, like that of a sky in a science-fiction movie. But I no longer got excited at this anaemic red balloon floating in the polluted soup. It was old hat. The full moon came and went, and it, too, was round and red when it was visible at all, but did not give out enough light for me to photograph it.

Another friend wrote that she could smell smoke in the Gulf Islands (west of Vancouver). She commented that it must be much worse for us, but in fact I rarely smelled it unless it was at choking level. One's olfactory sense rapidly ignores persistent odours. It is a defence thing so that you can be aware of new dangers.

One would think that this smoke would drive away the bugs. When it was very thick, there weren't any. But when it thinned a little, the blackflies loved it. They were dissipated by clear sunshine but as soon as a haze of cloud or smoke dulled the sky they attacked in full force. The smoke also moderated temperature. The forecast was regularly slated for thirty-two degrees Celsius but we had stayed around twenty-eight—although when the smoke eased enough to allow the sun to create vague shadows the day before, it warmed to thirty. In previous summers, temperatures in the thirties would often mean frosts at night. But the smoke modified that, too, and our mornings were around four or five degrees.

Like fog, smoke also magnified noise. I had thought fog conducted noise due to the moisture in it, but as smoke seemed to behave the same way, there must be another scientific explanation. Day and night, heavy trucks going up and down Highway 20 sounded as if they were in my yard and I heard them for many kilometres on either side of my place. I was at first puzzled at the apparent movement of so much heavy machinery, but to my amazement, I learned, by phone, that they were logging. Logging is usually stopped when fire conditions are serious and, this year, hauling had been halted the day before the fires started. There had long been a ban on any backcountry use—why the heck were they allowing logging trucks to work now? It wasn't as if they were hauling piles from fireguards either; this was a new area away from the fire. What loophole had the logging companies managed to get through to be permitted to operate at this time?

THE ONLY RELIEF FROM THE SMOKE WAS THE SCREEN. I BECAME AN internet junkie. I was hooked on the soap opera of the fires. First thing in the morning, I switched on the computer and checked the fire sites. Same after breakfast, and at noon, again in the afternoon, and before I went to bed. I was like a kid with an iPhone.

On August 4, my first cyberspace visit was to Fred and Monika's Facebook page. How relieved I was to see that they were still alive. It was interesting to note on the fire sites that the Precipice seemed to be the only blaze that received really strong winds on August 3. We had a good blow but nothing out of the ordinary and according to the websites, our fires did not spread far.

Every nuance of wind is so important in a fire zone. I had recently been sent a link to a fascinating site called Windfinder. It has a new colour scheme to learn. The shades are nothing to do with temperature, but with wind speed. When "particles" are activated, streaks swim around like little sperm. You can zoom out and see the great swirls over the ocean. Right then most of the Americas and Russia were a pinky mauve, which indicated very light winds. When I zoomed in to Kleena Kleene, I saw that the little sperm were barely moving. It was mesmerizing to look at. Like a TV program. But mountain winds are fickle. They are not always blowing in the same direction in the same general area at the same time. Often I have seen cloud layers moving in two, even three different directions when the ground wind bore no relationship to any of them. Windfinder can pick only one of these to demonstrate. That apart, the site seemed pretty accurate in its predictions.

To get a more intimate reading of the wind speed and direction, I erected a slightly less high-tech device: a piece of flagging tape tied to a stick. It was extremely sensitive. It fluttered when a puff of air was not even strong enough to move the grasses. I called it my flag-o-meter.

Now that the Precipice Fire had leaped ahead, there was serious concern that Nimpo and Anahim Lakes would be in danger. I doubted that any property would be damaged there, however—they were still a good distance away from the flames. It was also getting on for mid-August; surely the cooler weather must come soon, and there were now hundreds of firefighters in the area. I did, however, give a small thought to my pickup truck and trailer full of stuff that was stored at Stewart's Lodge. I never mentioned it to them, but Katie and Dennis were on the same wavelength and they offered to come up from the Bella Coola Valley to take the pickup down to their place. They would be able to drive there legally. I would meet them at the lodge. As far as I knew there were still no barriers between Kleena Kleene and Nimpo; nonetheless, I snuck out of my driveway with some trepidation.

Nimpo Lake was a millpond. A Cessna 185, the only plane they had not got out of there, was sitting on its perfect reflection by the wharf. Visibility might have been a kilometre here, but no one was flying. The lodge was quiet; there were no tourists. Two red Adirondack chairs sat on the deck facing the lake, the only splash of colour in a sepia landscape. They emphasized the loneliness of the fire zone; the sense of being cut off from the normal world. Katie told me that, as they were driving up the Bella Coola Hill, they met a truck going down carrying a snowmobile. Hardly the weather for snow sports so no doubt it was someone else putting their gear in a safer place.

Because of her asthma, Katie was wearing a heavy-duty industrial mask. We chatted briefly, but she needed to get into the clearer air of the Bella Coola Valley. Off they went, Katie driving the truck and trailer, and Dennis piloting their car. I was able to get home without being challenged.

Our Personal Fire

PRECIPICE, AUGUST 6–7

"LEE AND I ARE FINDING IT EXTREMELY DIFFICULT TO LEAVE WILLIAMS Lake for Vancouver today," Pat posted on August 6. "Although there is no way we will be allowed back into the valley any time soon, I feel a need to stay close to our Cariboo/Chilcotin neighbourhood. I feel more connected with our valley neighbours by being here in Williams Lake with other fire evacuees, sharing stories, living with the same confusing uncertainties and breathing the same smoky air."

Monika and I understood the desire to stay closer to the crisis. We had grown accustomed to our fire and its habits. We had become enamoured with it. Not as a friend but definitely as an entity of great interest. I felt bad for it in some ways because it paled in comparison to the much bigger, controversial fires that grabbed the attention of the media. It was our very own personal Precipice Fire. It seemed especially so when we were alone late at night with the smoke and the red glow in the sky. But we even had that feeling with the constant sound of helicopters. We felt guilty that so many people and so much money was being spent to fight our personal fire, even though we knew it was not just for us. When it sat idle to the west of us, I thought we would defeat it before it reached Anahim Lake. Now that it had passed us, I was not so sure.

When Monika reported the fire on July 7, they asked her for the colour of the smoke. "What in the hell for?" I thought. Now we study smoke intensely. We study smoke through a smoky haze. Black means hot and white cool. They asked what the size of the fire was. I thought it was silly to report the fire someone else must have seen and already reported. "Say a few hectares," I told her. Monika has a German accent, and the person at the other end of the phone must have heard "four." I later wondered how they knew it was four hectares then realized it is what we had inadvertently told them. It was our fire.

The daily Incident Action Plan (IAP) printed at the field office in Bella Coola called VA0778 the Precipice Fire. I was happy for that. The BC Wildfire Service website still called it the "Precipice Creek, Stillwater Lake, Hotnarko Fire." This did not please me. I did not want to share this fire with anyone. The Precipice Fire had become our very personal fire.

I craved getting the IAPs with their delightful and informative pictures on the cover and their poignant expressions. One showed the Atnarko footbridge in the park that they had worked so hard to save. Accompanying it was a caption: "The hardest thing in life to learn is which bridge to cross and which one to burn." Others included, "Safety is a state of mind—accidents are an absence of mind" and "Never Give Safety a Day Off."

I sought crumpled copies from pilots and firefighters with their details of equipment caches, helipad locations and phone numbers. I cannot say much about them as they contained official and confidential information, but a quick review of the number of helipads revealed how complex the fight against the fire had become—July 18 there were two; July 21, three; July 28, seven; August 2, ten; and August 5, eleven. The August 5 map update had the fire at 4,330 hectares. Our fire had grown from four to 4,330 hectares. Now we were losing it to others.

We craved getting these IAPs, but they were confidential so we only came across a few. Photo by Fred Reid.

The plans chief in the IC is the person who prepares the IAP for the next day's flights. He or she has to capture all the data, and work with the incident commander and the operations chief late into the night.

We had become so captivated by the fire and the battle against it that it was difficult to return to the task of haying. But the need to get it done was as urgent as ever. With the grass drying rapidly and the fire very hot and active, we needed to remove this dangerous fuel from the meadows.

The thick smoke persisted. Caleb phoned in the morning. "Can you see anything?"

"No, just too smoky, but Monika saw a strong red glow to the west at the bottom of the Hotnarko Canyon. I saw the same at 4:00 a.m. and could not sleep from that time forward." I was exhausted.

"I think we should start baling your south meadow," Caleb suggested. The grass had been cut just before the rank-five blaze struck and we had left it lying in the field, rather than raking it into windrows that could be more of a fire hazard.

I was reluctant, but conceded that we should. "If you can get through the fires between us you are welcome to come down." (But I was thinking, "Man… that guy is crazy.") "I will start raking at eleven. You should be able to come at one."

After our morning coffee, Monika and I headed to the greenhouse to water whatever needed it but neither of us had much enthusiasm for this day. The air was choking with smoke and we knew that the helicopters would not come. We expected it to get worse. I searched for the spot fires above the greenhouse but could see nothing. It was as if the smoke itself was suppressing them.

Raking the south meadow was agony. Heading west, in the direction of our house, I could see a column of black smoke darker than the rest of the thick haze in front of it. The fire was obviously very hot in the Hotnarko Canyon. Every time I turned round at the end of the field and headed the other way, my stress eased. A classic case of "out of sight, out of mind." But on the westward turn I faced that scary plume again and would think: "I should quit now. Damn, why didn't I turn the sprinklers on before I left home?" Then I would turn east and my worry would subside. In this fashion I nearly finished raking. Then Monika appeared in the meadow. My heart rate soared thinking something must be desperately wrong. I waved and she waved in return. It was a relaxed wave. I felt relieved and then saw the camera around her neck—more relief, or maybe joy. I finished raking while she took pictures.

Once home, I immediately turned on the sprinklers. I struggled with the pump, then it fired up and I felt a little safer.

It was the sounds of the sprinklers and pump that gave me the most peace of mind; for Monika it was the helicopters pounding at the fire. These had become relaxing sounds for both of us. I remembered being irritated by our volunteer's drone right at the start of the fire. We had come a long way since then.

With sprinklers pulsing near the house and the high-pitched whine of the Wajax pump by the creek, Monika and I felt comfortable enough to begin exploring the fire. One of its many fronts was in the pine behind the greenhouse. The smouldering ground fire spewed thick smoke but we ventured outside with our camera to capture some aspect of it. We laughed at the thought that a week or so ago we were petrified when we first saw flames cresting a ridge three and a half kilometres away. Now they were just a stone's throw away. We sat on upturned buckets waiting for individual trees to flare into flames, creating red glows within the dense orange-grey smoke. But like trying to get a picture of an elusive songbird, by the time we got the camera to our eye and focused it, the flame became another puff of smoke in the almost featureless wall.

Caleb decided not to come and bale hay at our place. Driving slow-moving haying equipment through the ever-thickening smoke with flames next to the road between us was just too dangerous. I was grateful for this because I could have more time with the fire. I was also grateful that Clemens had decided to stay for another night; I would not have to worry about Caleb being there on his own. They had no view down the valley and the smoke was often thicker at the ranch. Each day they drove ATVs up to a viewpoint above the Taylor house, or sometimes as high as Precipice Lake. But the higher they went, the denser the smoke became.

They became frustrated that they could see nothing and decided that the ATVs, which could travel much faster than the hay equipment, could be risked on the road between our places. They coaxed Monika and me to come see the fire next to the road. There was a dead pine leaning over it, burning vigorously when they had passed. They did not have a chainsaw and feared that it might have fallen across the road. We raced behind them with our chainsaw strapped to our ATV. The hills above the road were now a mosaic of green patches and areas of deep orange flame from candling trees cloaked behind orange and brown smoke. We stood by the burning tree. It had not yet fallen. It would be good to get it down and out of the way, but it was too dangerous to climb the steep slope to its flaming base. We had not seen firefighters come into the valley, but they had been there and laid hoses along the road from the river to past where the tree was burning. We undid a coupling and drew the hoses back to the green side of the road to prevent any chance of them being destroyed. The road was proving to be an effective guard and the fire had not crossed to the thick grass and willow below it. The fire was now moving rapidly uphill, where it had found new fuel. I was not tempted to try and stop it. The first rule of fighting a fire is to never attack it from the uphill side.

Back at home we did a few chores, prepared supper and went out to watch for candling trees. Miraculously we heard a helicopter. I always liked that scene from the show *M*A*S*H* when the characters stand on a ridge waiting for the helicopters to come in—you see the helicopters behind them and they all turn to watch. It felt a bit like that. We peered into the smoke. There it was, twenty to thirty metres above the trees.

Shane had flown Mark in to give us an update. This was their fifth attempt. Finally the winds had shifted just enough to give them an opening. They confirmed that the fire had grown a lot and was now well up in the hills above us but still to the west of the Taylor Ranch. Mark confirmed that they had bulldozed three fireguards between our valley and Anahim and Nimpo Lakes in case the fire should take a run at the towns.

I was not sleeping well at night—I was not sure whether it was the smoke and the stuffy room (we always kept the windows closed so that we could breathe) or the uncertainty about the situation we were in. Thick smoke with no discernible flame or plume addled my mind, confused and disturbed me. In the morning I would question my judgment when describing conditions that I could not accurately measure.

Early in the morning of August 7, I emailed Mark: "Temperature dropped from 9.8 to 9.6 degrees in the last fifteen minutes. The barometer has risen slightly. Less dew than yesterday. No teardrop formed on the truck's window with my diagonal finger test. The windmill that we use to generate power turned during the night indicating that a stronger breeze had come out of the ssw, but now it is very calm with a slight air movement from the south. The smoke is thick and visibility not good."

An hour later I had not yet heard from Mark and I stewed over my judgment. I emailed IC. "Hi Ken. I was out just now and the dew is still falling. More moisture on the grass. I would now say moderate to heavy dew. Temperature 9.4 degrees and you can really see your breath. No wind."

"Thank you Fred. I will print off your message for Mark so he can see it as soon as he gets here."

Lee was also up early talking with Caleb by phone. Caleb was concerned about having enough fuel to run the pumps. Lee emailed Mark and copied to me. "Hello Mark, Pat and I are now in Vancouver, keeping in regular contact with the valley. We are very appreciative of all the efforts of the structural folks in keeping our homes safe. Last night, Caleb expressed concern that we may run low on fuel, especially if he has to continue to replenish the fuel supply over at the Red Roof House. As a consequence, we may run short of both gas and 2-cycle oil. He asked me to enquire into the possibility of getting additional fuel and oil brought in. What do you think would be the best way to handle this? Would it be allowable to arrange with someone from Anahim Lake to bring some?"

I flushed with anger. It had been my domain to communicate with the firefighters, pilots and Incident Command. This was my fire. I was the one who could handle it. I emailed Lee.

"Lee. Please back off. These people have been nothing but helpful to us. When they say they will look after us they will. I talked with Caleb and we both feel that everything is fine here and there is no need to panic. Please let these people do their job."

Mark was unperturbed and replied: "I will look after this for you. Do you know how much he's looking for? Arlen is my right-hand man, and he will be driving/flying in to check on dozer lines and crews. I am sure he can line something up."

Faced with days of thick smoke and my unreasonable anger at Lee, I plunged once again into confusion and doubt. I woke up on Monday morning just past six. My throat was sore and I had a slight headache, but I had apparently snored loudly through much of the night so that might have been the cause. Monika had not slept well and was grumpy. The unrelenting worry and smoke was getting to us. I finished the morning weather report but then began to agonize about all the information I was putting out there.

My initial reports had felt so concrete and solid. "Three millimetres rain, broken cloud, eight degrees and no wind." Now I went out and searched for the finer clues and I was afraid to get them wrong. The staff at the wildfire office were always very encouraging, valuing this information from the ground, but this added to my sense of responsibility and need to be accurate. Was I reading the signs correctly? Was the windmill pointing to the ssw or the wsw? When had the wind been strong enough to swing it? The leaves on the trees were not moving but I could see my breath drift into the smoke— but in what direction? Overnight recovery of humidity, as estimated by the dew, was very important. But how was I to determine this? There was dew but should I measure it in the house meadow, where the grass was still green and lush, or where it was getting parched?

Thank god Mark promised to bring me a hydrometer for reading relative humidity. I needed a concrete number. The responsibility became agonizing on mornings when I felt this doubt.

Whenever I experienced these dark moments I wandered around to take pictures of the flowers, gardens and animals, reaffirming why I live in this beautiful valley. I engaged in the menial chores of the farm and tried to ignore the fire for a bit. I would post about these activities to alleviate my concerns.

"I harvested garlic and planted the last of the lettuce today. It was great to be on the end of a shovel with my back to the fire. But it is still there, only today it chooses to hide in its veil of smoke. The fire is taking its toll on us with its dogged persistence, yet it is reluctant to show its best hand and rage forward. Our nerves are getting frayed. Caleb barked at me yesterday and I barked and growled back at him. I snarled at Lee today, and he and Pat are frustrated with being out of the loop and wanting dearly to help. Mark berated us all for allowing Clemens to come in and help Caleb.

"I love them all dearly and we must stick together and keep things as normal as possible. I must do more gardening."

Losses were now faintly visible through the cover of smoke where the fire persistently clawed at the western edge of our property. The occasional tree would succumb and flare in an instant, resulting in a bright glow through the gloom. We mourned one pine two hundred metres from our property line that stood above the others. It was the harbinger of both early and late winter. When the sun passed low on the horizon at those times of year, its light would shine through a gap in the ridge and hit this tree's top and no other. It was a bright beacon of the changing season. Now when the smoke lifted enough we could see only its naked branches.

If the fire is a dragon, as it is often portrayed, then we are living in its stomach. However, we are encased within our green meadows and, like Jonah in the whale, seem to be indigestible. The dragon's breath was hot as it swallowed us, but it is cooler now. The dragon continues to consume the trees around us. We can hear the gurgling from within the stomach but can see nothing because of its thick lining of smoke. It also belches occasionally, annoyed with the resistant morsel that we represent. We wait anxiously in this stomach, anticipating our passing through its digestive system. Hopefully we will be deposited as a mass of green and not one of brown or black.

Because smoke hampered helicopter access into the valley, visibility became an important part of my weather reports. The pilots pointed out to us which ridges or trees would indicate a half kilometre or kilometre of visibility. I chose particular trees along these ridges. When I could see a certain one and not another I had a good estimate.

August 7 was a civic holiday—BC Day. No one involved with this fire was taking the day off.

The morning was unfolding into "another boring day with this fire. We are getting weary with the whole thing. It is tough to stay motivated in any way. The smoke forces us to stay inside and I find myself falling asleep while gazing out the window at it."

That afternoon, we had lots of visitors. Caleb and Clemens were the first to stop in. They were growing more anxious about the fire and were frustrated by the ever-increasing smoke. The structural protection unit came in by truck to test the sprinkler systems. Helicopters could not fly over the fire because of all the smoke, but Shane found a way round to bring in Mark and Kelly, the most recent ignition specialist, to update us regarding the fire-breaks between the Precipice and Anahim Lake. They had stopped in at the Taylor Ranch and noticed Clemens. Mark was angry with his continued presence in the valley and he assured us that no one else unauthorized would be allowed into the valley against the evacuation order.

In the late afternoon Josh, a young firefighter with a red shirt, chest pack and two-way radio drove into our yard. He explained he was responsible for the ground crew working east of us but he was going to take a look at the fire where it was bubbling away on our western border. Monika was worried that he might be trapped by an afternoon run. But Josh simply shrugged and smiled before crossing our island meadow and entering the forest. On his return he mentioned that they might have to do something there.

So we ended up having quite a social day! We even went over to Caleb's for supper. To my surprise the leaning pine still stood, though it was burned halfway across its base. It was eventually cut down by a danger tree faller. The road had proved to be a secure fire-break, and no trees were burned on its southern side. The fire had moved on from the spot we had first visited with Caleb and Clemens, and we were amazed at how much of the forest had burned on the northern side of the road in a relentless crawl to the Taylor Ranch. We assumed that the firefighters had been doing a ground back burn to strengthen the road as a fire-break.

I told Lee by phone that there had been a back burn between our homes, not realizing I was wrong at the time, and was soon to feel bad when Pat posted that night. "I cried when Fred told Lee about the back burn. It may be the best way to prevent the fire from getting out of control and racing up the valley floor and I am glad for that, but not having a chance to say a proper goodbye to this part of our valley landscape breaks my heart. I have passed that hillside—through winter, spring, summer and fall… To see these photos from Fred and Monika's blog tonight just made me sad for all the changes going on in the valley that I have utterly no control over. I thank the pine trees, the willow bushes, the wildflowers, the rose hips, the spruce trees, the bugs, the birds, the wolves, the coyotes, the foxes, the cows, the horses, the spiders and every other living thing that has made this hillside home. I loved seeing you, smelling you, hearing you and tasting you for all these years. I am forever grateful."

Pat later expressed all our angst with: "This fire is like having a new baby in the house—sleep deprivation, constantly guessing why the baby is crying, and then leaning in to see if it is still breathing when it is asleep. Never knowing what the next demand will be. So sleep when and where you can Fred/Monika even if it is while you are staring out the window."

The initial plume of the Precipice Fire on July 9. Photo by Katie Iveson.

Our cows resting on the hay raked from our hay shed. By July 13, the gable ends of the barn are draped in plastic to prevent embers from falling into the cracks. Photo by Fred Reid.

Downtown Kleena Kleene on July 10. The blackness of the smoke shadow is a huge contrast to the bright, hot day outside. Photo by Chris Czajkowski.

The awful sight of the Kleena Kleene Fire smoke rolling behind my house on July 10. Photo by Chris Czajkowski.

The Precipice Fire advances up the slopes on the side of the Hotnarko Canyon during the massive blow-up of August 3. Photo by Shane Groves.

On August 3, Fred's home and the surrounding green meadows are threatened by a rapidly moving rank-five fire. *Photo by Shane Groves.*

All the firefighters had left and taken their equipment with them by August 3. Mark Petrovcic is telling Fred and Monika that they have reserved a space in the last helicopter so they can leave. *Photo by Mark Petrovcic.*

Typical smoky sun before it simply dissolved into the brown soup, second week of August. Photo by Chris Czajkowski.

The fire at the edge of Fred and Monika's house meadow as it creeps toward the old homestead on August 10. Photo by Fred Reid.

The Kleena Kleene Fire on August 16. Shane wrote to Fred that the fire had doubled that day. It was not, however, the worst of the wind. That happened on August 18. Photo by Shane Groves.

Two IA crew work on the Spruce Bog Fire on August 18. Photo by Fred Reid.

Part of the four-person IA *team that works two days (August 18 and 19) to kill the greenhouse puffer.* Photo by Fred Reid.

The fire in the base of the Gentle Giant—one of the Three Sisters—on August 20. Photo by Fred Reid.

The Kleena Kleene Fire travels up a gully on Mt. Nogwon in early September. That evening the smoke turned orange in the sunset. Photo by Chris Czajkowski.

We Begin to Explore the Fire

PRECIPICE, AUGUST 8–9

ON AUGUST 8 MARK'S RESPONSE TO MY WEATHER REPORT WAS NOT encouraging. "Our weather man is still saying that the next three days look to be very similar. Thursday/Friday (confidence more on Friday) for the cold low that is in the forecast. You will see Pascal up there shortly to check on the pumps. Cheers."

Despite these and similar emails with IC, we were feeling out of the loop since the fire had passed us. No helicopters were flying in and out—the fire was too close and the smoke too thick. Then came a communication from IC with up-to-date information.

Subject: Situation Report—Precipice VA0778, 52
Importance: High

Smoke conditions prevail both at the Bella Coola and Anahim Airports as well as the Precipice VA0778 fire site. Helicopter operations are again being impacted during the morning period. A test flight will be made as soon as visibility is sufficient out of the Bella Coola Airport.

Contingency lines continue to be constructed on the west and east flanks of the fire... leading back to the Beef Trail west of Anahim Lake. Controlled burn planning continues with mixing sites being established. Small test burns will be conducted as required.

No significant changes are expected over the next two days. The outlook is for warm, dry and smoky conditions at the Precipice Fire site. Fire size mapped at 5,400 hectares (estimated).

- 20 per cent containment
- 41 firefighters
- 13 single resources
- 1 Structure Protection Unit (SPU)
- 4 fallers
- Support staff
- 9 helicopters
  - 2 type-1 bucketing
  - 3 type-2 bucketing
- 2 excavators
- 1 skidder
- 1 Cat
- 1 feller buncher
- 1 truck—water hauling
- 1 lowbed

The Precipice Fire was finally upgraded from a Wildfire of Note to an interface fire—one that threatened structures. I was not sure whether this meant us or the increased threat to the Anahim Lake and Nimpo Lake communities.

It was disappointing but not all that surprising to learn that our fire was only 20 per cent contained. It had managed to creep across the fireguard to our northwest and then rage by us. It had snuck down the inside edge of the fuel-free guard to our southwest and was now slowly advancing up the slopes above Telegraph Creek.

The southern flank of the fire above Stillwater Lake had held. The resources acquired for this fire were more than we had realized but still far below what would be devoted to a fire of this size in a normal year. Hard to believe that our fire was in fact one of the small ones. Even Kleena Kleene was bigger although it, too, was smaller than most.

If the predicted weather change came, it would undoubtedly mean more wind. More wind would mean less smoke but a more active fire. Despite this I wrote: "A change in the weather would be welcome. Almost any change really."

Neither Monika nor I bothered to wear masks. Around noon Monika went to the barn to milk Polly. She was returning to the house when she heard the whooshing sound of a tree catching fire. She turned and saw a pine candle at the very edge of our west meadow.

"Let's go out and look at the thing," I suggested, which was unusual for me. Normally it was Monika who wanted to venture farther from the buildings. Having seen Josh walk into the forest encouraged me to want to do the same. An element within me made me worry that I might have lost respect for the fire. A couple of times I had taken it for granted, thinking that it would easily be contained, only to witness it disdain the fire barriers and run. Whether it was due to a loss of respect, seductive captivation or pure naive fascination, we walked to the end of the west meadow and into the forest along the old Telegraph Creek Trail. The fire was sputtering away on the other side of the Hotnarko River. It was inside our property line, but to get to it we would have to cross a fallen spruce tree bridging the river and then crawl through tangled alder and willow. It lurked like an intruder rather than a guest. Smoke was drifting within the dense willow but flames were not visible from the safe side of the river. The desire to see the flames was strong. We ventured onto the log, crossing halfway over, but I began to feel that the fire had set some kind of trap. If we should climb down from the log into the thick willow brush we would not be able to move fast in the tangle of branches. The fire could suddenly flare up and ensnare us.

We circled back, and chose another route. We crossed our island meadow to a point upriver where the flow was very shallow. This intruder had been cloaked in smoke for so long. We wanted to see it more out of fascination than fear. We came to the very edge of it less than thirty metres from the property line. There it was, "bubbling away," as Arlen would say. Pockets of flame nibbled at the base of pine trees or slowly but relentlessly consumed stumps and dry logs. Other spots were smouldering hotly in areas of thicker grass. It was everywhere, and yet it seemed quite innocent. We studied it, fascinated by its methods of movement. The forest in this area was young, and many of the thin pines were not affected as the fire had stayed mostly on the ground. We could trace its crawl from the previous day to the points where open flame crackled happily. Its trails were much like that of a slug, but leaving ash rather than slime. It crawled on the ground through dry grass and along logs that had been dead for decades.

We ventured farther into the fire but became nervous while standing next to the larger open flames. The wind picked up and two trees rubbed, moaning ominously, making us jump. The wind was in the crowns but we could not feel it at ground level. The fire had not yet reacted to it but we knew it might. Having finally walked into the fire and confronted it, we became even more fascinated by it. But it was frightening as well. We hastily crossed back over the river and onto the safety of our meadow. Even there we found reminders that our intruder was trying to reach us, in the form of charred stems and leaves that had flown from the fire and fallen with the ash. Would they start fires spotting around us? We were not free of the fire by a long way yet.

Later in the day the wind picked up and it looked as though the fire would take an afternoon run. It also began to move the smoke. A message came from Katie in Stuie: "Chopper just headed your way, just as I wrote that there wasn't. Yeah!"

Arlen flew in with Lonny. Josh drove in from where he was working on the road between us and the Taylor Ranch. They had firefighting business to discuss so we stood back before joining them. Our conversations were more like gossip than business. We joked and talked casually about the fire as if it were some relatives dropping in. When will they arrive? What route will they take? Will they bring the mean uncle or teasing aunt with them? And most importantly: How long will they stay?

We asked if we could see the work the ground crew was doing. Until this time we had only had brief contact with personnel from a unit crew. Our request was ignored, but not refused, so we ventured by foot toward the Taylor Ranch, past the whining Wajax Forestry pump at the end of our big meadow, and down the road. We came upon part of the second unit crew—contractors from a private company on Vancouver Island. They were friendly and happy to be fighting the fire. They wore jerseys similar to those of the provincial firefighters but theirs were yellow instead of the red. They doused the fire using two-centimetre hoses that branched off the mainline. They were spraying water on logs and soil to create a thirty-metre fire-free zone next to the road.

The smoke had lifted enough to allow one of the heavies to drop water. We spotted it on our return to the farm. From a distance it seemed to be dumping it right over our house. I cursed that I had not turned the sprinklers on when we had left to explore the fire. But as we came closer we could see that the helicopter was wetting the very spot we had visited that morning. It was the first bucketing chopper we had seen for several days.

When we did not do an early Facebook commentary the next morning, Pat worried. She wrote: "Fred and Monika weren't posting this morning when I checked at 5:00 a.m. and then again by

8:30 a.m. and I began to wonder if they were okay. Then I think: 'Maybe they just need a break.' Facebook is our lifeline with them and they know that, but self-care during a crisis is crucial as well. I remember when my daughter, Sara, was first diagnosed with cancer and then again during the last ten days of her life—the ongoing phone calls and emails to update family and friends was exhausting. Sometimes I needed to isolate myself to recover and re-energize. My focus back then was all on Sara. Fred, Monika and Caleb's focus is on this fire.

"I finally gave in to my worries and phoned. They were drinking coffee and doing math puzzles."

Pat and Lee had lost their younger daughter to cancer when she was only twenty-six years old. The sorrow of that still haunts Pat. A memorial stands on a knoll above the Taylors' house. When Sara and her sister were young, they had read the Tolkien trilogy and one of their favourite games was to take their wooden broad swords onto the knoll and fight off evil demons. The memorial is composed of a sword stuck into a rock symbolizing Sara's spirit, which still very much infuses the place.

Later, Monika made one of her rare contributions to the Facebook dialogues. "I want you all to know how comforting it is for me/ us to open the computer and see your comments. There have been days when I was just glued to the screen. Knowing you are out there feels as though there is an invisible network of energy and support that is carrying us through the days. Days of anxiety and stress, waiting for the Unknown.

"So thank you all! I am grateful beyond words for all the love that is out there."

There was a new and unfamiliar noise at 10:20 a.m. while I was working in the greenhouse. It was the ground crew starting the pressure pump in our big meadow next to the Hotnarko River. As the fire moved, the sounds of the valley changed.

Sounds… When living within a fire your sense of sound is heightened—maybe out of fear or maybe because your sight is hampered by all the smoke. The sounds of a fire are many. The crackling of needles before a tree candles, and then the swoosh as it goes up in an instant. The fizz as flames consume a juniper bush. And most fearsome of all, the jet-like roar as it surges up a dry slope of pine.

In the afternoon, the winds picked up and the fire made another charge. It was rapidly climbing the south slopes in a rank-four rage. Josh came in to tell us that the ground crew had taken flight. He and two fallers would be the last to leave. We asked about Caleb. He had finished baling at our place, and he was taking the equipment back to Lee and Pat's. Josh had seen him and said he was probably home and safe by now.

We were now well versed in fire lingo. To the west, where the fire was mostly burned out, it varied between rank one and two. North, where trees were individually candling, it was a rank three. A rank four stormed above our southern border, spotting new fires east of us.

Our pump and sprinklers gave us a cloak of confidence. I had often thought of our little green meadows as an oasis surrounded by fire, but now it felt more like we were in the eye of a hurricane with the storm whirling around us. Yet we went to the balcony to take pictures.

A firefighter motto for safety is "Keep one foot in the black!" The safest place when trouble should arise is going to where it has already burned.

Late in the evening I went out to shut off the pump. Sounds are enhanced when darkness falls. There was the crash of a large tree in the Hotnarko Canyon to our west. I suspected a spruce—they are shallow rooted and vulnerable. Then there was the crackling of dry needles close to the ground that heralded the short whoosh as a tree candled. The wind goes straight up a candling tree. One firefighter called it "ladder ignition." I searched for the blaze. There it was on my left, at the bottom of the south slope. After the sound was gone the red flare remained for a few more moments, then faded into the smoke.

A jet flew over while I was outside one evening, probably a flight out of Vancouver International Airport. The sound was a little duller than the fire's and it droned from one horizon to the other. The fire did not care, I did not care. Once it was gone I continued to listen to the fire. Bubbling and crackling to the north. Popping and crashing to the south. Every so often an occasional whoosh.

Lockdown

KLEENA KLEENE, AUGUST 9–11

ON THURSDAY, AUGUST 9, IN ANTICIPATION OF THE WEEKEND'S FORE-casted winds, Anahim Lake and Nimpo Lake were put on evacuation order. The army would now be helping the police to man the barriers along the highway. For the first time, a barrier was placed west of me, on the far side of Anahim Lake. This would in effect cut me off from my refuge in the Bella Coola Valley.

That same morning, Monika phoned. She had some cheese and eggs that she could send out to the Anahim Lake Airport with an obliging helicopter pilot. Fantastic news! Storebought dairy gives me asthma, but farm milk products are fine. The taste is also far superior—and Monika's cows have a good proportion of Jersey in them so the milk is particularly creamy. I had not received any of her luscious dairy products since the fires had begun, and I drooled at this largesse. It would take me fifty minutes to drive to the airport; would I encounter any restrictions? More importantly, would I be prevented from getting home?

It was still calm and the smoke lay thick. My flag-o-meter hung motionless. I nosed cautiously onto the highway. I felt like a little mouse, sticking my nose fearfully out of my hole, all senses alert for the fire police, ready to jump back to safety.

Visibility improved somewhat as I drove north. A few vehicles sped by in both directions, but they were intent on where they were going and they ignored me.

The Nimpo Lake store was bustling. People were gassing up and some were filling spare cans. I topped up the van but refrained from taking any more—I didn't want spare fuel on the place should the unthinkable happen. Mick White was chugging diesel into an old flatbed topped by a huge, dented, rusty water tank. Mick is a workaholic—rancher, logger, carpenter, hunting guide—like most people in this country he does a bit of everything. He looked tired and very dirty, but happy. He would be raking in the bucks.

I grabbed a bit of hamburger made from local range beef. It is one of the very few non-processed items available in the area. Other people were stocking up as if for a siege but they were less picky than I was; there wasn't much else in the store that I would be able to eat. Richard and Leah, who own the store, run a great operation, but the store carries mostly convenience items. Up and down the fire areas, many people talked about the difficulty of getting food, but throughout the emergency, Richard's grocery trucks got through, and the Nimpo store kept going. And, unlike the few other business owners still operating in the fire zones, Richard never raised his prices throughout the whole summer. I eyed the dog food. My old dog's arthritis gets much worse if he eats kibble that contains corn. I still had about two weeks' worth at home. That would take us until the end of August. Would the fire situation be under control by then? Fire seasons were usually expected to end early in September due to the longer, damper nights, but in 2009 the Lava Canyon Fire, two hours east of Kleena Kleene, was still being fought until the end of that month. The roads were all open by then, though. I took a chance and did not buy any kibble. I had plenty of oats and rice in case of emergency.

Everyone I talked to was staying. The fire police were not present.

I guess they were giving people a few hours to get themselves organized before they clamped down the lid.

Anahim Lake Airport was a further twenty minutes west. The smoke was thicker here, wafting directly from the Precipice. A number of people milled around in front of the airport building. Several helicopters were parked, waiting, and a couple of groups of tired and grubby-looking firefighters in their red, flame-resistant coveralls were receiving instructions rather like hockey teams getting a last-minute brush-up from their coach. I knew the person who ran the office. Tamara has long been a friend of the Precipice people. She houses them on their way through if they need it, and she had billeted Fred and Monika's volunteers when they'd had to evacuate. Yes, she was staying, too. She didn't know anything about the dairy delivery. But as we spoke, a helicopter landed. After the rotors stopped spinning, the pilot climbed down and reached behind his seat for a box. Over to the office he came—and there was milk, cream cheese, yoghurt, hard cheese and eggs. Oh frabjous day!

I lost no time in getting home. Desultory traffic but no restrictions. I could clearly see Mount Nogwon as I drove south, but from its base a thick gush of smoke poured in the direction of my place, like water from a fire hose. Once again I plunged into gloom. As I arrived home, the wind died and the fire dragon tucked himself into his smoke blankets and took a nap to digest his meal.

I emailed Jaden to tell him about the evacuation order for Nimpo and the barrier west of Anahim, and said I was still going to try to go to Bella Coola if I had to leave.

"I want to go west as well," he replied. "I don't want to go through that hell back east again. Problem is, I need internet access for several hours a day because of my online business."

"Do you have a place to go in the Bella Coola Valley? My friends have several cabins. No internet at the cabins, only in or near the house, but they would welcome you and figure something out. If you need to bail out and I don't, I have a cabin with no internet, but you could have an office up in my attic."

"That's good to know. We'll see what happens. There was an official forest fire meeting at Tatla today. You didn't miss anything, a whole bunch of 'we are doing great and you are doing so great…'"

"I never heard about it."

"I didn't know about it either until my neighbour asked me if I wanted to go. It was a packed event. Very boring, though. They said the fire was mostly contained at your end and a little less toward the south (but supposedly still contained). They are a bit worried about the coming weekend winds, though…"

The next day (August 11)—me: "11:24. The wind's started. New, thick black smoke from Finger Peak directly toward me. Can you see anything?"

Jaden, 3:45: "It's not too different here yet. Just hazy smoke. It keeps raining ash, but it's not windy anymore."

Me, 6:31: "There's no ash here. Funny—we're so close, but it's always so different at each place."

HOW WERE THE COMMUNITIES OF NIMPO AND ANAHIM LAKE MAKING out with the lockdown? Patti, David J's wife, would be a good person to call. Her husband was now working on the Kleena Kleene Fire, and her son was in the opposite direction, on the far side of Anahim Lake, helping to construct a huge fireguard to deflect the Precipice Fire.

Patti manages the small recycling shed at Nimpo Lake, and she happened to be on duty a few days before the lockdown, when the army drove in. The camp had not yet been established at the Anahim Lake mill site, and arrangements had been made to put up the first wave of these firefighters in a couple of resorts. They drove down into one of the yards and were welcomed by the resort owner, who directed them to their accommodation. The boss, however, said he had not yet received official confirmation that they could use the facilities. "Well," said the resort owner. "The beds are waiting for you. I don't care about the red tape or getting paid." But the army boss said no. They would have to wait for the official word. It never came, and all thirty newcomers ended up sleeping the night in their trucks.

"And it was funny to watch," Patti told me. "The minute the vehicles stopped, the passengers all jumped out and fished out their cell phones and tried to get online. No one had told them there was no reception here." She also told me later that her husband had to show someone how to use a satellite phone. Personnel were flocking in, but they were obviously ill informed.

Patti had permission to stay in the area because of her men, but she was not supposed to leave her property. If anyone unauthorized was caught driving around, they got a bollocking from the cops. Patti got fed up with staying home, and she phoned a friend to see if she wanted to go for a hike. They favoured a five-kilometre circuit that ran mostly through back trails, but for a short distance they needed to walk along a gravel road leading to a resort. While on this stretch, they heard a vehicle. Should they risk it?—No. They leaped off the road and crouched down behind a bush. Sure enough, it was a fire official. Patti was wearing a red fleece and thought she would be noticed. But the official probably never imagined that a couple of stalwart citizens might be hiding in the bushes, and he passed them by. "It was sort of funny but not funny, if you know what I mean," said Patti. "It's horrible feeling like a criminal." Then she added: "Next time I go for a hike I'm going to wear camos."

RICHARD AND LEAH AT THE NIMPO LAKE STORE ARE GENEROUS WITH their time and assistance far beyond the dictates of their job, and as a result have become a focal point for the community.

Leah was forced to leave because of their young twin girls. If she had felt it necessary to stay, the girls would have been taken away from her. Richard was dubbed part of the Emergency Services (the gas pumps had to be kept open for the fire personnel and anyone wanting to evacuate) so was not expected to go. But he was not exempt from the fire police. He had obtained a permit to go to the dump, and on the way home he delivered groceries to a couple of people. A regular officer from Anahim, Sergeant Scott Clay, who was actually a friend of Richard's, found him there and said he was not supposed to be doing that. Scott was quite reasonable about it. He said that if people came to the store once a week or so, his officers would not harass them, but if someone was out and about every day, they would not be so lenient with them.

However, the following morning, another police officer came into the store. Not everyone had resupplied on the first day of the order, but when they came into the store on day two, this officer was far less accommodating. He ranted on about how they'd had a month to stock up and if they chose to disobey the order they had to stay on their properties or risk being forcibly removed. This showed a total lack of understanding of the situation. Like me, most people do the bulk of their shopping in Williams Lake. No one dared go to Williams Lake for fear of not being allowed home for over five weeks.

Richard was so ticked off, he sent round the following email:

Good evening!

Just giving everyone an update with the grocery situation. After this morning's chat with one of our local RCMP I was once again reminded that anyone who has chosen to ride out the evacuation order is to stay on their property. I even had this officer tell me that if he catches anyone driving around off their property without a permit more than once he would have them sent out of the evacuation zone. A conservation officer that I have known for quite a number of years was in the store at the same time, and proceeded to come back into the store afterwards and mention to me that shift change occurs at 7:30 a.m. and 7:30 p.m. every day. He felt that this would be a good time to make your way to the store. It was very nice of him to give this info but I still don't want to see anyone forced to leave due to poor timing. This conservation officer proceeded to go back to the detachment in Anahim Lake and blast the people there in charge for making this grocery situation such a bullshit endeavour. Currently with the fire situation around the Riske Creek/Lee's Corner area easing off, all of the eastern roadblocks have been taken down and the only ones up and running are located at Kleena Kleene bridge and at the Beef Trail [west of Anahim Lake]. This should stay the same over the next few days if anyone is looking to venture out to the store.

The grocery truck should come in on Tuesday as planned as it hasn't missed a single delivery this year. The fire at Riske Creek would have to be pretty incredible to stop him from coming. I have been setting up a way to get groceries brought in to certain areas around Nimpo Lake and Charlotte Lake, using people who have permits that live out that way. So if you don't want to risk coming to the store, please just email me or call me with a list of things you need, and I will have it shipped with one of these people to your area. This is still a frowned-upon way to get groceries, but it seems that CRD is determined to starve people out eventually. If there is anyone not on this email list please let me know or let them know how to contact me for groceries and we will make this happen. Also please keep this information from getting to our local authorities so that they don't shut this method down. Everyone stay safe and if you have any more questions let me know!

Living Within the Fire

PRECIPICE, AUGUST 10–11

WORRIED ABOUT THE FIRE'S RAGE ON THE SOUTHERN RIDGE, I RAN THE sprinklers for longer than usual before I went to bed. I had a restless night and got up early to email IC. "Your last day for this round, Mark. If I may quote Donald Trump, 'SAD.' Although you never know how he means that. Anyway, I mean it in the kindest way."

Mark responded: "Thanks Fred… you too, Monika. You are the definition of perseverance. I will say that it is quite inspiring that you both are OK with staying at your homestead while this wildfire is surrounding you. However, I hope you guys will reconsider repositioning since I think the next little while is going to be extremely active with even thicker smoke and a lot more flames. Confidence in the wx [weather] models is once again saying Friday/Saturday strong winds. The fire is going to show her fury very soon. I know that every time I mention my concerns you both look at one another and tell me, 'We're staying.' I look forward to reading your book once this fire is over! I will be back after some rest. You two take care. Keep me in the info loop. PS, Arlen has a portable wx kit that he will be putting up at the ranch. Cheers."

I was anxious about the higher than usual morning temperature. Did it mean another day of aggressive fire activity as Mark suggested?

Or was it hotter because we were now entirely surrounded by fire? I posted: "We survived another night. The fire was active later than usual but we woke up with it sleeping under its blanket of smoke. The fire can be as annoying as a cat rubbing at your legs when you are nervous and concerned with other things, and then it sleeps when you need its companionship."

Pat's response was immediate: "After Fred's 10:00 p.m. post from last night it took a while for me to fall asleep. I was awake at 3:00 a.m. and checked FB but no new news. I had to read myself back to sleep. I was late waking up. Holding my breath, I quickly opened my phone and I exhaled to see 'we survived another night...' Whew! Now I can pee and make coffee before we phone them."

Despite the somewhat ominous circumstances, Monika and I could not resist another venture into the fire. This time we climbed to the Sugar Camp Trail. The fire had burned very hot up there and was still very active.

A few steps from the greenhouse and we were in the black. It was more like grey and dirty brown, really, and it didn't feel completely safe. Mark and Rob (Mark's replacement) might have been a little annoyed or even pissed off if they knew how much we flirted with this fire. We had come to know it somewhat and I felt that we still gave it a lot of respect. True, "cool black" is the safest, but greys and browns were still smouldering and crackling away. They may not be hot but they were definitely warm. You would normally think of green as the colour of safety. The light greens of our meadows certainly are, but the dark greens of a flammable forest of spruce are definitely not.

VA0778 had its monster side, but funnily enough, as it bubbled and sparkled all around us on that day, it reminded me more of a young child just learning to walk. It was exploring its immediate world, oblivious to all else. Putting its feet in a puddle of water, splashing and giggling. Then suddenly raging in a fit of hunger or pain but easily distracted then nodding off to sleep.

"Envy. Jealousy. Brave. Crazy," Pat wrote. "These words come to mind as I read Fred's posts and look at all these fire photos. I envy his and Monika's courage. I am jealous that I lack that kind of fortitude. I see them being brave by walking toward the fire rather than away from it. I use the word crazy as a compliment. I love their joy for life and that they find humour and green amongst all the dark grey and brown. As their bond gets stronger I feel like Lee and I struggle here in Vancouver while we process, each in our own way, our fear of what may or may not come as our home awaits the serendipity of the resting dragon. Where next will its fiery breath strike? Will Sara's sword hold true?"

Pat's post left me numb. It was so raw and open, showing her to be more vulnerable than I had ever felt with this fire. Crazy we might have been, but we were not brave. We stayed mainly because we were naive. We had some fear in the beginning, but had grown accustomed to the fire's modes and methods of attack.

Monika woke me around 11:00 p.m. Exhausted, I had gone to bed early. "Anything to report?" I groaned.

"There appears to be a flame down on the meadow." She was surprisingly calm. I crawled from the bed saying we had better investigate.

I looked out our bedroom window and saw a small glow on the meadow where we had piled wood and other flammable debris. Maybe an ember had fallen into one of the piles, igniting it.

But in fact, the red glow turned out to be a reflection of the fire caught in the window of a battered old Nissan we had inherited from previous Precipice residents. The truck was sitting at the perfect angle to catch the fire's image. Panic over, we were wide awake now and mesmerized by the fire's nighttime activity. We stood for a long time just watching the fire crawl and smoulder at the meadow's edge. It seemed to be burning hotter into the night than it had in the past. Maybe it had always done so, but appeared worse because it was right beside us. Occasionally it flared from a hot spot where we had walked that morning.

My emotional swings continued; smoke always brought frustration and a sense of futility. The next morning it choked the valley. Trees on the very edge of our meadows could barely be seen. My weather report to the IC included, "Monika just informed me that visibility is not the greatest. A bit of an understatement, I would say."

Ken responded, "Thank you Fred. All this is going to pass, and you and Monika will have your oasis back again. I leave this morning for a rest and may be returning on August 15. I only got to meet you and Monika (and the hens) for a brief visit. The crews are always mentioning how kind you are to them during these difficult times."

On August 10, because of the threat of the impending winds, Anahim Lake was put under evacuation order. The fire would have to burn through the Taylors' summer range, endangering their herd, before reaching Anahim Lake. Pat's concern for friends, neighbours and their animals was almost paralyzing.

Late in the morning Monika drew me out for what was becoming our regular morning walk among the fires. I used the plural, for the conflagration had now become many fires in our minds. One part had crept dangerously close to the Three Sisters, fingering its way through the young pine surrounding the knoll where they stand. This north-slope fire was the most personal for me. This is an area that I have visited many, many times. It is "my" grove of pines, where, if there was need for a special size of tree for a picture frame, fence rail or building structure, I would go to look for it. Logs for our barn were from beetle-killed trees harvested entirely from this slope. The fire may have burned slower here because after each harvest I would pile and burn the debris. Monika and I had always debated whether or not it was better for the denizens of the forest (ground creatures, birds and soil fauna) to leave the debris or burn it. The fire has made that decision for us.

In the evening, Caleb phoned. "The rats are leaving the ship," he said.

"What do you mean?" I asked.

"They have taken everything. All the hoses and pumps. Even the bladder."

I explained that winds were forecast. "What should they do—leave everything to burn?"

Caleb had to concede that my logic made sense. It was, however, a pretty nerve-wracking situation for him.

When I posted about it, a friend commented: "Seems to me ridiculous if Forestry supplies you with fire protection when it's not a present threat but when it gets real serious they abandon you. That makes me mad. Them taking their equipment away when you most need it doesn't seem like the right thing to do. I hope everything works out okay and no structures are lost. Take care—I'm thinking about you all the time."

But the removal of the equipment cache on our big meadow made perfect sense to me. Firstly, safety of personnel was paramount. And why abandon equipment that would likely be destroyed? If the winds picked up and the fire raged no one would be able to get in and fight it anyway. They had not come in to take away the structural protection.

Barry (in Nanaimo) shared a Google Earth image. "As I read your stories, it looks like this image is not representing truly what is going on there. It's saying that the fire has burned out around your place, except to the south, and is now mainly eating the forest toward the north."

I replied that I had seen a different website that was more accurate. I was becoming annoyed with the various websites that were trying to represent our fire, often erroneously, it seemed.

Around noon on August 11, I shouted out over the internet: "The westerlies are coming! We actually have something you can call sunshine! We'll appreciate anything that mother nature can give us."

A typical equipment cache sits on our big meadow beside the Hotnarko River. Fuel containers are kept separate from hoses and pumps, each protected by a small ditch. Photo by Monika Schoene.

I was elated by the deep, deep blue of the sky. I had not realized how much the thick smoke had dampened my spirits. Helicopters were immediately back bucketing water. The winds stirred the plateau fires into angry turmoil. One pilot described a 360-degree view with five or more huge columns of smoke rising miles into the atmosphere. They were visible from over one hundred kilometres away.

The winds in the high country swept the fires eastward, where they took a run and grew rapidly, but our valley was almost four hundred metres lower, and here the winds had less strength. On the other side of the valley, the fire surged up Telegraph Creek but on the slopes next to our meadow it found no definitive direction. I watched it move on the ground and through the underbrush. It reminded me of a game of dodgeball. But rather than weave and duck to avoid a ball it twisted and turned to find new fuel. When it manoeuvred into itself and the flames dwindled to wisps of smoke, I cheered as if I had thrown the ball and hit the fire. I cheered from the green safety of our meadow. I was now confident that it would never burn. We had won this round, but the game went on. The wind was always changing in the valley bottom. Our windmill spent more time searching for it than actually generating power.

Shane, the pilot who always seemed to be in the air at the most dangerous times, sent pictures of the rank-five fire that had raged above our farm on August 3. I was frozen by the images. Scarier than I had ever imagined. My computer seemed to be frozen as well, its battery unable to recharge.

Late in the afternoon Pat posted: "Caleb says it is burning on both sides of our long meadow... It is now a short half kilometre to our ranch buildings and Caleb's cabin. We only have enough fuel to run the water pumps around our home, which is set back from the other building on the river, for another few days. This news fills me with concerns for Caleb and Clemens. Although Caleb still feels he can stay safe and keep most of our buildings intact, I will sleep with one eye open tonight. Sara, stand strong! If anyone can make friends with this fire-breathing dragon it is you."

I sat at the base of a pine in the middle of the meadow closest to the house and watched as two helicopters circled between the south slope and Airplane Lake. They had to come through the low-hanging smoke; I heard them before I could see them. They would appear like skaters gliding out of the fog on a winter pond. The first sky we could see in days seemed as ice above rather than below the helicopters. I ignored the roar of their propellers and just watched their grace as they emerged from the smoke, then dipped and slowed to swing their bucket in an arc above the fire. Then the bucket swung like a pendulum back as the water was released.

While I was posting about the helicopters, Monika ran in and shouted, "The fire is among the Three Sisters!" It had crept down the slope onto the knoll near the greenhouse and began burning vigorously in the needles and branches that had accumulated below the three large Douglas fir. Monika noticed it when it shot up the side of the magnificent tree that we called the "Tree-in-the-sky." She guessed that it had only burned the lichen hanging from the limbs but feared that the tree would be compromised. She was determined to do something. We were not the only ones who had noticed the flare-up, however. As we headed toward it, one of the heavies came out of the smoke, crossed the valley from where it had been working and dropped a bucket of water among the trees. Monika leaned on our baler and cried out of relief and happiness. The pilots' awareness of the fire surrounding us was amazing.

The bucket cooled the fire markedly but the branches of the giant trees dispersed the water and not much reached the base. The fire smouldered briefly but flames quickly sprung up and began licking at the base of the Tree-in-the-sky. I ran to the greenhouse for two twenty-litre buckets and raced toward the trees as the helicopter emerged from the smoke on the opposite side of our valley. I hid under the branches of a large pine near the knoll, not wanting to discourage the helicopter from doing another water drop, but the helicopter was once again concentrating on the south side. I scrambled up the steep, ashy slope and doused the base of the tree.

The fire sizzled an angry response but the flames were extinguished. I returned victorious to Monika knowing that we would have to go back to check on our efforts. It was our first direct action against the fire—two small buckets of water.

The fire was now within a kilometre of the Mecham Cabin. It was nearly 8:30 p.m. when a helicopter dropped onto our meadow. We were surprised by the visit as we had not had one for a while.

Fred throws a bucket of water at the base of the Tree-in-the-sky.
Photo by Monika Schoene.

Kerry and two others climbed out and crouched toward us. The propellers kept spinning. We all stood at the edge of the downdraft as the helicopter lifted off again.

"Rob and Arlen are going to start the Wajax pump at the Mecham Cabin," Kerry said. "Arlen has not started one for a couple of months and it has been over two years since Rob has, so I don't know how they'll make out. We have to wait here as the pilot needs a lighter load before he can land in the tight spot near the cabin."

The helicopter returned within half an hour. They did have difficulty starting the pump, eventually breaking the pull cord. The cabin would have to be left unprotected overnight. They had to leave immediately for Bella Coola because of the encroaching darkness.

Big Stick Lake

KLEENA KLEENE, AUGUST 12–14

SATURDAY, AUGUST 12, DAWNED CALM AND THE SMOKE HAD THICK-ened again—this time it had a noticeable smell, probably because new and slightly different material was being consumed. It was also a lot warmer than it had been—up to nine degrees at daybreak instead of four or five degrees. Warm mornings indicate more instability in the weather.

The first panic was no internet. How could I find out if Fred and Monika were still OK? The view through my window showed nothing but smoke. Visibility was back down to about two kilometres. I was too agitated to eat breakfast. But an hour later I was online again. What a relief. How dependent on this form of communication I had become. It made a mockery of my claim to be a wilderness dweller.

The forecast didn't look good. Another hot day outside our brown, stifling cocoon—and this time thunderstorms were in the offing. All we needed were a few more lightning strikes. Drops of rain were illustrated on the weather icons; Windfinder showed light winds for the time being—but they would be blowing directly from the new activity in front of Finger Peak so I could not expect to see much. I doubted that the showers would amount to anything here (and I was right). Still, it was clearer on the north side of my place and a few clouds speckled the sky. We even had a sunrise of sorts, the first I had seen for a long time. I rushed out and took several pictures. A moderately strong sun shone through the kitchen window as I did dishes, but soon it got dark again as the sun climbed into the smoke. I tried going for a hike but it was too buggy and smoky to enjoy being out for long. I heard helicopters working for the first time in about ten days. They were very busy, but all at the south end of the fire. I could hear no activity near me.

Jaden emailed at 12:49 p.m. "Last night I saw a red glow coming from the Finger Peak direction. The USDA Forest Service map shows crazy red in all the fires south of us." (Meaning lots of new activity.)

Me, 12:55: "Finger Peak was all red on the map last night; amber now. Environment Canada is advertising twenty-nine degrees for Puntzi [the nearest weather station, ninety kilometres east] but here it's only twenty degrees at the moment. Maybe the cooler weather is coming."

Me, 6:30: "Violent sw wind gusts started. Very dark. The whole quarter ssw to NW thick brown smoke with less than one kilometre visibility. Hope that's just a trick of the wind and not new fires."

Jaden, 6:33: "Oh man! No wind here. Just bugs."

August 13. Me, 11:57: "Smoke so acrid earlier I could hardly breathe. Strong wind and relatively clear now. I was just up on the south bluff. The fire has jumped out of the Klinaklini Valley as all of us locals predicted, and it is heading fast toward Big Stick Lake."

Jaden, 3:58: "USDA Forest Service and Google Earth maps don't seem to show any activity. Cannot be right at all; it's been soooo windy."

Me, 5:14: "I've had problems getting a reading, too. They are probably using the same satellite. The connection must be faulty."

Me, 7:16: "The wind has gone round a point or two. Lots of smoke from the Big Stick Lake Fire but I think it's turning back on itself. I heard a couple of helis over there earlier, but they didn't stay.

Maybe it was too windy to work. I sure hope they have ground crews doing something."

In fact the BC Wildfire Service had been aware of the activity near Finger Peak. Mike King and another pilot worked very hard to stop the fire from crossing the Klinaklini River but, as at Lee's Corner, the river itself was unsuitable for filling the buckets, and they had to resort to beaver ponds. They worked for hours and kept the fire at bay at first. There are apparently two kinds of bucket mechanisms. The visiting pilot had a bigger aircraft and it was using a bucket that could be filled more quickly, but its problem was that a stick could jam it. Beaver ponds are deepest closest to the dams, and sure enough, a stick was sucked in, preventing the bucket from closing. Both choppers landed, and while they struggled with the bucket, the fire got away on them.

It was now much closer to Christoph's Terra Nostra Guest Ranch. Christoph was galvanized into action. He and neighbours met at the Big Stick Lake Recreation Site, which is about eight kilometres off the highway.

The fire was well established on the far side of the lake, but it had jumped the water near the recreation site and about six hectares were burning there. The road was a small distance away from the lake, and Mike was already bucketing it. Doug Schuk on his Cat had already made short guards from the road to the lake on both sides of the fire. Christoph's crew used tanks and hoses to keep the guards wet, and that part of the fire seemed to be contained.

But the next day, the fire had jumped the lake in another place and was now going up the side of Mount Nogwon. Two Cats were working when Christoph and his crew arrived. They were starting to make a guard up Nogwon, hoping to surround the fire. Mid-morning, five pickups containing twenty people—a unit crew—turned up. They wore the Forestry red shirts; several were First Nations people from Anahim Lake.

Christoph went over and talked to a couple of fallers. "It's great to see you coming to help," he said. But the fallers replied that they had to wait to see if their boss gave them permission to work. One called his boss, then turned to Christoph and said they were not allowed to help because it was too dangerous.

Christoph was spitting mad. "But we have been working this fire all day already! Why is it too dangerous for you but not for us? Can't you even leave five people who could stay back from the fire and help with the hoses?"

But the faller said no. Christoph then lost his temper—emotions were all very high—and told them in no uncertain terms to get the hell out of there. And the five trucks and twenty people left.

A while later, a man and a woman in official-looking vests arrived. Once again Christoph hoped they were there to help. They also said no. Then they told Christoph and friends, and also the two Cat drivers, to stop working and get out of there. This made Christoph even madder—he asked who their boss was—he was going to complain. Then they admitted they were not firefighters, but representatives of Tolko, the company that owns of one of the sawmills in Williams Lake. Tolko has an agreement with the Tsi Del Del (Redstone) band to manage local forests, and BC Wildfire Services had given them permission to make decisions as to how the fire should be fought. It was not clear to the locals as to why Tolko might want this part of the forest to burn. I made several attempts to contact the company, but they hid behind a phone answering service and did not reply, and emails were not returned either.

The Tolko people went away and Christoph and crew returned home. But the Cat drivers stayed on. Doug told me he wanted to stop that fire. As a contractor, and therefore not bound by Forestry rules, he started work first thing in the morning and worked until late at night. He ignored Tolko's dictates and kept going.

Mike, who was working one of the choppers, later told me that Doug had started off in the wrong direction. Doug had been following ribbons that he had assumed had been laid by the guys marking the route, but loggers and hunters all leave such marks. The country was rough and heavily treed, so it was impossible to judge exactly where he was going. Mike tried to get Doug on the radio first, but received no answer. He flew low over the Cat; Doug saw him but simply thought he was being friendly and waved. His radio was on, but the racket from both the chopper and the Cat was deafening, and Doug was wearing ear protectors, so the background chatter was ignored. Mike tried another swoop—and got a second wave. Finally Mike tied a pencilled message to a water bottle and threw it on the ground in front of the Cat. Doug was pretty much oblivious to this manoeuvre, but suddenly saw the bottle on the ground. He got out, waved at Mike, and proceeded to drink the water! However, he had received the message and realigned his guard. He eventually took it almost to the treeline.

"Near the beginning of the guard, there was a bog," Doug told me. "Lots of black bear signs in there—the fire was only a couple of kilometres away. A team of flaggers had marked our path with tape, and indicated we were supposed to go right across it but when I drove onto it, the whole surface shook. We didn't have to follow the flagging tape exactly, but the Cat ahead of me, operated by a guy who didn't know the country, drove in and sank. Fortunately we also had an excavator along. The excavator operator cut trees and laid them in front of me so I had a corduroy road. That was how I was able to get to the other Cat and haul him out.

"Every night we would clear a safe area to store the machinery, and one morning I got to my Cat and in the newly turned dirt were fresh tracks from a medium-sized grizzly. The bear was walking funny. He must have had burned feet and was walking funny because it hurt."

ON AUGUST 14, CHRISTOPH AND CORINNE DECIDED TO RISK GOING TO the store. As owners of livestock, they had official permission to stay in our order zone, but it was such a long and tedious bureaucratic process to get a permit to travel anywhere that they figured they could probably get away with going as far as Nimpo without a pass. Unbeknown to them, while they were at the store, the order for Anahim Lake and Nimpo Lake was upgraded to evacuation alert. The last blow-up of the Kleena Kleene Fire had been fairly bad for us, but it was the Precipice Fire that would have threatened the twin communities, and it had not taken off as expected. Anahim and Nimpo Lakes had been on lockdown for only five days. Kleena Kleene was not so lucky, though. The barrier was shifted a few kilometres south; we were now the only community along the highway that was still blocked off. As Christoph and Corinne came home, they saw the new blockade being erected behind them. They had got through just in time.

Transition to Area Command

PRECIPICE, AUGUST 12—14

THE NIGHT OF AUGUST 11, IT WAS CLEAR ENOUGH TO SEE THE MOON. I took more joy in such things now. I checked on the Three Sisters in the moonlit morning of August 12 and then watched the surviving pines of our north slope emerge from the low smoke hanging over our meadows before sending in my weather report. The most important information was that the barometer had dropped significantly.

Now that we were surrounded by fires, my perception of them had changed dramatically. They are not always the raging inferno that is often depicted. That is their most destructive form, but they can also be a cleansing fire that clears the forest floor and speeds the recycling of nutrients. I had often driven through areas of old burns. Having not seen the fires in action, I would imagine that the forest had burned in a roaring inferno that was over in a flash. But now I know they are often a creeping, pernicious thing that moves very little for days, alternately sleeping under a blanket of smoke and wakening for a morning stroll or an afternoon run. Yes, they rage at times. That is when they will make the news.

Even in its fairly benign state, the fire still managed to ravage familiar territory between our place and the Taylors'. At its hottest, it burned some of Lee's large round hay bales and part of a log fence. An area I called the "magic meadow," a small grassy depression within the forest, was left untouched while the slopes around it were now grey and charred. The original homestead cabin (which was a ruin and not used anymore) was ash. The old cast-iron stove, once buried under the fallen walls and roof, had risen like a single tooth in a broken jaw.

The area beneath the Tree-in-the-sky had cooled. Had throwing water at its base been worthwhile when even the large buckets of the helicopters seemed futile? Our morning walk to the Three Sisters encouraged me that our effort may have helped. Only time would confirm if these three would survive.

Many expressed concern about these wonderful trees. Chris assured us: "Fir have bark specifically designed to cope with fire. That is why so many old firs have burn marks on them. A creeping fire won't harm them."

I was exhausted and went to bed at 2:30 p.m. dreaming that my last and only new post for the day would be that the fire took the day off and so did we. But no. I was awakened with a start.

"We have company," Monika yelled as she ran down the stairs.

"No helicopters," was my first thought. "They must have driven in—must be the new structural protection unit—Monika can handle it—after all, I and the fire are taking the day off."

My sleep broken, I got up anyway and followed the crowd to the creek where the two pumps rested on the muddy bank. The new crew, dressed in blue and very friendly, was from the Shuswap. The Comox people were introducing them to the layout of the Precipice. We learned that structural protection activity was being expanded to properties around Anahim Lake as well.

The day had changed dramatically in the one and a half hours that I had slept. The southwestern sky above the heads of the firefighters was erupting. A large orange, black and grey plume was building on the slopes above Telegraph Creek, and in the northwest there was a whirl of smoke without a well-defined plume. Would this fire ever end?

The fire now had many personalities. The north fire was on a relaxed jaunt up toward Hotnarko Lake. The Telegraph Creek Fire was still a bit too close for comfort and was definitely a little crankier.

The horizon seemed to be exploding in every direction but as soon as the smoke lifted, the helicopters were out in force. Helco and IC machines were first, circling and evaluating. Then the bucketing helicopters—the mediums and the heavies. Helicopters in the sky at two levels. We could just see the heavies above the horizon to our east, dropping water frantically near both the Mecham Cabin and the Taylor Ranch, trying to guide it by the buildings as they had guided it past us. Caleb and Clemens would get the show today.

While the sprinkler system ran, we looked in Monika's cabin. We had been warned about potential water damage when the sprinklers were first set up but had not bothered to check it before. To our dismay, we found that the floor had buckled, the heater stove had water in it, and cupboards and drawers had swelled. They had been so carefully made and we felt foolish that we had allowed this to happen. We could only blame ourselves. We searched for the cause and found that one of the sprinklers on the roof was spraying water into the chimney and through cracks where the lower roof came against the second-storey wall. The two teams helped change the configuration so water didn't pulse against the wall, and a garbage can was placed over the chimney.

In spite of the damage to her cabin, Monika was still happy with the fight against the fire. That night she wrote, "It's late and I'm a little tipsy. We finally opened Pat's Prosecco. We drank to the passing by of the fire. In spite of all that wind, there was not much activity near us. No helicopters landing, no bucketing close by. We feel fairly safe now, though I cannot quite believe it just yet."

But at the Taylor Ranch site, things were far from relaxed. The fire was spotting near the buildings and Caleb had to be vigilant. One ember landed in a pile of debris near the machine shed. Caleb laid a two-centimetre hose from his house and doused it. Two more fires were sparked in brush piles farther from the buildings. The helicopters quickly bucketed them, preventing flames from spreading into the pines near Lee's spring calving area.

On Saturday, August 12, Arlen emailed: "The fire is looking like it won't make its way to Anahim any time soon. On Friday it was trying to get up and go but didn't hit that threshold… thankfully." He had hoped to get in but didn't make it. "Sorry I haven't been able to pop over," he wrote the following day. "Things are transitioning to Area Command and getting more complicated."

We were unsure of what he meant by that, but later found out that the Precipice Fire was to be lumped in with the Kleena Kleene Fire in order to share resources. Administration would move from the Coastal Wildfire Service to that of the Cariboo. A large camp had been set up at the mill site near Anahim Lake. Although I was grateful for the news from Arlen, I was apprehensive as well. We had not heard good things about the way the Cariboo Wildfire Service approached firefighting, especially in terms of communication.

A story passed on to us by Chris was that a friend of hers, waiting for a plane at the airport, heard a fire boss speaking on his radio. A fire had broken out ahead of the Precipice main fronts, and it was right around the division line between the Cariboo and Coastal districts. The fire boss was trying to ascertain which district he would be working for. He couldn't send his crew in there before he knew who was going to cover their insurance and pay them.

There is only one road out of the Precipice, though each of our properties has its own branch. They diverge a little way up the valley side near the Mecham Cabin. We referred to our branch as the "bypass"; the other, down to the ranch, was the "shortcut." We decided to explore the bypass by car and see if we could reach the Mecham Cabin. We set off early, while everything was calm. The bypass had been ravaged four days earlier. Blackened ashy ground and pockets of open flame lay on both sides. We came to three charred trees, two pine and a spruce, blocking our way, and almost turned back but I had the chainsaw with me and we thought we'd try it. It was unnerving to have the car standing stationary while the forest smouldered above. Somehow it seemed safer when we were moving.

Fortunately there were no more problems. We found the cabin surrounded by green. It is close to a lake that looked as untouched and beautiful as ever. A pump had been placed beside the water, and numerous sprinklers were spraying the mainline and the building.

We did not linger, for we heard the first helicopter and feared a reprimand from the IC more than flames from the fire, which was beginning to move with the heat of the day. We went home via the shortcut to the ranch.

Clemens was preparing to leave. His truck was loaded with the pumps and hoses we had borrowed from Anahim Lake. The loss of this equipment gave us a lot of anxiety, though we accepted that the Anahim residents had their concerns. The Taylor home uphill from the ranch buildings was still covered, but protection of the ranch itself was weakened. At the onset of the fire Lee and the Red Roof House's owners had each bought two pressure pumps. I had David J's larger pump. Lee promised Caleb that there would be a replacement pump to protect the ranch site by the end of the day.

There were two critical burning areas near the ranch buildings. One was a group of dense pine next to the road (the calving area) and the other was a spruce bog just below the house that Caleb was living in. The IC dispatched three helicopters to dampen them. They occasionally shifted to hit the hotter areas next to the bypass where Monika and I had driven that morning. By evening Caleb thought the Spruce Bog Fire was out and passed the message onto Lee and Pat, but he, too, was to find that helicopters cannot stop a fire.

The winds had gusted all day but with no consistent direction in our valley. However, they blew the heavy thick smoke away. By day, hot spots could easily be identified by small plumes (puffers) of white smoke. There were many of them on all sides of us but they seemed almost friendly and none were alarming. We did not bother turning on the sprinklers.

Nighttime perception of the fire was markedly different, however. You could no longer see the puffers, but in two areas the night sky glowed red behind silhouetted trees. Close to us, the rank ones and twos were visible as small open flames on dead stumps or logs. Monika called them "campfires" because they resembled the spaced-out friendly fires noticeable in a structured campground.

While the winds were a benefit to us, they were whipping up the fires on the plateau with a vengeance. Chris commented: "Crazy windy at KK, but at least I could *see*. Spectacular pyrocumuli. USDA Fire Service map and Google Earth aren't working properly so I could not monitor progress at the Precipice. Please post soon. Looks like you guys can breathe easier—hope that's literally as well as figuratively."

In the morning of August 14, Chris emailed: "Frost up here this morning. No white, though—no moisture in the air to make crystals. I'm constantly amazed at your frequent references to dew. We never have any here. A broad band of smoke lies over the fire area so can't see what's happening there. I am very jealous of your direct contact with the firefighters. All I have to find out what's going on is my eyes—when I can see—and the websites—excluding the useless Wildfires of Note pages."

That day was to be Arlen's last with VA0778. I emailed IC, asking whether they still wanted weather information. Roland responded. "Hi Fred, yes we still would like reports. I will make sure Arlen's replacement touches base with you—thanks."

Although we were no longer in the front line, we were fully aware of the sounds of the helicopters bucketing at the Mecham Cabin and Taylor Ranch. I trusted that the firefighters would be able to guide the flames past all the properties in the valley. Guide? No, it was more like *herd*. The helicopters and ground crew seemed to steer the fire in the way that Monika and I would move cattle. Putting a little pressure on a confused calf so it will go in the right direction. When it moves, the mother follows. Then back off when it is going harmlessly in the right direction, even if it is running. This was how they moved the hottest portions past us.

The persistent puffers by our house were annoying reminders that we were still in the middle of a fire zone. But we now lived more in the black. The Taylors' place, with Caleb the lone defender, was still green. We were constantly reminded of Arlen's early prediction—"It will burn." He certainly was right because the fire continued to chew at the forest on all sides of our meadows. But he had also said, "you want it to bubble and not to boil," and he gave us confidence that all would be fine.

We walked on an old trail to Airplane Lake, near the Mecham Cabin, to try to determine the extent of the fire. It had snuck its way to the lake about a kilometre from the cabin. Two loons were on the water. One called a caution to its mate and continued muted warnings as they swam closer. Once they determined we were not a threat, the calling ceased and they swam away, content in their lonely smoky mist.

At the Taylor Ranch, Caleb was working on one of Lee's tractors. I marvelled at his ingenuity. He had designed a press to gently push a new sleeve into the engine's head. He had stored the sleeve in the freezer overnight to shrink it enough to fit into the block. He climbed onto the tractor many times to apply pressure with a ten-ton jack, cautiously measuring the downward movement of the sleeve as its upper end came close to the top of the block. If it popped rather than slid, its upper edge would drop below the top of the block and all would be lost. It was nerve-wracking to watch and I left while he was debating whether to file the last millimetre or try another push. I was amazed that he could concentrate on such a delicate task while the helicopters thundered overhead. They were dropping water on the spruce bog and the ridge above the long meadow— two mediums operating in tandem. The round trip to the water source took four minutes. They doused a hot spot every two minutes. Textbook stuff. To keep flames quiet they have to be hit within a three-minute interval.

The structural protection unit brought more fuel for all the pumps in the valley. David J was now working on the Kleena Kleene Fire but today he brought in a pump so the ranch buildings were better protected. At the Red Roof House, the Forestry pump broke and had to be taken out, leaving the buildings vulnerable.

I resented that they were devoting so much attention to the fires farther down the valley while our greenhouse puffer was active only thirty metres above the building, and another one persisted at the southwest corner of our property. No doubt ic knew what they were doing, but we still felt abandoned. We were tired—mentally and emotionally tired.

The Spruce Bog Fire

PRECIPICE, AUGUST 15–16

"5.6 DEGREES. GENTLE BREEZE OUT OF THE SOUTHEAST. SMOKY LIKE the good old days of a week ago. Fires are quiet. Barometer is steady. The dew is moderate. No rain."

Roland from IC replied, "Hi Fred, thanks so much. It's my last day here, not sure if I will be back to this fire or another one. Please keep your weather reports coming. We include them in our morning briefing."

Monika and I again ventured up the bypass to check on the fire. We went barely half a kilometre when we came to a newly fallen Douglas fir. But it had already been cut from the road. The firefighters must have been there before us. Flagging tape and more cut trees were evident farther along. But we never saw anyone. I felt a little like the cobbler whose shoes had been mended by the elves overnight.

We were travelling in the black but there were still campfires and puffers close to the road. Near the front of the fire we came to a very hot spot, a hollow beneath shallow-rooted large spruce trees. The area was still smouldering. One charred tree lay across the road and two more were dangerously close to doing so, their roots exposed, the rich duff burned out from around them. The road was wet, indicating that a helicopter had bucketed the site the day before.

Firefighting crews had flagged a path into the forest toward Airplane Lake, just in front of the fire's farthest advance. We saw no one, but realized they must be planning a direct attack.

At the ranch, we found that Caleb had successfully pushed the sleeve into the cylinder and ground it flush with the engine head. He was honing the inside of the sleeve in order to fit the piston. He seemed to work incessantly, sensing possible victory over the injured tractor. He still found time to ensure that all the homes and buildings were protected. Every available storage container at the Taylor house was full in order to have the lengthiest possible sprinkler coverage.

The helicopters came in the afternoon. While I was writing a Facebook post, I was counting the number of times a medium was dropping buckets on the south-slope puffer near the corner of our property and only three hundred metres from our house. I was at nineteen drops and the puffer was still very active when I got an emergency call from Caleb. The Spruce Bog Fire close to the ranch buildings had erupted again. It was getting dangerously hot less than one hundred metres from the nearest structure, and he could not get any of the pumps to draw water from the river. Monika and I dashed to our creek and lifted David J's large pump from the mud, waded through the creek and carried it to the car. I rushed over to the ranch. The pumping site was next to a channel of the river below a steep bank. A log fence crossed above the slope. The structural protection people had rigged a knotted rope from the fence down to the pumps as a safety measure. Moving the heavy pump through a fence and down the steep bank to the river was a challenge. We had to remove a rail of the fence to fit the large pump through it. We couldn't use the rope because our hands were fully occupied with the pump. Halfway down the slope we lost our footing and slid the rest of the way, focusing only on keeping the pump upright.

I set the pump among the abandoned ones while Caleb checked the sprinklers. I hooked on the suction hose and moved the mainline to David's pump and turned it on. My back was to the spruce bog, waiting for the suction hose to fill. I suddenly heard the familiar crackle of needles burning that happens just before a tree candles. As I turned, a large spruce burst into flames barely thirty metres away. It was the most dramatic and closest manifestation of the fire I had yet witnessed. The tree still stood, suddenly naked, its needles and small branches quickly gone. I thought of the uprooted spruce in the hollow next to the bypass and knew how vulnerable they were. I prayed this one would keep standing.

The pump, like the others, refused to work. It didn't seem to be able to suck water. I remained calm, shut off the pump, and assessed the problem. I felt it wasn't able to push and pull at the same time so I disconnected the mainline and pinched it closed against the water flowing back down the line. I stood on the mainline as I restarted the pump. It quickly filled the suction hose. As the pump started to spew water I quickly reattached the mainline. All sprinklers pulsed strongly. This was my second physical act in fighting the Precipice Fire and I had done it in the face of danger!

And yet I did not feel a strong sense of fear, nor did I feel particularly brave. I had grown accustomed to being near the fire and no longer felt directly threatened by it. Once I was charged by an angry bull and remember the paralyzing fear and my guttural scream. The bull veered away and broke through a metal gate at the last second. I shook with a numbing fear and it took real bravery to go among the cattle for the rest of the day as I sorted the calves from the cows. I never felt that type of fear the whole time we lived with this fire.

Again two mediums began bucketing hot spots next to the long meadow as well as the Spruce Bog Fire. The constant pounding seemed to have no effect. The fire was entrenched deep into the bog. Once we were confident that the pump and watering system were working, I went up to the Taylors' house and grabbed their last bottle of whisky. I brought it down to Caleb's cabin and we sat and watched

Danger tree fallers are the first in to cut a fuel-free guard. These two, from Vancouver Island, were the last to be flown out on this day. Photo by Fred Reid.

the helicopters as they passed directly overhead. As the sun set, the air cooled, smoke began to settle and the fire quieted. We walked to the fence and studied the bog. Flames began to grow along the edge and creep up another spruce but did not have the energy to cause it to candle. I thought, "This fire is like a teenage boy. It sleeps until the early afternoon. Then wakens with a ravenous appetite and plays video games until all hours." Caleb phoned the next morning to say he'd had a light show all night.

Monika and I finally met the firefighters working the bypass the next morning as we drove the bypass a second time. First were two danger tree fallers. Their job was to cut down anything that might block the road or be a hazard to those making a hose lay.

Then we came to a unit crew disembarking from pickup trucks. They were preparing to strengthen the defence line flagged the day before. We were self-conscious as we waited for them to get organized.

I was keenly interested in seeing how they fought the fire on the ground but was too embarrassed to ask many questions.

We drove the circuit to the Taylor Ranch. Caleb was exhausted. He had stayed up until 10:00 p.m. watching the Spruce Bog Fire and was woken by his dog barking at the fire at 2:30 a.m. He did not sleep after that.

The structural protection truck went by us on its way to our place as we visited with Caleb. We followed half an hour later. The fire was hardly noticeable but it was still active along Valley Bottom Road. It never ceased to look for fuel. Flames had crept to a dead willow, causing it to fall across the road. This must have happened after the structural protection crew had passed by. We were exhausted and frustrated by this most recent interruption to our lives. We stumbled from the car. I grabbed our chainsaw, which we constantly carried in the car, and cut the stems of the willow apart, throwing the cold branches to the green and the hot burning stems to the (soon-to-be?) black. We met the returning crew and they promised to cool this campfire.

And then, fantastic news: "We just heard that the evacuation order for Anahim Lake has been lifted!"

But it ain't over until it's over. The winds picked up and three puffers showed themselves on the north side of the fire—one directly above the greenhouse. We ran the sprinklers for the first time in three days.

Everything seemed to be reaching its limit. The pressure pump began to gasp for water. The flow in the creek was strong enough, but I had to dig the intake into the creek bed a little more carefully so as not to stir up sediment that would block the sprinklers. Caleb had run out of propane a couple of days before and took one from the Taylor house. We were low, but I still had a twenty-pounder in reserve.

The spruce bog continued to burn—more smoke than flame as the fire chewed though the thick organic soil. A rank four was active between our place and the Taylor Ranch. It was no threat to us and probably a day or two from the ranch. We were in a "just keep things running" mode.

For almost a week we had received only brief visits from fire-fighting personnel, and we missed Arlen deeply. We were not sure whether his absence was due to the transfer of administration or the complexity of the fight against the fires. Lonny was now our main contact. We latched on to him quickly. Far from my first impression, he had a keen sense of humour and was easy to talk to; still I was wavering and unsure who to send the weather reports to. On August 16, I never reported.

The response was swift. "Hi Fred. Can you please send your updates? They are very valuable for our daily planning as you are our eyes on the fire while we are gone for the night. Thanks so much! —Lonny"

Windstorm

KLEENA KLEENE, AUGUST 15–18

THE SHIFT OF THE ROAD BARRIER MADE ME FEEL MORE TRAPPED than ever. I could not even go to Nimpo now. I forwarded Richard's email to Jaden.

"That's crazy," he replied. "Keeping people safe by restricting their access to basic needs. When I was coming home from Vancouver it was 5:00 a.m. when I got near to Williams Lake, and I didn't want to hang about for the stores to open so I took the shortcut via Farwell Canyon and bypassed the city altogether. I never had a chance to shop. I have emergency food for many weeks. Boring, but I will survive. I have tons of millet, buckwheat and flour. Just no yeast—only baking powder. And while the power stays on I have veggies and meat in the freezer."

"I have solar power," I said, " so am not affected by the power cuts. I have a bit of freezer space if you need it in a hurry."

August 15 slowly wheeled by. The morning was again warmer than usual, the light brassy. My flag-o-meter fluttered a little, then fell still. Suddenly, violent gusts started. I had seen nothing of the mountains all day, and now as the air cleared around my home, I could see an enormous dark wall of smoke covering the whole ninety-degree quarter from south to west. It was so thick and formless I could not see where it originated. A hot ground wind puffed from the south-west, but the dark mass occasionally varied enough to show billows from the south. There were at least two layers of wind then—typical of unstable weather and thunderstorms. By 7:30 p.m. the gusts were less violent but still strong enough to sway trees. The fire websites hadn't caught up with this new activity yet so they were no help in finding out what was going on.

Then DriveBC showed that Highway 20 was once more closed at Riske Creek. The terrible fires had roared up there again. In the middle of the night I woke to a thick blackness full of a very acrid smell. It was dead calm and tons of smoke now blanketed my home. It was the worst it had ever been. Breathing was very unpleasant. If I would have been allowed back home again, I would have left like a shot. I shut all windows and doors and wound a scarf around my face, and was able to eventually go back to sleep. As daylight inched into the world, I thought, as all of us involved with the fires had so often done: "I have survived another night."

But the next morning was bizarre. I could *see*! There were the mountains for the first time since the last eruption twelve days ago. The Google Earth fire overlay showed that most of the fires in the province had not done much overnight. Their patches were still predominately yellow; even the Precipice Fire seemed to have been marking time. It was only the Colwell Creek area that showed new violence. It had almost doubled in size. It was now many kilometres downstream from the initial strike. One would think that the clear-cuts through which it now raged would have slowed the fire down, but apparently not.

Dramatic as that front was, more of concern to me was the activity around Finger Peak.

This mountain was now fully visible for the first time in a considerable while. The scrubby vegetation that had taken toeholds on the steep rock wall was brown. Puffers spiralled from several places.

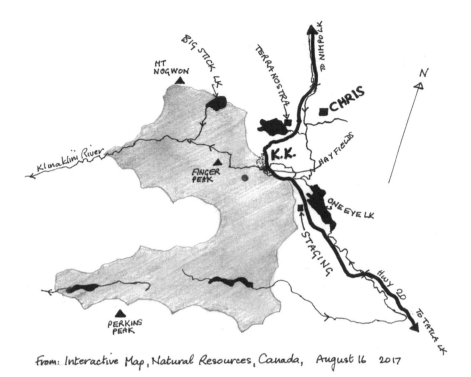

From: Interactive Map, Natural Resources, Canada, August 16 2017

The Kleena Kleene Fire's perimeter on August 16. Credit: Based on Natural Resources Canada's Interactive Maps, August 16, 2017. Drawn by Chris Czajkowski.

The peak is the hard, basalt core of an old volcano. Was it dreaming of its ancient fiery origins?

On August 16, I wrote to Jaden. "12:32: Wind started early and now there is huge smoke from the BSL [Big Stick Lake] Fire, plus pyrocumuli. The smoke is mostly travelling ninety degrees to the highway so is a little north of me. It is a thick and seemingly endless brown wall glimpsed between the trees. It will be blowing many kilometres past the highway. That is my way out. Hope a spark doesn't start another fire and cut off my escape route. For the first time I have heard several helis flying over there, but I don't hear them now.

It's been burning wild for days. Why wait until the wind is insane before they check it out?"

Jaden, 12:49: "I remember at the public meeting a week ago how they said that the KK Fire was fully contained there. Typical BS."

Me, 5:05: "Google Earth is horrifying. Shows the fire has surrounded BSL and is veering a bit south, heading straight for Clearwater Lake. Christoph and Corinne are still in there. I may have to leave."

Jaden, 5:57: "I will pack my car."

Me, 6:07: "If the fire by the guest ranch gets away, it might block the road between us. Any idea as to how to get hold of the structural protection crews?"

Jaden, 6:30: "No, I don't. My lot were here again this morning but they are based south of the fire and your crews are supposed to come from the camp at Anahim Lake sawmill. My people didn't seem to know how to get hold of them. Doesn't give one great confidence in their organization."

Later he added: "I was thinking that Peter Weiler's property would be a safe place to camp if we get cut off both sides. It is within walking distance of my place. There is a big meadow there, no trees, and the fire already burned through nearly a month ago. They have been using it as a helicopter base. We can go there if we can't go anywhere else."

We survived another night. On one weather forecast, winds were slated to reach forty kilometres per hour; another quoted sixty. We often got very strong gusts—sixty kilometres per hour would not be unusual. I watered the garden extra to its normal routine, in case it might be the last time for a while.

During the hot, gusty morning I was visited by another cop. She was totally different from the others. She had just arrived in the Chilcotin and was driving around getting to know everyone. She was not gloomy or critical. She said she did community policing in a rural area back home in Saskatchewan, and that made a huge difference to her attitude. She made a fuss of the dogs and of course I told her that Harry had just written a book. So she bought one! Harry seemed very blasé about selling his first book.

She didn't know how to get hold of the Anahim fire camp either, but when she drove out she must have told someone. A couple of hours later, someone came in to assess the situation.

At 3:08 I emailed Jaden: "Wind mostly moderate here with bigger gusts since noon. Lenticular clouds high up—they signify winds. Constant Cat and heli noise though I can't see much of what they're doing due to smoke. Sounds like they are bucketing."

On August 18, the wind became insane, swirling and battering at the buildings and blowing clouds of thick dust from my barren yard. I was packed and poised. I watched smoke and websites, and with every maniacal gust, my fear built. It was crazy to stay.

Jaden was also living on a knife blade, not knowing whether he should leave. He wrote: "Last night, I could see red beyond Colwell Creek. The fire must have crested the hill for me to be able to see it. It has made another huge run and is very close to the highway. This surge is quite a bit farther south than the one that threatened my house before and is of no immediate threat, but it might cut off my escape route in that direction."

He later sent me pictures taken from a small hill close to his home. In the foreground was the north end of One Eye Lake. The massive smoke banner from the Colwell Creek Fire ran from right to left across the water and for dozens of kilometres east; even the massive pyrocumuli towering above it must have been many kilometres long. It was later deemed to be a rank five, but in my opinion, looking at the pictures, it was off the scale.

A seething brown wall from the Big Stick Lake Fire roared along just north of my property. I judged it to be crossing Highway 20 pretty close to where my road joined it. That afternoon, Ken, an information officer who was currently based at the Anahim Lake fire camp, drove into the yard. He had visited often enough this last week that he had become something of a friend. I was very surprised to see him. He would have had to drive through the streaming wall of smoke to get here. He was putting himself in danger coming to talk to me. He had to raise his voice to make himself heard above the wind's howling.

"This is the worst it's been so far," he said. His face betrayed his concern. "You have to go."

"Will I be allowed home when the fire calms down?" I asked. I knew the answer, but I had to hammer home the point.

"No."

"Then I'm staying."

Ken's BC Wildfire Service shirt and pants fluttered and flapped. The wind thrashed the dust around and flung it in our faces. White ash was eddying in more sheltered pockets. Ken wasn't about to hang around. He began to walk to his car, then turned. He looked desperate. He blurted: "You're not the kind of person who plans on going down with the ship, are you?"

"No, of course not!" I retorted. "I'm watching all the sites on the internet. I also have a fairly good view of the fire from here. I'm checking out the Big Stick Lake arm like a hawk. I'm well aware that it might cut across my escape route. Otherwise I'm ready to go. I haven't really unpacked for six weeks. But the wind is supposed to die tonight. According to Windfinder. If I can survive that long, the worst will be over." I was touched by his concern, though. He was not just talking to me as an official, but as a human being.

As he drove off in a rooster tail of dust, I had to acknowledge that I did not feel as confident as I sounded. Logic told me I was right; instinct told me to flee. Every moment during this last several-day-long windstorm I had been dithering about going. The government kept iterating that the law about not being allowed home after we left was to keep us safe, but in effect, it put us in great danger, as it made us determined to stick it out far beyond what was wise. I had also inadvertently put fire personnel in danger, in the form of Ken, when he came to try and make me leave.

Google Earth's fire overlay showed that the south part of the fire had raced over high ground through a mountain pass toward West Branch, one of the two roads south of Tatla Lake, and the home of White Saddle Air helicopters. I knew people living down there. Not all were habitual internet users. Would they be aware of how close the fire was to them?

The day howled and battered on. The smoke-bronzed sun lowered behind the black plumes on Mount Nogwon and became a blood-red disc before dissolving altogether. Most days the wind dies when the sun goes down and I was hoping for that here. After all, that was what Environment Canada and Windfinder had both forecast. But where was our promised calm?

Although the sun was filtered by the smoke from my perspective, it shone above our earthly maelstrom, and the pyrocumuli above the Colwell Creek Fire caught its last rays. They billowed red. Pyrocumuli rarely last as evening comes; their enormous size so late in the day was a sign of the tremendous ferocity of the forces at work.

The smoke thickened as the light diminished and the temperature cooled. But wild gusts kept thumping and rattling against the building. Now that visual clues were absent I kept trying to evaluate them by listening alone. Were the winds in fact less furious or was that wishful thinking? I couldn't see any red glows that appeared to be all that close, though it was difficult to judge through the smoke. I dismantled the laptop and put it and the camera and all the other last-minute bits and pieces into the van. The key was already in the ignition. I fed the dogs and let them pee, then brought them into the house. I put leads on them before tying them to furniture. This was not normally necessary—they were pretty placid in the cabin at night—but I wanted to be able to grab them and run at a split second's notice. No evasive efforts from Harry, who might not want to get into the van. A last look out the windows. The red glows from the two main fire areas were obvious, but they were relatively constant, only rarely flaring into tree-sized flames. There were no stars or moon. All I took off to go to bed was my shoes.

That was when the phone call came.

Selma's voice.

This is an automated call from the West Chilcotin Search and Rescue. Evacuate now. You must turn off all appliances except fridges and freezers, and shut all windows and doors. Lock your house but do not lock gates. You must drive to the Emergency Evacuation Centre in the Boitanio Mall in Williams Lake and register there... YOU MUST EVACUATE NOW!

This message was not for me, I argued to myself—I was already supposed to be out of there. This new flare-up, however, was threatening Tatla Lake, which was being upgraded to evacuation order. I was still simply on the automated phone list. Mind you, the northern part of the fire was now just as serious.

Why do they always wait until the end of a day to send these messages? By mid-afternoon, Google Earth's fire overlay had shown an unprecedented expansion of our fire. If I can see the seriousness of the situation by 3:00 p.m., surely the desk jockeys in their offices can do the same. Instead of telling people to up and leave when it is still daylight, they wait until it is dark, when things are more difficult to find, and after many people in this ranching and logging community have gone to bed.

Mike King's helicopter base was in West Branch. He told me later that two police officers arrived by ATV at 2:30 a.m. telling him to leave. It would have taken them two hours from Tatla Lake on those vehicles instead of one hour by truck. They wanted to go to his brother's bed and breakfast next door, and a neighbouring ranch, where all the pilots were sleeping, and get them out of bed. Mike was askance. "We are all working maximum hours. How can we do our job properly if we are not allowed to sleep?"

The worst thing, I knew, was to leave at the last minute. That is how people get trapped by fire. If the law had been different, I would have been gone long before. Instead I hung in there, prepared to flee at any moment. I leaped up every time the wind roar increased. And every time I checked the night for any increase in the red glows through the smoke. I was as stretched tight as a guitar string about to snap. *Do I stay? Or do I go?*

The Ground Battle Starts in Earnest

PRECIPICE, AUGUST 17—19

MY FRUSTRATION WITH THE FIRE WAS COMPOUNDED WHEN MY COM-
puter finally quit after weeks of difficulty keeping the battery charged.
It had been dying faster than the fire. I had to switch to Monika's laptop, which had a German keyboard, and I got the *Z*s and *Y*s mixed up.

"Lonny, the thought that zou are at the other end of these weather
reports gives me some peace. 9.4 degrees, barometer rose somewhat,
moderate dew, smoky but relatively good visibility. The fire on our
south side is active and the smoke is blowing gently with winds out
of the southwest. No rain. Promises to be another exciting day."

We had an email from Katie at Stuie. She and Dennis had gone
down the inlet in their sailboat to try to escape some of the smoke.
"We are listening to the rain on our deck above, and wishing we could
send it your way... High winds are just starting, too, which we'll try
to hold back, but they have a mind of their own, I'm afraid."

With the fire seemingly past us on the north slope above our
greenhouse the remaining threat was now from the southwest. Here
it was still very hot and the dominant winds blew it more directly at
us. The continued bombardment of it by helicopters had kept it out
of the crowns but I was, once again, becoming angry with VA0778 as
it crackled away at our south slope. We could hear it through our

bedroom window all night. I was hoping that the trees on this side of our valley would be spared but was beginning to think not. We ran the sprinklers late.

These days it was not the smoke that was most discouraging. It was the sound. Crackling and popping at a relatively high volume for a puffer, and occasionally the soft whoosh of a tree candling and the crash of another one toppling. Trees will be falling for a long time after this fire has passed. So much soil lost, roots damaged and stems weakened. They will be falling all winter when the slopes will be covered with snow. Chris has mentioned how sound seems to be amplified and carried farther by smoke or cloud. But maybe it is only our senses that are heightened, on their nervous edge, when we cannot see...

Monika called me to the greenhouse to listen to a crackling, sizzling sound, like a live and broken power line fishtailing on the ground. She thought it was just above the greenhouse hidden in the thick smoke. It seemed to cover a large area—snaking or dancing through the rocks. We searched for it, eventually finding its source over a hundred metres away. The fire was eating into a squirrel's cache of Douglas fir cones.

Frustrated with my ailing computer, I slipped into a sudden, deep, dark depression and felt so alone. Was it post-traumatic stress? I could not say but I briefly stopped communicating with everyone. I did not go out to meet with Lonny, and could not even talk to Monika, though we had laughed together through most of this fire up until now. But I had a strange need to share my experience with everyone and could not stop writing. I wanted everyone to know how I felt about my relationship with the fire. I felt alternatively like a host with many guests; like a student on a field trip; like a birdwatcher trying to catch a photo of a rare bird (in this case a candling tree); like a voyeur out of place while watching those who were fighting the fire, looking from the outside, as if there was a window in between us. I never felt like a firefighter or a hero, just an observer. I could not stop taking pictures and I could not stop writing.

My darker emotion didn't last more than a day and my fascination began to shift from the fire itself to the methods of fighting it. Earlier I was enthralled by the helicopters' role. The air battle was still going on but now the ground battle was becoming intense. A Caterpillar was contracted to put fireguards across the centre of the Precipice. The operator was Frank Gladden, who grew up in the valley and knew the country well.

I was impressed by how much Mark, Arlen and now Lonny had learned about the landscape since they had been dealing with it. Every trail—new and old. They also knew about fire, where it liked to run and where it had difficulty. They made the decisions on where the guards should be located. In one day Frank pushed a fuel-free three-metre-wide strip from the western end of Lee's long meadow to Airplane Lake. These locations made secure anchor points at either end. Five pickups and a first-aid truck were parked at the eastern end of the long meadow. A unit crew was already laying hose and setting sprinklers along the green side of the guard. At the same time, one IA team was working on the fire in the spruce bog and a second battled in the dense pine at the edge of the meadow near the ranch bridge that crossed the Hotnarko River. Members of the IA teams dragged six-centimetre hoses into the bush and slung the nozzle ends over their shoulders to beam a high-pressure spray of water deep into the soil.

Others tended the pumps and maintained a lookout position for the safety of their team members. Always cautious that the fire would not sneak up on their partners.

Monika and I felt a little neglected by all this activity, but when we returned home from one of our excursions to the Taylor Ranch we found that one of the mediums was bucketing our south slope. This made us feel better. After doing a few chores we returned to

A member of the Initial Attack crew douses spot fires. Photo by Fred Reid.

Caleb's for supper. It was nearly dusk yet two firefighters were standing in the long meadow. We asked about the day's activities. They were danger tree fallers waiting for the last ride out by helicopter. They explained that they had fallen trees for a handmade guard only to have the Caterpillar come through and negate all their work. But the men were not concerned. That is the way things happened sometimes while fighting fires.

Monika climbed over three large boulders onto the new machine guard while I took pictures. It was an impressive mess of rocks, earth and trees that had been piled into a tangle of stems and branches on the green side. A hose lay extended down the length of it, from which sprinklers branched off. The sprinklers were already running. We

Monika climbs onto the new machine guard. Photo by Fred Reid.

said goodbye to the fallers, joking: "We hope the pilots have not forgotten you."

Caleb was up most of the night watching trees candle on the ridge behind the spruce bog, but later it began to rain.

We only had one millimetre and I could still hear the ground fires crackling, visibility was fairly good and I was upbeat. My August 18 morning report included: "Everything is relatively quiet. Good luck."

Lonny responded: "Thanks Fred. We will be working the lines hard today. Good to see some precipitation!" (There was no trace of precipitation at Kleena Kleene.)

Monika and I visited the Taylor Ranch and were very encouraged by the activity. The IA team continued to work at the spruce bog. Two mediums were still bucketing water in the canyon and on the slopes next to the guard. A line locator began flagging the path for the next section of fire-break, which would begin just behind the ranch buildings and extend up to the dirt road above the Taylor house. The line locator was an Australian firefighter, so far from home, but shouting out, "I will find a way!" before disappearing into the forest. The danger tree fallers followed shortly, smiling broadly, with their large saws slung over their shoulders. The swampers and buckers hung around a helicopter piloted by another Australian. Everyone was eager to get at this fire.

Back at home we hiked back into the fire on the north slope above the greenhouse. It was still smouldering and puffing and had many campfires, but we could see what all the bucketing had achieved. The fire had stayed on the ground. Most of the trees should survive. Some impressive flames blazed in the core of a couple of fallen Douglas fir. It was like looking into the heart of a coal furnace. It seemed they would last forever but after a day they choked themselves out of oxygen.

Pat wrote, "Seems so odd to me that we have all these people in the valley at our place and I am not there to welcome them and offer them coffee, cake and a soft place to sit. For that is the Chilcotin way. The Kleena Kleene Fire has closed Highway 20 again, so unsure of when or how we can get back home."

The wind's vagaries would dictate the nature of the fire, and I added these observations to my morning weather report. I would check the windmill to see if it had swung round, then stand in the smoke of morning and breathe deeply. It was cold enough for my breath to be visible and by its direction I could tell if the wind had shifted. Comfortable with my assessment of the wind and visibility, I went in and made my weather report—my contribution for fighting this fire on this day.

Monika and I were again up to our mischief. We began poking around the parts of the fire that remained around our place. We checked out the puffer directly above the greenhouse. Ten metres

A medium helicopter buckets the greenhouse puffer, keeping it cool until an IA *team can come in and extinguish it. Photo by Fred Reid.*

below the Sugar Camp Trail it was burning actively over roughly one hundred square metres. It had crawled along a log (now just ash) to the base of a Douglas fir that had broken in half decades earlier. A four-metre-high snag still stood; the remainder lay as a decaying log below it. The half-tree was riddled with squirrel and woodpecker holes—rotten to the core. The fire was licking at the base and I was interested to see how long it would last. We took pictures, hoping to document its demise.

In the afternoon, we wanted to tour the work being done to the fireguard across the valley. The car would not start. The ATV had begrudging ignition. It sputtered awkwardly and finally growled into life.

An IA team was putting out fires and cutting down dangerous trees along the bypass. Sprinklers, fed from a huge bladder, were watering the machine guard between the bypass and long meadow. We could hear the unit crew working in the thick brush but could not see them.

Caleb was mowing in the big meadow as we headed for home, but we did not stop, not trusting the ATV to restart. We had kept it idling all the way.

At the Taylor Ranch we sensed there was real optimism that the fire could be stopped mid-valley. Two mediums were pounding it in the canyon between our place and the ranch, keeping it cool and giving the firefighters time to complete the guard and lay hose above the ranch. They called this section "Caleb Trench." It connected to a helipad and pump site on a place they called "The Flats." Beyond the helipad, the machine guard continued up the hill with branches toward Precipice Lake, the phone tower and Hotnarko Lake. To make them, the Cats ran over fences and pushed them aside.

Lonny was at the ranch. We mentioned the greenhouse puffer and the half-tree—he promised to deal with it and went on to mention the Caterpillar that was making the machine guards in the

A member of the IA crew extinguishes the greenhouse puffer. Photo by Fred Reid.

valley was spewing oil badly where a hydraulic hose had cracked. We would later hear that it just made it onto the flatbed to be hauled out; fortunately, all its tasks were completed. He also mentioned that close to eighty firefighters were now working in the Precipice.

One medium continued to quell the fire on the south slope. It occasionally passed over the greenhouse to hit the puffer above it. In the afternoon I picked peas, oblivious to the noise, then turned the sprinklers on and went into the house for a nap. Monika awakened me with a start—the pump had stopped. Fearing something more was falling apart, I went out to investigate.

But all was well. An IA team of four had come to put out the greenhouse puffer and they had turned off the pump to connect a second one into the mainline just below the greenhouse to give them the extra pressure needed to pump water up to the fire. They had laid out one hundred metres of seven-centimetre hose that ended just below the puffer. The hose was wound around the base of a large tree so that it would not slide back down the steep slope. Above the tree they had installed a *Y* so two hoses could be worked at once. I marvelled at these young people. How well they worked together as a team, changing roles without a hiccup, always polite and never pushy. Two people, hoses over their shoulders, spraying into and under burning logs and dousing flames at the perimeter of the puffer. Another pulled up the slack from weighty water-filled hoses and a fourth broke apart logs with a Pulaski to expose embers. I had to step carefully around open flame and areas of deep hot ash to watch them work. They kept their distance from the half-tree, which now had flames pouring out of the holes in its bark. I became concerned that I might be a distraction for the team and left—the half-tree was still standing. The following spring, while harvesting morels, Monika and I returned to the site—the half-tree was all but ash. I was disappointed at not documenting its demise, but I would later learn that many firefighters have lost their lives by the collapse of similar old snags. In retrospect I am surprised that Lonny did not scold us for being there. Neither of us had hard hats, fire-resistant clothing, proper boots or radios.

It took the IA team another day to kill the greenhouse puffer.

It rained again in the night, and I wrote, "The rain on the roof sounds peaceful. No click, click, click of the pulsating sprinklers."

CHRIS

Calm

KLEENA KLEENE, AUGUST 19–21

AND SO FIRST LIGHT PULLED ITSELF OUT OF THE MURKY DARKNESS ON the morning of August 19. We had survived another—and most terrible—night. It was still quite windy. Nowhere near as bad as before, but the flag-o-meter was far from relaxed, and warm, wild gusts periodically made boisterous noise, like an exhausted child reluctant to let go of his tantrum. The day had a brown cast; the smoke was settling again. Ash drifted down, coming to rest on my solar panels like flakes of snow. I even found some snagged in a spider's web tucked deep in a bush where it had been sheltered from the wind. I could not see the mountains; Internet Hill was a very vague shape. But there were no obvious close fires.

I phoned Christoph. "It was horrible!" he said. "Horrible!" Google Earth's fire overlay showed the perimetre to be only one kilometre from his house. He and Corinne were exhausted, smoked in, but everything was still intact.

Oddly enough, the Kleena Kleene Fire was the only one to get this violent windstorm. The USDA Forest Service map showed our effusive red blobs of activity, but all the other fire masses in the province were yellow. Even the Precipice seemed to have experienced nothing out of the ordinary. Some wind, yes, but all it did was clear their smoke, and the boundaries of their fire stayed very much the same. However, how much can be read from the websites remains a moot point. The virtual information for the Precipice Fire showed almost no activity at all for the last few days, and yet apparently nine helicopters were bucketing and dozens of ground crew workers were still operating. If there were helicopters flying over our area yesterday I did not hear them. It would very likely have been too dangerous.

THE CLINIC AT TATLA LAKE HAD BEEN IN FULL OPERATION SINCE THE equipment had been moved back on July 27, but it was now closed again. This time Patrice and Doctor Rob didn't transfer stuff into the hall. Both habitually carry enough equipment for most emergencies in their vehicles, and they re-kitted out the SAR first-aid truck (which had been replaced at staging by a Forestry vehicle) and took that home as well. Their house was under evacuation order, but the nearby Tatlayoko Valley was only on alert (with an escape route via Eagle Lake) so there were still plenty of people in the area. Patrice and Rob had permits to travel, and the Tsi Del Del (Redstone Reserve) and Ulkatcho (at Anahim Lake) clinics were both open.

LATER IN THE MORNING, TWO MEN DROVE UP TO MY HOUSE. Accompanying a new fire boss was Gord, the man in charge of the structural protection units. (Yes, the very same Gord who had designed the sprinkler system in the Precipice.) He eyed the water still sitting in the shallow pond below the house but figured that trying to use it might create too many problems because silt and sludge would clog up the pump. They could have laid hose to the river—in other areas a half kilometre was deemed a short lay—but Gord thought it easier to bring in a bladder. Around 4:30 p.m., Badger, my faithful visitor-alert dog, barked, and into the yard came an SUV sporting insignia from Comox Fire Rescue. Following it came a dusty little red fire truck whose sides, and the coveralls of its occupants,

The structural protection crew sets up the bladder in front of my house.
Photo by Chris Czajkowski.

were emblazoned with Ferndale-Tabor Fire Department. Out of the suv came a large orange bundle of sturdy, tarp-like fabric. It was unfolded and laid out, the fire truck backed up to it and a roaring chute of water poured into the bladder. The water had been sucked out of the river near the bridge. Men held onto the sides of the bladder until the weight of the water could support its shape. I have rationed water all my life. To see so much being casually poured so quickly was a bit overwhelming. The first truck didn't hold enough to fill the bladder, and soon a second came, this one from Logan Lake Fire and Rescue. The capacity of these little trucks wasn't great, but a large vehicle would have been useless in twisty, narrow bush roads such as mine. The men were all obviously (and very justifiably!) proud of their vehicles and the service they were performing.

The sprinkler men from Comox smiled when I mentioned Monika and Fred. They'd had a great welcome down there.

One of them showed me the handwritten notice they would put up at the end of my road. It identified my property and listed the structural protection equipment used.

Sprinklers were set up about ten paces from each of the four corners of my house. The firefighters liked the fact that my roof was metal, and also the way the lower part sloped steeply down, delivering water to the bottom of my walls. A big old pump was hauled out. If things hotted up (literally) the crew would likely be in and out but I asked for starting instructions in case I had to run it on my own. I was used to gas motors, but the pump proved to be a lot more complicated than my generator and chainsaw. The operator took several tries to start it—then it backfired alarmingly. After a lot of fiddling, it finally performed, and jets powerful enough to cover my whole roof area and all the land around the house shot out from the spigots.

I mentioned that I had no spare gas, worried that the pump might run out. "Oh, that's not a problem," Gord explained. "The water will run out long before the fuel. There's enough here for two hours." He smiled at my obvious dismay. *Two hours only!* "If there's a need, we'll be in to run it," he said.

The firemen turned off the pump. Pity—I would have loved to give the garden and dust bowl around the house a really good soaking! Off they drove—and wouldn't you know it, but as soon as they left, it started to rain. Not very much—just a tiny dribble. But it lasted all night—enough to give everyone a bit of breathing space. The air smelled sweeter at first, but as it started to move, the scent became underlain with the reek of wet bonfire.

Not long after this, Fred posted a picture of a bladder along one of the hose lays at the Precipice. He referred to it as "one of the biggest bladders I have ever seen." I countered with: "My bladder is bigger than yours..."

Violent five-day windstorms, where the nights are only minimally calmer than the days, are not uncommon in this country. When these storms quit, I feel quite discombobulated. As if I am perched at the edge of free fall, with nothing to stop me from tumbling over.

The wind finally gave up while the sprinkler crew was still here, and it became deathly quiet. There had not been enough precipitation to settle the smoke and now it was building up again. The silence was eerie. I decided to walk to the river. My every step was tentative, as if the dragon might be waiting, hiding behind a tree, ready to pounce.

There is an open field below my property, which was cleared when a now-defunct homestead was operating. My absentee neighbours' buildings at the bottom edge had a distinct air of abandonment, but they were unharmed. The grass in the unkempt meadow was short and sparse from the drought; my eye caught an unidentifiable darkness trapped between stems. I bent to look; it was a charred aspen leaf. Then another; and more. Some still bore the marks of the "circuit-board bugs," the leaf miners that chew amazingly regular, geometric tunnels between the skins of the leaves. Any one of the leaves could have been burning when it fell. Any one could have started a new fire. If it had, there would have been nothing to stop it.

"I must confess," Fred emailed later, "that I think you were crazy. Mark and others always told us that to contemplate leaving at the last minute was the worst thing to do. You are likely to be caught in the fire. We never thought we would try to leave at the last minute. Instead we had safe places to go like the ponds in our meadows. Leaving at the last minute is so dangerous."

"If the stupid law had been different I would have been long gone," I retaliated.

After a moment's thought, I sent a second reply: "We all thought you were crazy to stay in the Precipice on August 3!"

The Anahim Lake fire camp emailed to ask if it had rained and how much. I replied that I had no rain gauge, but that as soon as the dribble had started, I'd turned the wheelbarrow upright, and by calculating the difference between the areas at the top and the bottom of the container, I could estimate we'd had three millimetres. That afternoon someone came by with a cheap rain gauge that you stick in the ground. They placed it in the open area in front of my house and dog Harry promptly peed on it.

I had other visitors. The Comox sprinkler crew came back—but it was not to do anything with the pumps. They had been into the Nimpo store and seen *Wildfire in the Wilderness*, the book I had written about the 2004 Lonesome Lake Fire. They had purchased every copy and had brought them to me to sign! "Let us know if you want anything," they said as they headed back to their vehicle. "Anything at all from the store, and we will bring it." Although, in fact, their two-week shift was to end in a couple of days and I never saw them again.

A new fire boss came by. (It seemed only days since the last "new fire boss" had introduced himself.) This man was from the Lower Mainland. I at once complained, as I did to all my visitors (who now came two or three times a day) about the ridiculous law of not being allowed home in an evacuation order area when the fire died down.

The man was not at all patient. "Far too difficult to manage," he snapped. "Besides, what would you do if you wanted to escape and there was a tree across the road?"

"Cut it out with my chainsaw!" I snarled back.

He looked taken aback, and then had the grace to look contrite. Obviously his city-generated models do not factor in seventy-year-old women who habitually carry—and use—chainsaws.

And finally Ken turned up once more. He had earlier offered to bring food. I had explained that I was far from starving, just getting low on a few specialized treats like miso, which the Nimpo store didn't stock. As Ken approached the door this time, he held his hands behind his back. Then he brought what he was holding to the fore. "Miso!" I exclaimed. "Where on earth did you find that?"

"I have a colleague in Bella Coola," he replied. "She found it down there. She came up the Hill yesterday and brought it to me!"

I heard this same kind of story from everyone who was stuck on their properties. All the fire workers they encountered were so helpful and friendly, bringing anything they could to help ease the prisoners' lot. There had been so many things to feel bad about these last seven weeks—fear, both of the fire and the authorities; lack of information; frustration with bureaucracy and their increasing restrictions—now here was a little group of feel-good incidences; they were worth so much more than just a favour. I lead a solitary life by choice and would go crazy without the necessary amount of aloneness. But I found these small human generosities in this difficult time very touching.

THAT OTHER WORLD—THE WORLD BEYOND THE FIRE—WAS FULL OF the news of the impending solar eclipse. On August 21, we could expect an 80 per cent blockage of the sun at about 10:30 a.m. I wondered whether I would be able to see it. But despite the smoke cover, the sun was far too bright for me to look at it with the naked eye, even though it was not strong enough to cast shadows on the ground. More disappointingly, my not-very-fancy camera couldn't cope either. The only picture I was able to get was about halfway through the eclipse when a small cloud partially obscured the sun. It did, however, get creepy dark.

I was busy drying kale at the time. I had been avoiding the task as it is a two- or three-day process, and I had never been sure if I was going to have that much time at home. But now the whole character of the season had changed. It was calm, damp and cool. I picked baskets full of kale, blanched it, hung it up to drip, then transferred it, leaf by leaf, to drying racks propped outside. This took several hours, during which time I kept stopping to take photos of the eclipse. And just when I had got the kale all set up, it rained. Just a light sprinkle— not enough to do much good regarding the fires, but just sufficient to screw up my drying plans. There was barely room in my house to set up all the racks. I had to live with them in there for the next three days. The ranchers also threw their hands up in frustration. Most of them had been prevented from haying because of the fires; now they had to wait for the rain to stop.

The Three Sisters

PRECIPICE, AUGUST 20—24

ON AUGUST 20, 3.5 MILLIMETRES OF RAIN FELL OVERNIGHT. THE winds picked up as the low-pressure system intensified but we continued to feel safer every day as the fires around us cooled. The IA team came back to finish extinguishing the puffer above the greenhouse. We had a visit from Alan, branch director of the Area Command. He emphasized that they still wanted us to obey the evacuation order, but had been grateful for our co-operation when we stayed. We asked about the length of time he expected the order to remain. With a nod toward the south slope, he said, "As long as you have a hanging fire near your place, the evacuation order will not be lifted."

"Hanging Fire": that was a new term and I liked it. It could mean a fire that is on the slopes above you or a fire that hangs around. In any case, we are victims of our own design. We did not want them to burn our side slopes as a fire-break for our buildings. Arlen had mentioned early on that that was how they would normally protect a property in this situation. We were grateful that he had respected our wishes; the scarring would have been very visible from our house. But as a result we had to now live with these slow, persistent ground fires.

All the guards held and all the fires in the Chilcotin began to cool. However, some were still dangerous and we began to lose helicopters to where they were more urgently needed. We were lucky to have had them when the other fires were too hot to be attacked.

In the afternoon Monika and I took the ATV up the bypass to explore the edge of the black on what they called the Mecham cabin hose lay. The path of the hose lay merged with the machine guard, which was still being dampened with sprinklers. I was amazed how close they placed a hose lay to the front of the fire. The black was at the very edge of the hose lay and there was even a small area of open flame on the green side. We were too tired to try and put it out. The vegetation around it was damp and green. There was no nearby source of water in any case. Some weak smouldering continued inside the black. The guard ended at the edge of Airplane Lake near a charred tree we had noted a few days before. We counted the hoses on our return—eighteen thirty-metre lengths. There were kilometres and kilometres of hoses going everywhere.

We then tried to drive up the machine guard next to the hose lay. As we bounced over the large angular exposed rocks in the guard we became aware that one of the ATV tires was getting flat. Another bit of machinery falling apart. We wished for this epic to come to an end; we were running on empty. But it was by no means over. A spruce at the edge of the bypass candled as we drove by. At the Taylor Ranch, Caleb commented that a few more pine at the back of the spruce bog had gone up in flames. But we all agreed that the fire was definitely cooling.

The previous night Monika had noticed what she thought was a campfire behind the Three Sisters and in the late afternoon we decided to investigate. We hiked up to the charred forest behind the large firs and saw no sign of it. But as we turned back, we spotted flames searing out of the base of the biggest one, just behind the Tree-in-the-sky. After our first firefighting on this knoll, we thought the fire to be dead, but the heat had hidden beneath a deep blanket of ash and for nine days it had burned unnoticed, a very lowly rank one. It had gnawed along two large roots like a slow-burning fuse to the base of the tree, leaving small channels where the roots had lain. It was now burning intensely into the core of the tree. This was fire at its most sinister—hiding from view, yet finding the weak spots in the forest. Its appetite seemingly insatiable.

All trees must die, but we were not ready for this. After our commitment to its sister, the Tree-in-the-sky, we could not abandon this gentle giant. It was not as easy a task as dousing the surface flame had been and there was no helicopter support. We carried eight buckets of water 110 steps from the greenhouse to the base of the knoll and another thirty much shorter steps up the slope to the tree. We first poured water onto the soil and stones at the base of the tree until it was cool enough to approach the fire. We had to be careful not to step into deep hot ash, which would have quickly poached our feet. When we could finally throw water into the red-hot core the fire hissed angrily back at us. I had to go back to the greenhouse to get reinforcements—shovels, grub hoe and more water. We continued throwing water and dirt into the hollowed-out base of the tree until we could see no more flames. But we could still hear the crackling of latent fire as smoke drifted from deep inside the tree. Finally we packed stones and soil into the tree's gaping wound until the fire was suffocated and no more smoke seeped through the cracks. Our actions seemed futile, because the tree was gravely and probably fatally wounded. It had become a danger tree that always had to be approached from the back because it leaned toward our meadows. I watched Monika plaster the last bits of clay and mud over the wound as though she were caring for an ancient elder. She then placed her ear up to the tree as if monitoring for a heartbeat. But she was listening for a sound that she did not want to hear: the crackling or hissing of fire inside the core. The silence gave her confidence that the fire was out. But we resolved to check later.

Caleb resumed baling at the Taylor Ranch. Pat wrote how glad she was that their balers used chains rather than belts inside the drum. With the latter, sticks can get caught between belt and metal frame, causing friction and igniting dry grass. Balers with chains are less likely to do that but all balers must be constantly cleared throughout the haying process. She asked Caleb and I to be vigilant.

The next day, a new pilot worked our south slope puffer. Monika noticed that the helicopter was making a longer circuit than usual to the fire. Lonny was able to stop in, and she asked him why the pilot was working that way.

He smiled and shrugged. "She is an Australian pilot and a little more cautious in these mountain winds. She likes working independently so we have her working your puffer. She is actually very good. We try to let most pilots do their own thing."

He confirmed that a baler did catch fire on another ranch, near Anahim Lake, and it was this same pilot who had put it out. She had spotted it as she had lifted off the staging area, and she had diverted to drop a bucket of water on the flames. The baler had been lost, but the surrounding hayfield suffered no damage.

"The mountain winds and variable updrafts can be too much of a challenge for some of the foreign pilots," Lonny mused as we watched the helicopter make another wide arc over our valley. "We had to send a French pilot home. He was just too uncomfortable with these conditions."

We visited the Three Sisters again. Our Band-Aid at the base of the gentle giant seemed to have held. The ground around the tree was still warm but there was no smoke. We could only wait to see what the fate of this tree would be.

Caleb drove an ATV to the top of the rim rock to check on the fences that had been destroyed when the machine guard had been made, and he told us that the herd was beginning to trickle back into the valley. This increased our urgency to get the haying finished.

We were now in full-tilt boogie. Caleb began mowing at noon and I started raking about an hour later. I could not help reflecting on the last time I had done this. Then, the sky to the west was alive with fire and smoke. I was nervous every time I turned toward it. Today, I also felt tension as I turned west and looked up at the sky, but this time it was concern about rain. A few sprinkles fell. How welcome they would have been two or three weeks ago when I kept having to look at the wall of white, black and orange smoke. At that time I had thought, "Why am I bothering with raking? I should be home protecting the buildings from fire." Now the fire was all but stopped. There were still the puffers and campfires on our south slope, the remains of the hanging fire. The hottest portion (occasionally flaring to a rank three) was along Telegraph Creek. The fires in the canyon between our place and the Taylors' still persisted.

By August 22, things began to heat up again. I posted: "When the fire was coming directly at us, it was being fought with twenty-five firefighters on the ground. They did amazing work but they were not enough. Now there are seventy-two ground crew, with more expected tomorrow."

Monika and I drove up the bypass in the late afternoon. We heard the whine of small backpack Forestry pumps placed in any little swamp or pond with enough water and we could see firefighters approaching puffers through thickets of trees. On our return trip we bumped into Lonny, standing alone, two radios in hand, listening to both the air-to-air and ground-to-air channels. He had been co-ordinating the movement of equipment and crew all day. He must have been tired but it did not show. He was excited about how well the fight was going. He was arranging the safe departure of all the crews for the day. As we chatted, their transportation helicopter swooped in and landed.

We did an inventory of what it took to protect all the buildings at our place. One pressure pump with suction hose and one-way valve. Seven seven-centimetre mainline hoses thirty metres long and thirteen that were fifteen metres long. Nineteen fifteen-metre and three three-metre hoses two centimetres in diameter. Thirteen pulsating sprinklers and seven fan sprinklers. Various *T*s and *Y*s and valves to fit. All this and our lush green meadows to protect twelve structures. If any embers landed close to the buildings we did not notice them; they would have quickly died in the moist grass. It was the meadows that probably saved us, but it was the sprinklers that gave us peace of mind. We were so grateful to those who came early to help build the system when we didn't have a clue of what we were about to face.

The next morning an IA team of five was waiting by the greenhouse. Lonny came by helicopter and flew off with the team leader to check things out. The plan was to attack the persistent ground fires nearest our home—all with the hope of getting the evacuation order lifted.

The fire nagged at us. As Caleb and I took a break from haying, a column of black smoke sprang from the slopes between the long meadow and Airplane Lake. Caleb groaned that the fire would go on for a long time yet. The scouting helicopter was quickly there, buzzing in frantic circles to see what could or should be done. Then the medium was up and starting to bucket. Strangely it did not drench that hot spot, which died down after a few anxious minutes. The people in the helicopters saw the fire a lot differently than we did because they were looking straight down. They also had a lot more experience.

I was almost giddy as I completed raking in the big meadow. I met Alan as I drove the tractor home. A thought crossed my mind: in the past we would be startled when we saw a foreign truck, but meeting a strange vehicle was commonplace now. Alan asked me to tell Caleb not to worry about the couple of puffers near his house. They were not serious and the fire crews would look after them in the morning. A helicopter was bucketing by the ranch for the first time in three days.

Caleb and I had a repair to do on the rake, and afterwards we sat in front of Caleb's house to sip on the bottle of Lee's dwindling whisky and watch the Spruce Bog Fire heat up. It was just smoking but there were some threatening crackles. The firefighters dared not go in there without falling trees first. Those remaining upright, dead or alive, have had most of the soil burned from around their roots.

At home, smoke drifted eastward across the face of our south slope. They were unable to put out the hanging fire. We felt safe from it, but it refused to let go of its grip over us. Like a lingering cold, it hung on. We were not confined to bed anymore. We could go to work but we would not be free of our affliction until the fire finally died.

The Meeting

KLEENA KLEENE, AUGUST 23–24

THE CARIBOO REGIONAL DISTRICT ANNOUNCED IT WAS GOING TO HOLD a meeting at Nimpo Lake on August 23 to address various fire issues. Some locals from the Nimpo/Anahim area had put together a proposal that they would be presenting to Donna Barnett, our MLA, the chair of the Cariboo Regional District and others. Here are a few extracts from the proposal:

- The evacuation order [*i.e., the Anahim/Nimpo order*] was issued long before it was necessary.
- The order covered a much larger area than was justified.
- Those of us who decided to stay were essentially put under house arrest. We were not able to leave our homes to get food or medication, or to check on our neighbours' homes, many of whose houses are empty due to seasonal occupation. We were unable to set up sprinklers in the neighbours' yards or organize as a community to make the place more fire-smart.
- The First Nations population issued their own permits to any individual that wanted them. When one community member complained about this over the phone to the CRD, the chairman replied that they could do nothing about the

Ulkatcho people as they have an autonomous government...
We would be justified in thinking that the CRD has deliberately
set out to cause a racial rift in our community. [*Powerful
stuff! Not all of it completely accurate. And what ire from a
community that was under evacuation order for only five days!*]

- The authorities cut off all information about the progress
  of the fires, preventing us from making informed, rational
  decisions. [*Not quite true—certainly we received very minimal
  information—but I think that was because the various levels of
  bureaucracy did not know what was going on either.*]

The following proposals I certainly endorsed:

1. Those of us who decide to remain in spite of an evacuation
   order should be allowed free movement within the community.
   There is no justification for house arrest. If anyone is caught
   looting, s/he should be arrested, as at any other time. Since
   there is always such a massive buildup of RCMP and military
   force in the area once an order comes down, that should be
   easy. Why should due process of law be suspended? Would
   anyone tolerate being arrested just because they *looked* like
   they might commit a crime? If necessary, we are open to the
   requirement that every citizen who wishes to remain under an
   evacuation order and does not want to be under house arrest
   must attend a firefighting certification course so long as those
   courses are made available to every community locally and on
   a regular basis.

2. Residents should be given timely, accurate and complete
   information about the progress of wildfires beyond the sparse
   and often many-days-old bulletins posted by Cariboo Fire
   Centre, so that they can make informed, rational decisions as
   to whether they remain during evacuation orders or leave. It is

the responsibility of the Cariboo Regional District to provide this information to those who elected them.

I WANTED TO GO TO THE MEETING. I PHONED THE CARIBOO FIRE Centre in Williams Lake to find out how I could get a permit. They gave me the chairman's phone number, whose voicemail message announced that he would call back as soon as possible. I received no reply, and several days later I phoned again and this time was able to get hold of him. I explained where I lived and that I would like a pass to go to the meeting and return home afterwards. Kleena Kleene was now the only area along the highway still under evacuation order. Without even considering it he rattled off the mantra that if I was in an evacuation order area and left, I would not be allowed home. By the tone of his voice it was obvious that he had said this many hundreds of times during the fire season.

Friends suggested that if I was part of the firefighting endeavour I might stand a chance. I was, after all, sending daily weather reports; maybe I could see if that carried any weight. I wrote to the person who was receiving the reports; he duly made the effort on my behalf, but all I got was another categorical no. I contacted several radio stations, resulting in three phone interviews. They wouldn't get me a permit, but at least I was able to voice my protest. I wrote to Donna Barnett, our MLA, but got no reply. I was informed by email that the meeting would be filmed and posted on YouTube; I would be able to see it then.

Maybe I could risk going anyway. What could they do if I left my dogs and computer stuff at home? I was willing to bet that Christoph would be there, with or without a permit, but he had his rancher status backup. I had not been caught before; it seemed like a first offence might just be a warning and it was only the second offence that would result in being "forcibly removed." And how would all these officials—the CRD chairman, Donna Barnett, etc.—get to the meeting? They would have to drive through the fire zone and drive back through it again. To put a cap on the whole ridiculous situation, I heard that *tourist fishermen*, for goodness' sake, were being given permission to go through the zone to Bella Coola and return. If looting was the concern, what was to stop any of these people from reading the flagging-tape code on the highway and doing the deed if residents were not home? What on earth was the difference between them driving both ways on the highway and me doing the same?

The meeting was to be held at two in the afternoon. David J, who was still working on the Kleena Kleene Fire, called and said he would pick me up. As a first responder, he could travel freely. Sometimes, he told me, the people manning the barrier didn't count heads; at other times they stuck to every letter of the permit law. The dribbles of rain were keeping the atmosphere damp, but the wind got up a lick or two late morning and David J contacted me again, by satellite phone, saying he had to be at his work station so wouldn't be able to come. I dithered about taking the law into my own hands until the last minute—in the end I stayed home. (Funny, really—normally I would have done anything possible to *avoid* going to such a meeting...)

The CRD posted the meeting on YouTube as promised, but it was even less satisfactory than I had envisioned. The Nimpo Lake community hall is a small, windowless log building renowned for its poor acoustics. A stage area occupies one end, and a camera had been set up to focus on a lectern and six officials sitting there. Several other officials were apparently present, but they were all off camera. The audience was invisible and, for the most part, inaudible. A couple of mics were up front, but even when the speakers used them, their diction was often hard to understand.

The emcee was a woman who had appeared often on the CRD's little YouTube videos that had been posted throughout the fire. This film started in the middle of one of her sentences—she no doubt announced her name and status, but that had been cut off. The MLA, Donna Barnett, spoke next. She thanked the community for approaching her so that she could help organize the meeting. Then she praised the firefighters, for which she got a big round of applause. She explained it was the BC Wildfire Service's job to fight fires and provide information to the Cariboo Regional District. The regional district works under the auspices of the Local Government Act and initiates emergency and social services, which are in fact staffed by volunteers. She stressed the "volunteer" bit, but no one reacted to this. If the rest of the community was like me, they would think: "So what?" Nothing goes on in our communities that is *not* run by volunteers.

Based on the information received by the BC Wildfire Service, Donna continued, the CRD puts out the evacuation orders. In response to the hundreds of complaints she had received since the fires began, she explained that it was her job to support both the BC Wildfire Service and the regional district.

She was to enlarge on this later, but she first introduced Tony from the BC Wildfire Service. He talked about the drought, and the excess of dead material due to the pine bark beetle infestation that had lasted a decade and had resulted in large quantities of flammable material being left on the ground. Since 2010 there had been no serious wildfires. The lightning storms in July of this year had been far more extensive than they ever could have imagined; nearly a hundred fires were started on the same day. The BC Wildfire Service was simply overwhelmed. They very much appreciated all local groups that had geared up to help. As of today, there were 1,816 ground firefighters, 60 aircraft and 180 pieces of heavy equipment employed. Right now, he added, all the fires were looking pretty good. The only ones left uncontained were the north and south ends of the Kleena Kleene Fire. (This was not in fact the case. No mention of the Precipice Fire, and the Elephant Hill Fire had a big run on August 30, when it clawed its way to the shores of Sheridan Lake.)

He talked about the Plateau Fire, which was the name given to a number of conflagrations north of the highway that were deemed to have joined on August 12, "making it an unprecedented size in BC's fire history." When fires join they immediately become far more powerful. Runs of twelve to fourteen kilometres a day were recorded.

I found these figures puzzling. Either the USDA fire maps or the BC Wildfire Service was in error. Sure, the boundaries of this multiple-fire complex now enclosed an enormous area. But the USDA fire map showed a very large space complete with lakes in the middle of the complex that was not burned at all. Would the fire still be just as dangerous? Or was the BC Wildfire Service trying to make their job seem more impressive?

Tony continued: "People have been annoyed about the increased area of evacuation orders and alerts, especially those given out for the East Chilcotin on August 12. This was done, however, because of the weather forecast. A cold front was expected, and these are often preceded by cold, dry winds. The BC Wildfire Service's first priority was public safety, but most residents felt the ruling to be over the top." Obvious parallels to the Nimpo/Anahim Lake area here.

I looked up the dates later, and in fact there was a major blow-up on August 12 (the same day our fire galloped to Big Stick Lake). *CBC News* published an article about it on April 26, 2018. The meteorological storm, which started in Washington state, flung up four massive pyrocumuli over the East Chilcotin. They created their own thunder and lightning comparable to a moderate volcanic eruption. Smoke was sent into the stratosphere, travelling round the globe. "It was the biggest pyrocumulonimbus event ever observed," David Peterson, a meteorologist, was quoted.

The Riske Creek Fire jumped the road that leads to Chilko Lake in the south part of its range, providing a few scares to the people from Nemiah who were driving past. Its most gruesome recorded detail was the burning of ten wild horses. A ranger subsequently photographed them—the picture was published in the *Province* on August 23. Trees, ground, charred carcasses, all are black as soot. The horses' heads are thrown back, teeth bared and their legs are flexed. This is a natural result of the intense heat, but it adds to the drama of the picture. The only divergences from the funereal hue are white streaks marking some of the horses' flanks—faeces left by avian scavengers.

The audience was firing questions, and Tony was having a hard time. I could hear very little of what the audience commented on, but Tony kept saying things like: "Yes, we could have done better at this"; "Yes, we tried to get local help but that information was not always passed on." I had an experience of this. A fire boss asked me for weather reports and I sent them faithfully for a week. Another fire boss came by and politely wondered why I had not been sending the reports—turned out the recipient of my information had finished her shift and left but had not bothered to give me a new email address or pass the reports to anyone else.

A query was made as to why firefighters had to report to staging early, then wait for a fire boss, then wait for a safety talk (why would this change every day?) and then do stretches before they were allowed to work. British Columbia was the only province that insisted on this. Albertans and Ontarians who were fighting our fires did not have to comply with these regulations—nor did the Australians, New Zealanders or Mexicans who had been brought in. "Thank goodness for the foreigners," someone said. Tony muttered something about fatigue being a concern. Fair enough, but I knew that many of the locals worked over seventy-five days straight without a break, starting early in the morning and quitting when they felt they could do no more.

One person asked about the hoses that had been abandoned in the bush after many wildfires in the past. Tony said that all equipment was packed and evaluated for use in the future. But I can attest to the wastage: when sprinklers were set up around Nuk Tessli in 2009, crews came in and parcelled up a lot of the equipment after the fire. The following year, however, about half the hoses were discovered buried in the bush. They were frayed by weather by that time, and useless.

Another question addressed fires in provincial parks. The Precipice Fire started in Tweedsmuir Provincial Park, and the audience member stated that—because Parks' policy is to let fires burn naturally—it would never have got so out of control and affected their communities if it had been fought right away. But Fred has iterated that the Precipice Fire was fought very early on. In fact the first priority was to protect the new walking bridge that had recently been built inside the park. They had ground crews and structural protection people there before they came to his place. Tony replied to the audience member by giving an answer he was now resorting to quite frequently: "This is beyond my scope..."

Reg Stuart of the BC Cattlemen's Association then came to the microphone. Tall, lean, silver belt buckle, large cowboy hat—he was right out of Central Casting. But what he said was clear and concise. He talked about the recovery process, which was already underway for people who had lost hay crops. Thirty thousand cows were so far accounted for; many were still missing. It was going to take a lot of work to get it all sorted out and would take time, but it was being done. Claim forms were available at the back of the room.

Ashley was next. She represented the Red Cross. She was almost impossible to understand, even with the mic. I looked at the Red Cross website and found that evacuees were to be given six hundred dollars per household for every fourteen-day period away from home. They would also receive three hundred dollars on their return to help with costs such as food replacement and cleaning materials. I had been under an evacuation order for most of seven weeks. But I had either stayed home or sneaked in and out. Because I had solar power, the contents of my freezer were unharmed and I had no food loss. Running up and down the Bella Coola Hill cost me extra gas money, and the whole summer had been a colossal waste of time, but I didn't feel it necessary to try and claim any of this. Let those who were in real need reap the benefit.

That more or less finished the first hour-long video. The second jumped in when a speaker was already talking. This was a large man referred to as Phil, representing Transport Canada—it was he who made the decisions as to when to close the roads based on information given to him by the BC Wildfire Service. He was asked many questions and he spoke clearly (without the mic) and with great confidence at first.

"How were you able to drive through the evacuation order zone?"

"We had permits."

"Was there any danger anywhere along the road?"

"Not at all!" (He didn't realize that this comment was putting him at a disadvantage.)

"Why is it safe to drive one way through the fire zone but not the other?"

"That only happened at the beginning, to facilitate evacuees."

"It's been happening for well over a month!"

"Oh, I didn't know that... um... ah... I'd have to look at my notes to confirm that. I don't have my notes here..."

"Why is it so difficult for most people to get permits?"

"It's not at all difficult. You just have to send a picture of your area on your phone..."

"How? There's no cell phone service here."

"Oh, um, by computer is fine. Then a permit will be issued."

"Why was a person living in Kleena Kleene refused a permit to come to this meeting?"

"No permits are being refused."

What?

"What happens if you are in an evacuation order area and wanted to come to this meeting and return home?"

"If anyone living in an evacuation order leaves, they will not be allowed home. That law exists until the state of emergency is declared void."

The emcee, who was unfortunately still holding a microphone, said: "And that will be August 23." Someone turned quickly to hush her, obviously telling her it already was August 23 and Kleena Kleene was still considered to be under a state of emergency.

An audience member spoke up. "Four days after the evacuation order was announced for Nimpo Lake, I went to the store. In front were five pickup trucks with their families—some of them kids— all going to Bella Coola for fishing. 'How come you're able to drive through here?' I asked. 'Oh, we have permits,' they said.

"Adults have been allowed to stay in evacuation order zones, but kids never. Why were they given permits?"

"No idea how they got permits." Phil's confidence was eroding. "All news to me. You'll have to ask... um..." He pointed to the chairman of the CRD, sitting behind him. "It... er... falls out of my purview..."

He was glad to leave the stand.

The next to contribute was Sergeant Scott Clay of the Anahim Lake RCMP detachment. He was a tall man, and his flak vest seemed to bother him as he kept hooking his hands into it, as if he were try- ing to drag it down. I never have anything to do with the police, and had never met him, but Scott was well known locally and generally considered a fair person. He had worked in the Cariboo/Chilcotin for thirteen years, but like all RCMP personnel, had to move frequently.

He had been stationed at Anahim Lake for eight months. Quite a lot of the information written below was collected during an interview with Scott after the fire, but I have mixed it in with my observations of the CRD YouTube video.

On July 10, Scott was commissioned to deliver evacuation orders to the residents of Kleena Kleene. He had only two locally based constables and two Fisheries officers, who had volunteered to come up from Bella Coola, at his disposal. He asked for more help and was sent ten more constables, all from the Lower Mainland. Most had either no or very limited experience of rural life. Scott appreciated their city ignorance very well—he had grown up on Baffin Island. More constables arrived until he had a total of twenty-five under his command. Eventually, the first group of tactical troop (TAC) members came. They were from Alberta and had worked with the evacuations during the devastating Fort McMurray Fire in 2016, when large portions of the town burned. Their primary job in the Anahim Lake/Nimpo Lake/Charlotte Lake/Kleena Kleene area was to provide evacuation planning and support. Two members from E division (British Columbia) TAC were present at the back of the room.

Scott knew that the roadblocks were a sore spot. They were staffed by one or two officers plus military, either regular or rangers. The latter had their own chain of command, but they received guidance from the RCMP. Some of the rangers were from the Cariboo/Chilcotin, and extremely familiar with both the country and the fire's history. Many, however, were rookies who didn't know to question people like the fishermen when they waved permits at them. Worse, they were letting through people who simply wore red shirts and stated that they were part of the firefighting response crew. When Scott found this out, he told his staff to smarten up and question people. However, it was a difficult line to draw as to what might seem a reasonable query and what might seem heavy-handed. It was a definite learning process for all involved.

One audience member asked: "Why was it that as soon as the evacuation order was pronounced, decent upright citizens were suddenly being treated like criminals?" Scott maintained he would never have actually forced people to go. But why were people threatened with expulsion if it was not going to happen? Why did Jaden have such a bad experience with the cops who evacuated him? Maybe cop training should include a course on speaking to people in rural areas. After all, given British Columbia's fire history, it is undoubtedly going to happen again.

Scott said he followed the state-of-emergency rules as best he could. The main goal—and Scott's personal number-one priority— was to ensure that all community members were safe and accounted for. He also stated that the rule enforcing people to not leave their properties was so that if an emergency happened, the authorities would know where the residents were. This made sense—but why had no one bothered to explain it to me before? Why had looting been the only concern mentioned? At the beginning, the SAR took care of our whereabouts; when the command centre was moved to Puntzi, no one knew where anyone was anymore.

When asked why the CRD were issuing permits through order zones when locals couldn't get them, Scott said that the CRD would have to answer that. He had no powers to alter CRD legislation. All he could do was work with them as best he could.

Donna Barnett, the MLA, got up again. To comments that the legislation disallowing residents to come and go through evacuation order zones should be changed, she replied that the Emergency Protection Act has been in place for many years. I looked it up. People bandied about those three words throughout the meeting, but in fact, the British Columbia Emergency Protection Act refers only to crimes against people. The correct term is Emergency Operations Act, or on some websites, Emergency Program Act. In 2004, when the Lonesome Lake firestorm caused the community of Charlotte

Lake to be evacuated, people were allowed to go home once the fire had calmed down to tend to gardens, sprinklers, etc. They could go only in the morning and had to be back out by 11:00 a.m. A darn nuisance, but everyone could work with that. Now, apparently, that option is no longer viable. Donna Barnett said that once legislation has been instigated, it would take years to change. She said it doesn't have to be changed. We just have to work with it. She suggested communities get together and develop a strategy for such events and this would go a long way in reducing friction. (But Tatla Lake had had a strategy in place, and it had been disbanded when Forestry moved in.)

The chair of the Cariboo Regional District got up for a brief talk. Even though he was using the microphone, I could hardly understand a word he was mumbling. He did say that we should not be accusing the RCMP of putting us under "house arrest."

There was no excuse for the chairman's poor diction. I heard the next speaker loud and clear. The Swiss accent was unmistakable. It was Christoph. He came up to the podium clutching a paper, saying: "Excuse me, Mr. Chairman—I am a rancher living in Kleena Kleene and I need you to sign my permit so I can go home tonight…" The audience laughed and gave a great clap. Even the chairman had the grace to smile but he directed Christoph to someone at the back of the room for the signature. I probably could have gone with Christoph, and ridden home on his permit.

The young woman who was acting as the emcee then started to say "thank you" in an effort to bring the meeting to a close. But immediately there was a big outcry from several audience members— they hadn't finished yet. However, that was where the YouTube video quit. I heard that the meeting got quite rowdy afterwards, and CRD didn't bother to publish that.

And the most ridiculous thing was, as far as I was concerned, the very next day, August 24, at 4:00 p.m., the evacuation order for

Kleena Kleene was downgraded to evacuation alert. According to the emcee's inadvertent comment, the ending of the order had been imminent on August 23. Would it really have hurt the CRD to give me that permit? Or was the communication between all the departments so bad the CRD didn't even know that the state of emergency was about to be lifted?

Mischief with the Fire

PRECIPICE, AUGUST 24–26

IT RAINED TWO MILLIMETRES ON AUGUST 24. IT INTERRUPTED HAYING and allowed me to reflect that such a light rain seemed to magnify the puffers. They fought back against the moisture. Possibly kicking up more steam than smoke. It was harmless smoke—the white stuff, not the black, angry kind. It rose lazily from the ground rather than rushing skyward as if to escape from the forest. The lazy smoke would rather linger in the trees as if to caress each one before it drifted off. It could go either way; I saw smoke drift in different directions at the same time.

Wind and rain were double-edged swords. Good regarding the fire, but I would have to rake the hay one more time. I felt more like a rancher than a firefighter those days (fixing rakes, smelling tractor diesel and going round and round). But when the wind picked up, I found myself casting an anxious eye in the direction of the puffers.

I have not mentioned wildlife much in regard to this fire. I had visions that creatures would be scurrying across our meadows ahead of the flames but it had not been so. The squirrels were as annoying as ever and sightings of the larger animals were as rare as always. There were the deaths of Cactus and Fossie, but they were natural deaths unrelated to the fire. A young fox was found, badly burned and starving. Mercifully it was killed by a firefighter. A black bear had used our meadows as sanctuary—feeding on Cactus in company with a family of ravens. He had been seen often from the helicopters and we came across many of his resting places. The fire may have deprived him of much of his normal diet and we felt he was welcome to the horse.

Some of Lee's cows had trickled back to the ranch—they usually come home on their own in the fall. One of the calves was wounded in the hindquarters next to the tail (a gouge and claw marks). The calf, though limping, should survive. Two of the cows that had returned were not accompanied by their calves. We feared that they might have been killed by predators, and that we would be bothered by this fire for some time to come because of the disruption to wildlife. I posted: "We are not free of this fire yet. I almost hate going on with this story. It feels like a speech that has gone on too long. A toast that is incoherent to those other than the immediate wedding party.

"We were told that the firefighters would have to put out all the puffers in these hills and slopes around us and then scan the forest with infrared cameras in search of hidden hot spots before the evacuation order would be lifted. Kleena Kleene, we heard, had just been downgraded to alert."

Monika and I were keen on meeting the Mexican firefighters, so on August 25 we went up the bypass to a large staging area. Six white crew-cab pickups were parked neatly in a line. The Mexicans had already left for the day's work. We walked the edge of the black along the hose lay, now a well-beaten trail. There were a few very small puffers and even some open flames inside the black but they presented no danger. By Airplane Lake, the trail abruptly climbed onto a knoll that had burned very hot. The ground was completely covered with a layer of ash; only a few charred stems of pine protruded upward. We had hoped to catch the Mexicans, but I needed to get back to rake hay so we turned for home. Scott from New

Brunswick, who was their crew boss, was at staging. He explained that the Mexicans arrived between six and seven in the morning, and left in the afternoon around five. (They were accommodated in tents at the Anahim Lake fire camp. In addition to their ten-plus hour work days, they would need to drive for over an hour each day.)

It was dry enough to start raking in the early afternoon. On the way to the Taylors' big meadow, I met Lonny. He was all smiles, and confident that they had won the battle. He was nearing his last day and had elected to drive rather than fly into the Precipice in order to get a better sense of the land. He offered me Gatorade powder to add to my water. Dehydration is a major risk for firefighters. The Incident Action Plans often expressed warnings like, "Hot! Hot! Hot! Continue to monitor yourself and your coworkers for dehydration." Lonny's departure would be one of the sadder changes of the guard on the fire lines. We had met so many friendly, kind and caring people. The operations staff had changed from Kiwis, to Albertans, to British Columbians and Australians. We had hardly noticed a ripple in the battle to put out this fire. Just a sad goodbye and an introduction to the next person who would be looking out for us.

Lee and Pat came back north to the Precipice. As they turned west onto Highway 20, they had again been awed by the devastation between Riske Creek and Hanceville. They had passed a crew convoy near there flying a Mexican flag. They waved and gave them a thumbs-up. The skies grew smokier as they travelled toward the active fires near Kleena Kleene. Puffers and firefighters in their ranch meadows greeted them as they drove into the valley. Then late in the day we got the news of our evacuation order being lifted. It was much sooner than we expected, and we were jubilant. We had been under the pall of this order for forty-seven days. Probably the longest evacuation order in the province.

It would be three more days before we got official confirmation from the Central Coast Regional District. "Hello Fred and

A unit crew of twenty Mexican firefighters sets off to work. Photo by Monika Schoene.

Monika, Troy and Lorrein, and Pat and Lee. In case you are not already aware, the evacuation order for the Precipice area has been downgraded to alert.

"Please note that BC Parks has their own closures within the evacuation area and the closure of Tweedsmuir Park (South) still applies. Let me know if you have any questions."

The next morning, Monika and I planned to be at staging along the bypass before the Mexican crew arrived. They were parking their rented trucks as we pulled up. We asked if we could take pictures of the crew and they kindly lined up for us. Scott radioed Lonny that we were with the crew and were about to hike into the fire zone after them. Lonny asked us not to, citing that he wanted to meet with us later in the day. We took the pictures and, like a dog with its tail between its legs, we headed home.

We found some mischief anyway. The fire had crept slowly down our north slope to the edge of our road near where it crossed the Hotnarko River by way of a ford. A hanging fire was still on much of the slope. It had burned actively through a large rotten log and had reached the base of another large Douglas fir about four metres above the road. We had buckets in the car and started to carry water the short distance from the river. Monika hoisted up the full buckets and I scrambled on the steep slope to kill the hotter portions of the fire. Our efforts seemed small and feeble. We stopped the fire where it clawed at the Douglas fir but did not take the time to douse areas farther up the slope.

Two crews of five were still working on the other hanging fires on our north and south slopes. They with their pumps, axes, grub hoes and chainsaws would have to be the ones to completely kill the fire, which was a cool, weak and spotty image of its former self, but still dangerous if winds, low humidity and higher temperatures should excite it. Lonny flew over from the Taylor Ranch to say good-bye. He had to do one more flight around the fire and invited Monika to join him. She was delighted and this time remembered to take the camera.

In the past I had not wanted to share VA0778. It was my personal fire, I alternately defended it and railed against it. It was now Pat's turn to embrace it, or rather the fight against it. She posted: "Sunday, August 27, 5:15 p.m. Lots of helicopter action (the pilot is Steve today) right over my head as I walked over to check the haying in the big meadow after spending a few hours weeding our garden. Fred, Caleb and Lee are working hard to get the hay gathered and baled. Continued puffers in spruce bog, canyon, and round meadow, which are waking up again with the sunnier weather and wind action. For me, the newbie fire-watcher, that is always a bit worrisome. They are dropping buckets of water on it as I write. Andrew, the new operations chief, feels all is manageable."

Chris read the post and added her two bits: "Multiple puffers at KK. Two months ago puffers like that would have had us freaking out. Now they are so common we hardly notice them."

It had been an effort to keep up the normal in a very abnormal summer. I now had to focus on our homesteading routines. I picked peas and fed the bolting cabbage to the cows. We had been unable to sell our crops in the summer because of the evacuation order.

The day before had been quite different. It was eerily quiet all morning. No reassuring early helicopter flight. No sounds of pumps or chainsaws of the ground crews. I stopped at the Hotnarko River ford to dump ten or twelve more buckets of water around the base of the Douglas fir, and pulled some burning fence and pieces of smouldering decaying logs from the forest, throwing the hot ones into the river. With my morning firefighting done (a joke, really) I proceeded to the Taylor Ranch for a day of raking. Heat radiated off the tractor and on to my legs whenever I turned into the sun. I cast a cautious eye to the temperature gauge to ensure that the tractor was not overheating then surveyed the hills to the south and west. The puffers were definitely heating up. They began bucketing the one next to the spruce bog. Caleb and I parked our tractors in the field and watched for a while before we resumed haying. When I got home, Monika reported that they had been bucketing around our meadows as well.

The Trip to Town

KLEENA KLEENE, AUGUST 26

AUGUST 24, THE DAY THE KLEENA KLEENE EVACUATION ORDER WAS lifted, was a Thursday. On Friday I drove to Nimpo to gas up, and on Saturday I went to town. I left early so I would be able to return as quickly as possible, hardly daring to believe that the road might not be closed again. It was an emotional trip.

It was still dark as I drove through downtown Kleena Kleene; no sign of flames, but heavy smoke cut the power of my headlights to feeble beams. I was relieved to emerge into much clearer air around Tatla Lake—it was the first time I had been even this far east for seven weeks. It seemed odd to be driving without having to feel guilty.

Daylight came, and with it a spectacular sunrise that never seemed to end. The emerging land was softened with smoke haze that grew thicker as I approached Alexis Creek. A new sign graced the highway: *WATCH FOR LIVESTOCK AND POOR VISIBILITY. DRIVE WITH HEADLIGHTS TURNED ON.*

Just past Alexis Creek were the first burnt trees visible along the highway after Kleena Kleene. It is not far from there to Lee's Corner, where the restaurant used to stand. Fire had blasted both sides of the road. The gas pump was untouched; it was swathed with police tape. It stood like a lonely metallic finger amid a flat plane of destruction. Close by were a couple of heavy concrete troughs. They had been placed to define the parking space, but the maker of the delectable carrot cake had always prettied them up in summer by growing a blazing show of petunias in them. Behind the troughs was a small level shelf and then—nothing. The restaurant must have been built over a basement dug into a bank. I walked over to the troughs; below was a yard containing a few wrecked and burnt vehicles. Oddly enough, a couple of conifers were still green. It was a constant marvel to see these islands of green remaining after such a long conflagration tossed every which way by wild winds. Perhaps the most poignant sight was that inside the troughs, a few petunias were still blooming. The plants were stunted and wizened, but they had survived.

I had heard that the owners had been well insured, and I knew they were ready to retire and hoping to sell, so after the initial shock wore off, they would be all right.

Not far past there was the field in which Miriam and I had been told to wait on July 7, and the logging road along which we had escaped. The sun was shining, that particular spot was unburned and it held nothing of the drama we had been presented with on that fateful day.

Several other houses had been destroyed in the Lee's Corner/ Riske Creek area, and I was at first puzzled that I couldn't see their remains. But then I realized there was nothing left of them to see. Burnt trees stood, but homes and barns had largely vanished without trace and were simply part of the overall black. I spotted a brick chimney in one place; a blackened, twisted metal roof in another. The tow-truck driver's house had been stuccoed; it had always been a tidy property; now the house was soot blackened, but it must have been usable, for there was a light on inside and a clean pickup was parked in the yard. Behind it, frighteningly close, were the twisted remains of the burnt forest that now could not conceal the quite extensive pile of unclaimed vehicles that had existed among the trees. The fire-scabbed cars and trucks, sans windows and headlights, squatted low on their tireless rims. Ed, the tow-truck driver, told me later that he had been working with a neighbour just up the road when the fire became dangerous. This was on July 15. He rushed home to turn on the pumps and sprinklers that he and the Terrace firefighters had already set up. Within minutes, it was too late for Ed to drive back to the highway and he escaped by running across a field. The fire roared by with the speed and noise of an express train—and then it was gone. The house and shop that his son had sprayed were saved, but a log barn, a pumphouse and two storage sheds—the latter only two metres from the house—were consumed by the fire. "It is impossible to describe what it was like to anyone who hasn't lived through this kind of thing," Ed told me.

Now I was driving through the long stretch where the power poles had been destroyed. New ones marched along the road, some tied to their charred predecessors, a few of which still supported the phone line. Fencing contractors were working furiously, for this was not open-range country and the cows had to be kept from wandering onto the highway. Bizarrely, green grass sprouted energetically along the verges, no doubt a result of the copious amounts of water that must have been dumped there to help keep the highway open.

Fires were still quite active along one stretch of road. Smoke lay in slabs from these when I went east; by afternoon when I returned, it was puffing up vigorously. Logging trucks had accompanied me on my morning journey—that was to be expected—but suddenly I met a whole convoy of road users—there must have been well over fifty vehicles. Never in my life have I seen so many together on the Chilcotin highway at one time. Usually I won't encounter anywhere near that number during the whole three-and-a-half-hour trip. Some components of the convoy were private pickups, some the plain white rental vehicles, both sedans and trucks that I had grown to identify with fire personnel, and some were chunky army vehicles, bristling with shovels and other tools. They trundled along at a sedate pace, no doubt heading for their staging area. Their camp was based on a field that was visible from the road. I got quite a chuckle out of it. The army portion had a row of large tents lined up side by side with military precision. Next to them was a gaggle of small tents of every shape and colour, strewn haphazardly along the ground. Here, presumably, were the civilians. The haphazardness made sense—the occupants would be seeking the most comfortable spots in the uneven ground; they would have to lie directly upon it. The army probably had cots.

Becher's Dam is a spot where I often draw off the road for a break. This man-made pond used to have a picnic table and a couple of wooden outhouses on the far side. It was a good place for bird-watching, and a nice spot for the dogs to run if they were travelling with me. The forest was severely burned—it is fir there rather than pine—but close to the water were a few singed deciduous trees and one tiny patch of green conifers, just three small trees. Another mystifying oasis that the fire dragon had failed to digest. I found one of the outhouse sites—just a hole in the ground almost hidden by a fallen tree. To my utter amazement, the other outhouse was intact. It was hidden by the three living firs. And yet a couple of residences not far from the pond had been annihilated.

Half an hour from town, the highway drops sharply to the Fraser River. There I came upon five happy-looking cows munching at the roadside. No open range here; these cows must have wandered a considerable distance. One report said that eleven thousand were still unaccounted for from the Plateau Fire, and some that had been discovered had to be put down because of burned feet. A moose was apparently shot for the same reason. No one knows how many other animals, wild or tame, had succumbed.

A helicopter drops water on puffers by the Kleena Kleene hayfields.
August 25, 2017. Photo by Chris Czajkowski.

Town was unbelievably normal. The occupants had been home for over a month and most of the people I talked to had well-established businesses that had not suffered greatly in the long run. New enterprises had not fared well. Any outfit catering to tourism had to write off the whole summer. The forested hill where I had seen the first lightning strikes looked green and untouched, innocent under an almost clear sky, even though the fire from up there had swooped across Highway 97 just south of the city.

I had one surprise in town. At home, during hot weather (and, when I forget, in the rain) I leave doors and windows of my vehicles wide open. Now of course, I had to close and lock them. Town was hot; the first time I reopened the door I was knocked back by the heavy reek of old smoke. The smell must have been deeply embedded in the fabrics.

I was out of town early enough to drive home in full daylight. At Kleena Kleene, the rancher was raking hay next to the far fence; a very short distance behind him, a number of puffers were sending up smoke signals. A chopper was dousing them. It had no bucket, just a long tube with which it sucked up water from a nearby pond into an internal tank. The machine had to squat very close to the pond's surface to fill up, and as it did so, the rotors stirred up a fog of glittering spray. The light was behind the helicopter as it flew to the puffers and I took several dramatic photos of the shining slabs of water cascading down.

We Venture Out into the World

PRECIPICE, AUGUST 28–SEPTEMBER 2

ON AUGUST 28, I WENT WITH LEE TO ANAHIM LAKE. LEE WAS DOWN TO his last barrel of diesel fuel and we were almost out of propane. It was my first trip there in over two months.

I was shocked by the changes on the bush road out of the Precipice. A helipad had been cleared near the valley bottom. Trees had been piled in tangles at its edges. Two machine guards had been pushed through the forest. One extended to the old fire-break that had been constructed for the Lonesome Lake Fire in 2004. A long stretch of road also bore edges of ripped and piled trees; it must have been widened to create a fuel-free guard. Where our bush road branched off the logging road, a large sign hung in the trees: "Precipice Fire, VA0778," with an arrow pointing down.

Kappan Mountain logging road was graded and expansive to my eyes—it seemed so uptown, so modern, but it was just the normal gravel road, though it had been well used by the firefighting traffic. Along it, two more machine guards had been pushed through the forest toward Hotnarko Mountain. I was dazed by all the work that had been done, and this was just a fraction of it.

I was nervous about going to Anahim Lake. I felt different, as if the fire had changed me. I was also wondering how I would be

289

received by my neighbours, many of whom had complained so bitterly about the way they had been treated throughout the fire. But after a few hellos and "How are things?" I began to feel at ease.

The next morning Monika drove me to my tractor, which I had left at the ranch. Only one helicopter was bucketing. Ground crews had arrived around 7:30 to attack the hot spots. A Forestry pump whined beside a large pond below the road (the pond would be drained by the time they had quelled the puffers on the slope above it). As I raked Lee's big meadow, Monika and Pat walked to the Red Roof House to check for rodents because Jade, Ryan and the kids would soon be coming home. They chatted with Steve, an older, very seasoned and skillful pilot from Calgary on his last day working this fire. Monika had witnessed him extracting water from a spot in the Hotnarko River barely wider than the bucket. No other pilot had attempted removing water from such a narrow area.

When I returned home from haying, there was a pickup in the yard. I thought it must belong to an IA crew, but when I peered in the side window and saw the children's car seats, I knew it was Jade and Ryan's. Monika came bouncing out the door with excitement. Our valley was full again.

The fire seemed excited about the day as well. Ironically, it had been many days since it had raged so. Columns of dark smoke were once again billowing up just beyond our southern ridge. Alan rushed over on an ATV to tell us that though the fire was definitely angry, it presented no real danger because there was plenty of black between us and the intense burn. I felt that he was a bit self-conscious to have such a fierce fire blow toward us just after the evacuation order had been lifted.

Thick smoke drifted overhead and ash began to fall. A helicopter was called to bucket it. It would have been disastrous and embarrassing for those who had just lifted the order if the fire had breached the ridge and spotted fire onto our buildings. Monika and I had seen it charge the ridge during its most dangerous days, but we felt no threat this time. We had a picnic in the yard with the family and feasted on chicken noodle soup.

The fire peaked in the late afternoon. It became a bit nerve-wracking to once again hear the jet-like roar as it surged up a slope just beyond our ridge. I also started wondering if the lifting of the order had been a bit premature. I briefly turned the pump on to show Ryan how these difficult and noisy two-stroke Forestry pumps worked in case he was confronted with the need to start the one at the Red Roof House. The creek, which was barely a trickle, still carried enough water to run the sprinklers. Despite our constant worry, it had never failed us.

Since Lonny left I was receiving no replies to my weather reports. On August 30 I sent my last one and no one commented. My usefulness in that regard was done.

Haying was near completion and I was able to take a much-needed day off. Crews began flying in to the Taylor Ranch at 8:30 a.m. A Forestry lookout was positioned on the rim rock above our valley to watch for any violent fire behaviour. Smoke was still quite thick. Monika and I were well adjusted to it but Pat's throat was irritated and she stayed inside as much as possible. She made a note to herself: "Do not bake a pot roast in the oven for three hours when it is thirty-three degrees Celsius outside and you can't open the windows due to smoke."

Pat's Facebook posts continued to rail against the fire and the way it had disrupted everyone's lives, but on August 31, I retaliated: "We do fire an injustice. All the dramatic pictures and sensational news. We highlight its destructiveness and its cost to human infrastructure. And yet human infrastructure has been the more damaging. What cost to wildlife habitat, and air and water quality, has rampant urban sprawl and excessive resource extraction caused? We highlight the dramatic pictures of raging fire and burnt-out cars (I am guilty of this myself as I wait like the paparazzi for a tree to candle) but there is much more to a fire than that.

"Certainly there is human suffering and sometimes great individual loss. But fire also has a cleansing effect. I am certain that the result of this fire will be an increase in biodiversity and an enhancement of the forest surrounding us."

The next day Monika and I decided to visit the south slope to see what was happening. We headed toward the sound of a whining Forestry pump, knowing that the ground crew would have cut a path from the pump next to the river up the very steep slope to reach the fire.

The hose lay made the hike up the rugged slope much easier than it had been for us in the past when we had explored this portion of the forest. The fire had been extinguished on the slope, but when we reached the top of the ridge we were surprised how active it still was up there. Campfires and puffers were scattered over a rocky bench of land. Five professional firefighters in yellow Forestry shirts were working on it. They had been stationed there for over a week. Their object was to kill all puffers and campfires for thirty metres into the black.

In the evening it began to rain. A cool fall rain with a heavy sky. The following morning, while I was picking peas, a Forestry pump started. Then a truck's horn blared—some crew members trying to get the attention of others. The sounds angered me. Katie and Tabi's drone had annoyed me at the start of the fire; during it, I welcomed the helicopter racket and the whine of pumps; now I was back in wilderness mode and resenting these urban intrusions. There could have been no threat from the fire anymore, but the cleanup continued.

After the day of rain, Monika and I felt safe enough to hike deeper into the black, to where the rank-five firestorm had raged on August 3. There were moments of amazement and sadness as we

Fred hikes up the ridge into the black. Photo by Monika Schoene.

climbed. The lower slopes next to the Sugar Camp Trail had not burned so hot and many trees had survived. Just above the trail the slope steepened, and we tramped up to a ridge. On the windward side, the trees had not been so lucky. They still held red scorched needles but they had no green ones and would not recover.

At the crest of the ridge, the landscape was dramatically changed. It was there that winds had blown embers over half a kilometre ahead of the front. No trees survived the flames, which must have roared with the power of a blowtorch. There was no deep white ash that is common with a ground fire. The char on the trees was thin. Even the stately, large Douglas fir were killed—every needle blasted from their branches. Only the stems and larger branches remained, leaving deformed sculptures of death.

From the top of the ridge, we could see across the valley to where the fire was still burning on the slopes of Telegraph Creek. It appeared very active, but we knew it was no longer dangerous to us.

We continued to Crazy George Lake, hiking through bare stems of pine. Almost total devastation. There were only small pockets of green around occasional ponds. We had no need to keep to the path we once used, for the charred forest was now wide open and we wandered aimlessly in shock and awe.

Crazy George Lake had long been a favourite hiking destination. We had explored the rock bluffs above it and built a trail around the east side where we had found the remains of an old cabin. We had built a campsite and hosted many wiener roasts. The logs we had used as benches were completely gone. The stack of firewood, gone. The bucked logs we had used as tables and chairs, mostly gone or just charred images of what they once were. A large spruce had fallen directly over the fire pit. The saddest thing was there was no shade. Not a single tree had survived. All was black now.

We didn't circle the lake to check out the old cabin. Instead we hiked over the rock bluffs toward Precipice Lake following the path of the fire. It had lost some of its potency as it climbed the bluffs east of Crazy George Lake (we had too). Areas of green appeared, and there was new regrowth already beginning—willows, ferns and grasses. The bottom of a shallow gorge between two rock bluffs was still lush—a green oasis in a desert of grey ash and black stems. A young marten checked us out from his safe haven among the shrubs, grass and rocks. It was heartening to see the survival of a creature in the midst of the devastation.

Bushwhacking in the bluffs had never been so easy now that the understory with its tangles of alder and fallen logs were gone. We saw only three small puffers along the way and no open flame. The fire had again burned very hot in the rock bluff on the west side of Precipice Lake. It had exposed some old campsites we had not seen

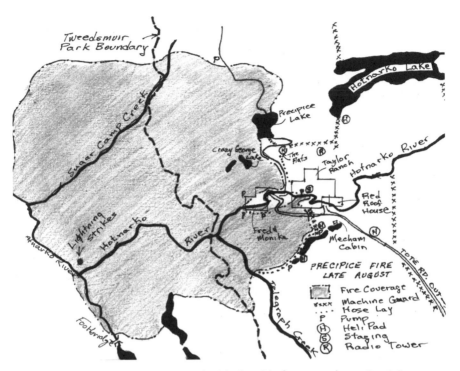

The Precipice Fire was stopped with the aid of our meadows, Precipice Creek and Precipice Lake. *Drawn by Fred Reid.*

before—tin cans and broken glass. The fire had been unable to cross Precipice Lake, and, on this side of the valley, that is where it had met its end.

I had a sudden panic as we descended from Precipice Lake to the Taylor Ranch. A fluttering of orange flame. "How had the fire sparked into this green area?" I thought. Then I realized it was only orange flagging left by one of the firefighters. I first felt relief and was grateful that the firefighters normally use baby blue and pink for their communication. We read the message: *Start; POC; Sept. 02/17; McColl #2; "SILVER." Access—Driving & Walking; VLR/LOD 1,* then north and west co-ordinates. Another flagging at the same location gave the distance to a helipad, known as the Flats, a short way down the fire-break. We would come across a number of such communications as we further explored the burn.

A structural protection crew (volunteer firefighters from Swan Lake) had been to check the sprinkler systems around our buildings while we were gone. They would be removing them in the next day or two. Alan announced another change of personnel and said his goodbyes to Pat and Lee. Two others from the BC Wildfire Service came to the Taylors'. They told Pat that the military would be coming in to "mop up" the hot spots over the next few days, but in fact they never materialized. Another example of the rumours and confused policy coming out of Area Command.

Monika and I were too tired to notice, but the Taylors saw the plane that uses infrared to check for hot spots fly back and forth over the valley during the night. They watched it zigzag across the moonlit sky as we slept.

Visiting the Precipice

KLEENA KLEENE, AUGUST 27—SEPTEMBER 15

THE WEATHER BECAME COOLER AND OFTEN DULL; IN OUR PART OF THE world, the fire dragon had lost his sting. We could begin to relax. It would, however, be a while before life returned to normal.

The sprinkler crew had come while I had been in Williams Lake, and they had taken the hoses and bladder with them. A small runnel of mud close to the woodpile was the only indication that anything had been there. On the following Monday, August 28, we had our second mail delivery in two months. Our post person has a school-aged child and she helped carry the pile of parcels and letters to my van. Term was supposed to start on September 5, but Tatla Lake, where the school was situated, was still under evacuation alert and the schools would not open under those conditions. However, the alert was lifted as far as the school buildings on September 4.

I persuaded Jaden to accompany me down to Bella Coola to meet Katie and Dennis, and help me pick up my truck. I had been up and down the Hill several times that summer, but in my new-found freedom, it seemed as though I was looking at the road with fresh eyes. We stopped to look at views. We ran around the valley a bit enjoying the new feeling that we no longer had to rush, or sneak around, to get home.

Chris's mail is delivered to the Kleena Kleene post office for the first time in a month. Lindsay Gano helps to carry it. Photo by Chris Czajkowski.

I needed the pickup before I could go down to the Precipice—the road is too rough for my van—and that's saying a lot as the van has been treated like a tank throughout much of its life with me. The logging road south of Anahim Lake is fine, but the tote road needs more clearance. The top of the tote road was emblazoned with flagging tape and a crude board bearing the legend: VA0778. Apparently this had been left to mark a place where crews needed to come in to block off the hose lays and fireguards.

The tote road is narrow and in previous times shrubs would have squealed against the paintwork on both sides of my little truck, but bulldozers had flattened all this and chewed up the edges. In one place a rare flat bit of ground had been bared to the earth, but roughly, like a badly ploughed field. This would have been a safe spot to store vehicles at night.

Fred has lived at the Precipice for only eight years, but he has made the tote road his own. Literally hundreds—maybe thousands—of balanced stone sculptures have been erected. Regular visitors like me look forward to the changes among this population of rock people. I have a hard enough time balancing a bit of wood on a chopping block to split it, and I am amazed at Fred's ability to make these sculptures stand. Sadly a good many had succumbed to the heavy machinery, but a large fresh monument stood by the side of the road. Solidly built, it somehow did not have Fred's delicacy of touch; sure enough, it bore a small sign: "to Fred from BX," which was apparently the insignia of one of the fire crews.

The tote road was drowned in trees and, apart from the machinery marks, there was little sign of the fire along it. Just before the road made the final drop to the rancher's hayfield, there was a view across the valley, and one could see pockets of burned forest. Beside the farm road that runs along the valley bottom, brown areas were evident, but they were kept cool and gentle so that the fire licked up the grass and twigs on the ground and did no extensive damage.

Precipice residents Lee Taylor and wife Pat, and Monika Schoene and Fred Reid stand victorious after the fire. Photo by Jade Dumas.

Many of the standing trees were also killed, but this area should regenerate quickly. Aerial watering had been copious, and new green grass, not normally seen so late in the year, was growing abundantly.

From Fred and Monika's house everything looked much the same as when I had last been down there. The fire had come so close—but all seemed green. From a distance, even the forest behind the greenhouse looked untouched. Smoke climbed from Telegraph Creek and the air was thickly hazy, but otherwise, very little of that devastating fire could be seen. In front of the house, Monika's flowers were blooming and the market garden stood behind them, its long green rows of late produce ready for harvest. It was hard to realize that such a major drama had been played out around them.

The other residents of the valley, Lee and Pat Taylor, Jade, Ryan and the kids (Caleb was never a social animal) came down for lunch and we had a silly sort of celebration. Not much beyond pleasantries was said; none of us needed to elaborate. We were all feeling a little odd. It was almost as if we were suspended in a vacuum. Our enemy had been vanquished and we had nothing left to fight against anymore. Our minds and bodies could move freely, without restrictions, but we didn't know where to go. It was an unexpected end to our ordeal. It is hard to know how to put this feeling into words.

Fred and Monika had received nothing like the hard frosts that had already razed my more sensitive plants to the ground, and I came away with an armload of greens and some fresh dairy as well.

VARIOUS FLARE-UPS HAPPENED THROUGHOUT SEPTEMBER. THE FIRES farther back from the highway were left to burn and we once had a spectacular sunset where all the smoke plumes billowing up from Mount Nogwon turned orange.

Jaden invited me on a hike with his friends up the Miner Lake road toward Perkins Peak. Part of the attraction was to go through some massively burned and still burning areas; I don't doubt we should not have been there, but although we heard helicopters and heavy machinery constantly, we met no one along the way.

The fire devastation was horrific. Huge areas were blackened and smoking, through which one could now see lakes that had previously been hidden. One or two fires were still quite aggressive; where these were burning, small trees candled into flame, one by one. The country was an appalling mess. Fireguards had been punched through, some bare to the yellow dirt, but some a tangled jumble of smashed trees, all blackened when the fire had jumped them. The biggest mess was the result of one of the few misjudged back burns. That was when I had arrived the second time to water my garden and had to leave again in a hurry. Even the clear-cuts, on which very little but grass and stumps had remained, were totally black.

The others took the main road, which goes right to the treeline and beyond—there were once gold mines near the summit and the roads are favourite places for ATVers. Jaden, who knew the country well, recommended a different destination for me. I followed logging roads through older clear-cuts where young trees were already starting to grow. The fire had bypassed these, but the roads had been newly widened—this would be the route to Colwell Lake and I imagined Doug Schuk and company churning their way through there. In places, the machines had chewed up the roads, making it a bit tricky for my little truck, but I found the creek that Jaden had instructed me to look for, and parked.

I started up a steep slope and at once entered a totally different world. Not only was the forest still green, it had also never been logged. This is a very rare sight in my neighbourhood. Moreover, because it was at quite a high altitude, it was composed of incredibly twisted whitebark pines, the same tree that defined the forests around Nuk Tessli. I love this plant. It grows at upper elevations only, and has been very much a part of my mountain life.

The greatest attribute of this hike, however, was the complete lack of smoke. The wind was quite fresh and blowing in my face; the huge sprawl of smoke, flame and helicopter noise was at my back and it disappeared completely as I climbed over a ridge. The world in front of me was brilliant. It was as if I had finally wiped the dust and smears off my glasses and could now see the world without a film over the lenses. I had forgotten what a haze-free landscape looked like.

A short climb and I came into a wide-open space with low hills on either side. The top of Perkins Peak showed above the south ridge; it was already greyed with the year's first snowfall. Only a few bonsai trees grew on this plateau; the rest was covered by scrub birch that was just on the point of turning colour. It was all so bright and fresh. My sinuses were unused to these great drafts of clean air. Small hills on either side would have given me wonderful views of the area around my home, but I didn't bother to climb them. I knew all I would see in that direction was devastation and smoke. I would come back here again, when the fire was done.

Mopping Up

PRECIPICE, SEPTEMBER 3–30

FROM THEIR VANTAGE POINT IN THE RED ROOF HOUSE HIGH ON THE eastern end of our valley, Jade spotted a sleeping fire on the south side of Airplane Lake. The black puffer, awakened by the increasing afternoon heat, shot up from a group of spruce next to the lake. It could have expanded under favourable winds and temperatures and taken a run, but a helicopter began bucketing it right away. We might have been near the end of the fire season, but the BC Wildfire Service was still keeping an eye on us.

From September 5 to 9 a couple of helicopters ferried in crews who rolled up many kilometres of hose, folded bladders and retrieved pumps. We were busy with the last of the haying. The days were humid but not hot. A puffer reignited in the canyon and a helicopter bucketed it. On September 8 the Spruce Bog Fire became active enough for an IA team to spend a couple of hours dousing it. Jessie, the operations chief, announced that they would have the firefighters on the ground for only one more day but they would keep sending helicopters to watch for flare-ups.

Lee's herd continued to trickle in from their summer range. The fire had stopped just short of it. A second calf sported deep gash wounds on its hindquarters. By September 12 most of the cows had made their way home; two more calves had injuries. Wolves were determined to be the culprits. The herd had suffered very few attacks over the years so this was unusual. One cow and five calves never returned from the range at all. Three of the four injured calves did not survive.

Wolves' hunting patterns had no doubt been greatly disturbed. The fire may have pushed them onto Lee's range this year, but the area's overall ability to support wildlife will probably increase. We will live with the consequences, both good and bad, for a few more years yet.

The BC Wildfire Service's priorities for the Precipice Fire shifted from fighting to rehabilitation. A team began to visit the valley on a daily basis to assess the damage caused to roads and forest.

On September 14, on their daily walk, Lee and Pat "were greeted by grouse, deer tracks and sunshine. Perfect! Lots of birds and bees flitting and buzzing since the smoke has cleared. And the Fox is back."

One evening, Monika and I walked to our greenhouse under a star-filled sky and gazed for a while at the glow and campfires still burning to our southwest. It seemed so peaceful. It would take snow to put out the final flames, but we hoped that was still a ways away because there was much to do before then.

On September 15 we received an email from the Central Coastal Regional District: "As of this afternoon and pursuant to the BC Emergency Program Act, the Evacuation Alert in the Precipice area has been lifted by the Central Coast Regional District at the Emergency Operations Centre. Attached please find the Evacuation Rescind and the map showing the area that has been lifted."

Caleb had come into the valley to look after the ranch when Lee had injured his leg in the spring. He had stayed throughout the fire, and his dedication and resourcefulness were huge contributions to the saving of our valley, particularly the Taylor Ranch. But he had another job waiting for him. We had a farewell dinner, and the next day Monika and I drove him to his new home. We travelled through an area where a fire had raged ten or so years earlier. The white stems looked so barren compared to the lush green beyond the boundary of the fire. I could not help but be thankful that we do not have slopes like that around our valley. We can hike into the black and witness the damage but we do not have to look at it daily.

Monica and I were twenty kilometres from home and eighteen kilometres from Anahim Lake when we got a flat tire. The car had not been out of the valley for over two months—the spare was flat. We had no option other than walking to Anahim Lake. We would stay with Tamara and Paul and get our vehicle sorted. We kept up a good pace, as we wanted to reach their house by ten. We looked at the forest differently as we tramped along. We saw it as potential fuel for a fire and not potential wood for a mill. We argued about what would burn and what would not. The eighteen kilometres seemed endless. A glow on the horizon as we turned with the road invoked memories of the fire—but it was the northern lights. We laughed at our new perspective. Finally an electric glow through the trees— the airport. Then the lights of the power plant—bright, blinding us, causing us to bump into each other. Two more kilometres and we reached Tamara's house. We made it by ten minutes to ten.

The next day with our vehicle rescued and refurbished, we were home by 2:30 p.m. We were exhausted from the walk the day before but rains threatened. With rubber legs we rushed to put in the last of our hay. It seemed there would be no time to relax from the mental and physical strain of the summer.

We launched ourselves into the fall work. Monika was preserving vegetables and I was cutting firewood. Initially I tried to salvage burned trees from the edge of the long meadow. The fall colours of aspen and shrubs were enhanced by the backdrop of the blackened slopes. I piled the discarded branches and set them alight. While I was doing this, a helicopter passed overhead a couple of times.

Rather than feel relief that those in the helicopter were looking out for our safety, I was more concerned that they would be pissed off that I had a fire. I was grateful that the helicopter did not drop onto the meadow to see what was going on.

For a break from cutting firewood next to the long meadow I hiked onto the ridge next to it. Suddenly I spotted a small plume of smoke rise from the willows by the river on the other side of the ridge. I was jolted that the fire was still there. A sleeper, deep in some organic soil. In the cool fall temperatures it would never find enough strength to amount to more than a harmless puffer, but it was a reminder that the fire was not yet dead.

We were going through a kind of withdrawal and at times the fire caught us off guard. A new puffer ignited east of us, racing briefly up a hill. The slopes around Telegraph Creek were still riddled with them. On a return trip from Anahim Lake I smelled fire on the bypass—only faint smoke from some smouldering remnants in boggy areas—but it triggered a visceral adrenalin lurch. We would not be free of that kind of thing for some time.

We had a nostalgic moment when a helicopter circled over our house and made the approach for a landing. We rushed out to meet its occupants and were very happy to briefly relive those exciting days when the helicopters were constantly hovering like humming-birds (both are hard to resist taking a picture of), buzzing in and out of our yard. It was Mike King with a couple of foresters. We invited everyone in for a coffee and got an update on what was happening. Crews, now based at the Puntzi fire camp, were doing the mopping up. The fire season was rapidly winding down for everyone, but as predicted by the IC in the early days of the fire, "It will be with you until the snow flies."

October 14 was the last day we saw any evidence of fire in the valley. There were two very small puffers—steam mostly—drifting up from deep organic soil next to the long meadow.

I made my last fire-related post on November 4. "Like most people in the interior of British Columbia, from Prince George to Hope, our summer plans were either forgone, delayed or compromised. Since the evacuation order was lifted we have put up firewood, sorted cattle, harvested the garden, started building an equipment shed, and visited family and friends on the coast. All of this done in a frantic rush before the onset of winter.

"Of course, winter had different ideas and just to frustrate us further, came a lot earlier than it usually did. Much of the work had to be completed in wet icy conditions. We finished harvesting leeks, carrots and beets on October 10 in the snow."

IN LATE OCTOBER THE CARIBOO REGIONAL DISTRICT HELD POST-FIRE meetings to get communities' input about improving future emergency response. They informed us: "We are hoping you will share your experiences and challenges moving forward, in a respectful and candid way, which will ensure we are prepared for future emergencies and help us improve how we communicate during those emergencies... Consultations are notoriously difficult, and we are hoping these family-friendly meetings will allow all residents who experienced the many challenges of the wildfire season to have a voice."

On November 4, I viewed the BC Wildfire Service website in preparation for the meeting. The Precipice Fire was still listed as active, though any activity would have to have been in the far reaches of Telegraph Creek. It had covered 7,367 hectares and was one of the smaller fires in the province. The Plateau Fire, which was an amalgamation of many fires that came together, was an enormous 521,012 hectares. The Hanceville/Riske Creek and Elephant Hill Fires covered 239,298 and 191,865 hectares respectively. The Kleena Kleene Fire burned 25,558 hectares. It had been British Columbia's biggest fire season to date.

I attended the meeting in Anahim Lake on November 7. They asked us: What did we do wrong? What did we do right? What could we do in the future? There were some heated comments regarding the road closures and evacuation orders. Agencies were there to offer services and money for recovery from the fire. These meetings were held in all affected communities; Chris went to the one at Nimpo Lake the following day. She complained bitterly about the legislation that would have prevented her from going home if she had ever left it. She told them that such a ridiculous law actually put people in danger, for they stayed long after they should have gone. The following spring, the findings of these meetings were published. One document was fifty pages long, the other seven hundred pages. They addressed a lot of things—but made no mention of Chris's complaint.

During the Anahim meeting, I sat quietly thinking how glad I was to have stayed with our very own Precipice Fire. When I finally spoke it was to offer my thanks and gratitude for those in the BC Wildfire Service, who were so respectful to us, and who did so much to protect our lives and property.

Afterword

THE FIRES OF 2017 BROKE ALL RECORDS FOR THE HECTARAGE BURNED in British Columbia.

The 2018 fire season was even worse.

Although 2018 was such a terrible fire season overall, the West Chilcotin was largely spared—at least from the flames, if not the smoke. But things had changed. One small fire between Chris's and Jaden's properties was ignited after a horrific lightning storm, but when the fire was called in, the Wildfire Service was there instantly. Chris had heard that there had been a big restructuring as to how firefighting resources were deployed. Each crew now has multiple skills—and they were completely ready to go.

Two major fires occurred farther north. The Tweedsmuir Complex was an amalgamation of seven wildfires (all started by lightning strikes in Tweedsmuir Provincial Park) that grew to over three hundred thousand hectares and threatened the old Ulkatcho Village. People from the Ulkatcho First Nation went in to save the remaining structures and gravesites before the Wildfire Service finally arrived to set up structural protection.

David J, his son and son-in-law, as well as Clemens, scrambled to move equipment across country to protect ranch sites on the

Blackwater River against the Blackwater River Fire that grew to over 8,300 hectares.

The frustrating restrictions on travel throughout the West Chilcotin during the 2017—and almost every—fire season were greatly exacerbated by there being only one road between Williams Lake and Bella Coola. For years people have been suggesting an alternative route north of Anahim Lake, which would end up in Vanderhoof. Much of this route of bush and farm roads is swampy and impassable for much of the year, and there is concern that it might affect the mountain caribou migration. Many things will have to be discussed, but promises have been made that this route will eventually go through.

The BC Wildfires of Note website now has a large disclaimer pop-up, saying why it is impossible to be accurate with their information. Fortunately there are many other informative websites available.

The gentle giant, one of the Three Sisters near Fred's greenhouse that was patched with mud, survived; however, more of the surrounding forest than expected died. The creeping ground fires initially seemed to spare them but many had damaged bark close to the ground and could not sustain sap movement.

Although we stayed in the face of the Precipice and Kleena Kleene Fires, the tragic loss of life in the California fires of 2018 highlight the need to obey early evacuation calls in urban centres when confronted by wildfire.

Acknowledgements

VERY GRATEFUL THANKS TO ALL THE PEOPLE INVOLVED WITH FIGHT-ing fires everywhere.

For the Kleena Kleene Fire we can acknowledge Sergeant Scott Clay, Dr. Rob Coetzee, Christoph and Corinne Gisler, Patrice Gordon, Katie Hayhurst and Dennis Kuch, "Jaden," David and Patti Jorgensen, Miriam Koerner, Ken, Rylan Schuk, Karin Satre, Richard and Leah Simon, Duncan Stewart, Gord Schneider and his crew from Comox Fire Rescue.

Special thanks to Mike King and his crew, Gerald and Johanna Kirby, Selma Padgett and Doug Schuk and all the "Chilcotin Warriors."

—Chris

FOR THE PRECIPICE FIRE, SPECIAL THANKS TO KERRY PHILLIPS AND the Bella Coola personnel of the Coastal Division of the BC Wildfire Service.

Our valued contacts with those fighting the fire included Mark Petrovcic, Arlen Kanary, Kate McLean, David Pascal, Demitri Vaisius and Lonny Turnbull. You all made us feel so protected and looked after. Your generous communication kept us well informed and taught us so much about wildfires and the methods of fighting them. You figured larger in our lives than this book could ever fully acknowledge.

Special thanks to pilots Jim Henderson, Catherine, Rob, Randy, Tyler, Evan, Sean, Shane and so many others. Like comrades in a crisis we only got to know many of you on a first-name basis.

Local fire heroes include David Dorsey ("Hoss"), David and Patti Jorgensen, Troy and Lorrein Gurr, Pat Roach and Clemens, who all worked frantically in the early stages of our structural protection. Tamara Lowrie and David Chamberlin, at the Anahim Lake Airport, co-ordinated the ferrying in of supplies and sent us a few treats of their own. And, of course, "Caleb," who committed so much of himself to the crisis.

I give a special shout-out to Comox Fire Rescue, whose team worked diligently to complete our structural protection in the face of a rank-five firestorm.

Pat Taylor figures largely in our story and I am so glad that she shared our experience through her Facebook posts and allowed me to use them to flesh out the emotional trauma experienced in such a crisis. Lee, although you were in the Precipice for only a short time, you were with us in spirit throughout the whole situation.

I thank Katie Iveson, Tabi Magnan, Jim Henderson, Shane Groves, Mark Petrovcic, Arlen Kanary, Kate McLean, Jade Dumas, Graham Smith and Pat Taylor, who shared photos, maps and information to help fill in some of the details in our story.

A special thanks to my co-author Chris Czajkowski, who encouraged me to write our story and did so many early edits of my work, and to those above and many others who also encouraged me to put our experience into a book.

My most grateful thanks to my partner, Monika Schoene, who stayed in the face of the Precipice Fire under a greater stress than I was aware of at the time.

—Fred